£19.50

D1222705

SPEND FOR EMPLOYMENT

Employment, Capital and Economic Policy
Great Britain 1918–1939

Employment, Capital and Economic Policy Great Britain 1918–1939

Alan Booth
and
Melvyn Pack

Basil Blackwell

First published 1985

Basil Blackwell Ltd
108 Cowley Road, Oxford OX4 1JF, UK

Basil Blackwell Inc.
432 Park Avenue South, Suite 1505,
New York, NY 10016, USA

British Library Cataloguing in Publication Data

Booth, Alan
Employment, capital and economic policy: Great Britain, 1919–1939.
1. Great Britain — Economic policy — 1918–1945
I. Title II. Pack, Melvyn
330.941'083 HC256.3
ISBN 0–631–13804–8

Library of Congress Cataloging in Publication Data

Booth, Alan, Ph.D.
Employment, capital, and economic policy, Great Britain, 1918–1939.
Includes index
1. Great Britain — Economic policy — 1918–1945.
I. Pack, Melvyn. II. Title.
HC256.3.B62 1985 338.941 84–28442
ISBN 0–631–13804–8

Typeset by Banbury Typesetters Ltd
Printed in Great Britain by The Bath Press Ltd, Avon

Contents

Preface

Although the subject-matter of this book is firmly rooted in the interwar years, the stimulus to investigate this area of the policy debate lies very much in the 1970s and 1980s. We have been much influenced by one of the most celebrated of current political slogans – 'There is no alternative'. We hope that this volume not only throws light on the interwar debate, but can also begin to illuminate more recent discussions. We would like to thank many colleagues at the University of Sheffield and Leicester Polytechnic for their help and advice in the preparation of this book.

Introduction

This book is about the debates over economic policy in interwar Britain. Much of the already voluminous literature on this topic has approached the study of policy from the history of economic thought and has attempted to link the evolution of policy to the contemporaneous changes in economic theory which we have come to call the 'Keynesian revolution'. From this perspective, the policy debate becomes a clash between competing economic theories; an anti-expansionist Treasury orthodoxy in conflict with a developing Keynesian system with expansionist policies at its centre.[1] This dominant Keynesian historiographical tradition rests upon two very interesting assumptions, neither of which looks very robust in the 1980s, when mass unemployment again disfigures British economic and social life and when Keynesian policies are widely believed to have failed British policy-makers.[2] The more basic assumption is that 'Keynesian policies' offered a solution to Britain's interwar economic problems. The questions of what constitutes a 'Keynesian policy' is somewhat vexed, and is taken up in chapter 8, but the dominant perspective in British economic historiography has presupposed that interwar governments could have cured the unemployment problem simply by creating additional monetary demand, most easily through public works programmes. Recent improvements in historical statistics and mathematical modelling have at last allowed historians to begin to test this proposition, and the weight of current opinion is that the Keynesian premises are

[1] There is, of course, work of outstanding scholarship in this tradition. See, in particular, Donald Winch, *Economics and Policy: A Historical Study*, London, Hodder & Stoughton, 1969; Susan Howson, *Domestic Monetary Management in Britain, 1919–38*, Cambridge, CUP, 1975; Donald Moggridge, *British Monetary Policy: The Norman Conquest of $4.86*, Cambridge, CUP, 1972; Susan Howson and Donald Winch, *The Economic Advisory Council, 1930–1939: A Study of Economic Advice During Depression and Recovery*, Cambridge, CUP, 1977.

[2] See, for example, Robert Skidelsky (ed.), *The End of the Keynesian Era*, London, Macmillan, 1977.

false.[3] The interwar economic problem was much more intractable than Keynesian historians have been wont to admit.

The second serious objection to the tradition which sees economic ideas as the most crucial element in economic policy is its immense weakness in explaining actual tactics or strategies in economic policy. Interwar governments, supposedly in thrall to orthodox, anti-interventionist principles, introduced a range of policies to aid industry, deliberately managed credit, and managed the exchange rate.[4] More recently, the years between 1945 and 1975 are often termed the 'Keynesian era', yet only a brief examination is necessary to see that the main objectives, institutions and initiatives established at the end of the second world war owe very little to the economic theories of Keynes, whose *General Theory* contains surprisingly little policy advice. As we shall see, many of the initiatives in 'planning' and the enlargement of the public sector which governments have introduced since 1945 *did* appear in interwar writings, but in programmes of political parties and economic interest groups rather than in the theoretical works of academic economists. There was a great reappraisal in the interwar years of the role of the state in the economy and Keynes undoubtedly played an important part, but the dominant Keynesian economic historiography has exaggerated his role and has almost totally forgotten the decisive contributions made by non-academic, partisan groups. Proposals for the mixed economy *plus* the regulation of aggregate monetary demand *plus* big government *plus* extensions of the state's welfare responsibilities (that is, the broad thrust of policy which has evolved between 1945 and 1975) *were* formulated before 1939, but in the neglected programmes of the political and industrial critics of interwar government policy.

Of course, the acid test of any economic strategy is in its ability to provide realistic answers to the economic problems it has been designed to confront. The power to anticipate later developments in policy or institutions pales into insignificance beside this crucial requirement. However, we have already cast doubt upon the established Keynesian analysis of the interwar economic problem, so we must begin by reassessing British economic performance.

---

[3] Sean Glynn and P. G. A. Howells, 'Unemployment in the 1930s: The Keynesian Solution Reconsidered', *Australian Economic History Review*, 20, 1980; T. Thomas, 'Aggregate Demand in the United Kingdom, 1918–45', in R. Floud and D. N. McCloskey (eds), *The Economic History of Britain since 1700*, vol. II: *1860 to the 1970s*, Cambridge, CUP, 1981.

[4] The best introduction to the basic element of 'orthodox' economic thought is B. Corry, 'Keynes in the History of Economic Thought', in A. P. Thirlwall (ed.), *Keynes and Laissez-Faire*, London, Macmillan, 1978.

BRITAIN'S INTERWAR ECONOMY

The ability of an economy to provide full employment clearly has both a current and a historical dimension. A buoyant economy will have a balanced economic structure, with a good representation of industries in secular expansion, and a strong market sector able to compete effectively both at home and abroad so as to finance the investment and import needs of the whole economy. These are the long-run preconditions for full employment. In the short-term, there needs to be sufficient home and foreign demand for British goods and services to provide the full employment of British labour. It is important to distinguish between these two elements and to recognize that they may not coincide.

It is clear that the most basic long-run problem for the British interwar economy was the effect of Britain's changing position in the international economy.[5] Britain's economy had prospered during the nineteenth century on the basis of a narrow range of specialized export industries. The need for structural change was apparent before 1914, but progress was limited, especially in the Edwardian years. Labour, particularly skilled labour, was cheap by comparison with the more dynamic economies of this period, thus production remained skill-intensive and there was insufficient demand for the breakthrough of the twentieth-century growth industries of the age of high mass consumption.[6] In 1913, the British economy was prosperous, aided by export demand for low-technology coal and cottons, but it was vulnerable.

The precariousness was fully exposed when the first world war smashed the network of world trade and payments upon which nineteenth-century prosperity had been built. After 1918, Britain was heavily committed to the production of goods which other countries increasingly preferred to produce for themselves or buy from Britain's competitors. Thus Britain had throughout the interwar period a hard core of unemployment which was increasingly concentrated in the export industries of coal, cotton, shipbuilding and, to a lesser extent, iron and steel. These industries were constrained by their lack of competitiveness, with obvious consequences for investment and employment. Employment tended to fall more rapidly than output, giving reasonable productivity performance, but the gap between British and best foreign performance in these industries was only

[5] A fuller treatment of this approach to the economic history of the interwar years can be found in Sean Glynn and Alan Booth, 'Unemployment in Interwar Britain: A Case for Re-Learning the Lessons of the 1930s?', *Economic History Review*, 36, 1983.

[6] C. K. Harley, 'Skilled Labour and the Choice of Technique in Edwardian Industry', *Explorations in Economic History*, 2, 1974.

maintained, not closed.[7] To regain competitiveness, British producers needed to take further the substitution of labour by capital and pay lower wages.

On the other hand, reducing wages, and hence domestic demand, could only have handicapped the expanding industries geared to the domestic market. Vehicles, public utilities, light engineering and retailing all experienced rapid growth in output and employment between the wars. Labour was used quite extravagantly, with labour productivity performance relatively modest. Though demand for these goods and services was increasing rapidly, it did not grow quickly enough to produce full employment. Demand still lacked social depth, with the result that the pace of structural change was again very modest.[8] Thus policy-makers were faced by a dual economy, each side of which required careful treatment, but in which the remedy for one implied adverse effects upon the other.[9]

This basic economic problem was compounded by geographical factors. The declining industries tended to be located on the old-established coalfields of Scotland, South Wales and northern England. The expanding industries concentrated in the Midlands and the south-east of England. For a variety of reasons, population mobility was low, leaving the social and political burdens of unemployment concentrated upon a very narrow range of communities.

Superimposed upon these domestic regional-structural difficulties were problems requiring action on the international plane. The peaks of unemployment in 1921–2 and 1929–33 were associated with slumps in the international economy, and export values throughout the interwar years failed to reach the 1913 level. Protection began to spread during the 1920s, and in the 1930s autarkic trade practices were very common. Interwar financial arrangements were little better, with the efforts to reconstruct a gold exchange standard bedevilled by arguments over reparations and the unwillingness of America to play an international role commensurate with her economic power. The 1930s also witnessed the breakdown of multi-lateralism in international finance, though new attitudes began to emerge at mid-decade. As a result, world trade was less dynamic than it had been before 1913 and it failed to keep pace with world production. There were

---

[7] B. W. E. Alford, 'New Industries for Old? British Industry Between the Wars', in Floud and McCloskey, *The Economic History of Britain*, p. 314.

[8] N. K. Buxton, 'The Role of the "New" Industries in Britain During the 1930s: A Reinterpretation', *Business History Review*, 49, 1975, pp. 219–22.

[9] Glynn and Booth, 'Unemployment in Interwar Britain', p. 338.

obvious ramifications for a trading nation such as Britain, though these factors explain only part of Britain's difficulties.[10]

Interwar governments were faced therefore by a formidable, multilayered economic problem. Such was the commitment of resources to the staple industries even in 1938 that no effort to cure the unemployment problem could ignore their troubles. Government had to find ways both of restoring confidence and vigour to international trade and payments and of improving the competitiveness of British exports acceptable to the international community. Transfer of resources out of the export industries was imperative, and this meant that demand had to be expanded to foster growth in the home-market industries. However, this expansion of demand, presumably begun by increasing employment in the non-market sector, had to be achieved without weakening the competitiveness of the market sector.[11] It was imperative to hold wages in the staple industries and to accelerate labour productivity growth in the expanding industries. In these circumstances, some form of industrial and incomes policy was essential on both sides of our dual economy. There are two final twists to the story. First, the British authorities were operating between the wars on very narrow margins in the balance of payments on current account. At the exchange rate prevailing in 1913, Britain could have financed 30 per cent more imports. After 1918, not only had this safety net disappeared, but the authorities had to choose between an employment and an exchange rate target as objectives in short-term policy. Secondly, such were the disruptions of the interwar economy, particularly in international trade and finance, that a clear-cut solution to Britain's economic problems was never really likely. Amelioration rather than cure was the target.

In broad terms, therefore, the radicals had (1) to find ways of defending the balance of payments at higher levels of economic activity either within existing institutional arrangements or under a modified system; (2) to evolve policies which would absorb at least some of the unemployed but which would not prejudice the search for higher efficiency and lower unit costs in both sides of a dual economy; and (3) accelerate the pace of structural adjustment, either with the support of private investors and businessmen or by fulfilling their functions in alternative ways without inhibiting the expansionary potential of the home market sector. In the following chapters, we hope to measure the alternative strategies of the interwar period against these needs.

[10] The evidence is succinctly summarized by Derek H. Aldcroft, *The Inter-War Economy: Britain, 1919–1939*, London, Batsford, 1970, pp. 246–7.

[11] The terminology is explained in Robert Bacon and Walter Eltis, *Britain's Economic Problem: Too Few Producers*, London, Macmillan, 1976, ch. 5.

1

The Economic Policy of the Labour Movement, 1918–31

Of all the alternative economic strategies of the interwar period, those generated within the Labour Party are the most difficult to evaluate. Labour recognized before most other groups that unemployment was more than a temporary problem of adjustment, and that fundamental structural changes directed by the state would be necessary to restore prosperity. Many of the initiatives pioneered by the interwar Labour Party have been introduced since 1945, and elements of Labour's strategy were taken up by radicals of a very different political hue. No one can dispute that the Labour Party possessed valuable insights. Unfortunately, there were also serious flaws in these programmes. In the interwar period, the party's economic strategists had not yet fully come to terms with capitalism, and this prevented them from applying their analyses to the management of the existing system. On the other hand, the leadership was unwilling to make the party an instrument for the overthrow of capitalism within a specified and limited period. Moreover, when it did come to power, Labour betrayed a depressing tendency to drop the more incisive parts of its analysis in favour of rigid orthodoxy. As we shall see, these problems were inherent in a party hoping to achieve 'socialism' by gradualist, parliamentary methods.

THE FIRST WORLD WAR

Despite its encouraging electoral successes after 1900, the Labour Party did not issue a major policy statement on economic (and other home) affairs until the publication of *Labour and the New Social Order* in 1918. Before 1914, the party was 'opportunistic, narrow, moderately reformist (and even reactionary)...It was pragmatic and influenced by other social classes, "labourist" and weak in theoretical precepts.'[1] It was a loose alliance of trade unions, in which a strong liberal, anti-socialist ideology was firmly rooted, and socialist societies committed to the achievement of socialism by constitutional methods.[2] The nature of the alliance meant that the socialist objectives had to take a back seat to retain trade-union participation. But, even in the Independent Labour Party, the strongest of the socialist societies, there were pointers to the problems to befall the Labour Party between the wars over the interpretation of 'socialism'. The ILP's inaugural conference committed it to the collective ownership of the means of production, distribution and exchange, but the ILP's programme was made up of interim demands such as the eight-hour day, minimum wages and the right to work or maintenance.[3] These prosposals could be presented in two not necessarily consistent ways. First, they could be tactical objectives on the road to socialism, part of a wider campaign of propaganda and agitation. Secondly, the ultimate aim of such proposals could be a more humane capitalism – amelioration and redistribution in favour of the working class, yet retaining private ownership across all or most of the economy. This latter reformist strategy implied a considerable effort to investigate and correct the defects of the system as it existed, and a campaign to secure limited changes which could be accommodated by the system. The former strategy might best be termed the 'convinced socialist' path, whereas the latter is a 'convinced reformist'. Even before 1914, the ILP had experienced the tensions which inevitably accompany those who wish to change society by constitutional, that is by reformist, methods, particularly over unemployment policy and the right to work.[4] The portent for the Labour Party before the wars was ominous, but the difficult questions could to some extent be avoided in the continuing debate about the inadequacies of the Labour Party's performance in Parliament and the relative merits of industrial and political action in furthering the interests of labour.

The war exerted a decisive influence on the economic strategy of the Labour Party, by creating the conditions by which it, too, was brought to advocate socialism by constitutional methods, largely under the guiding hand of Sidney Webb. At the outbreak of war, the War Emergency Workers National Committee (WEWNC) was established as a body to

[1] David E. Martin, 'The Instruments of the People? The Parliamentary Labour Party in 1906', in David E. Martin and David Rubinstein (eds), *Ideology and the Labour Movement: Essays Presented to John Saville*, London, Croom Helm, 1979, p. 142.

[2] For a brief period, the Marxist Social Democratic Federation had been affiliated to the Labour Representation Committee, but soon retired from membership to take up a more overtly 'class war' position.

[3] Robert E. Dowse, *Left in the Centre: The Independent Labour Party, 1893–1940*, London, Longman, 1966, pp. 5–6.

[4] Kenneth D. Brown, *Labour and Unemployment, 1900–1914*, Newton Abbot, David & Charles, 1971, chs 3–6.

speak for the entire labour movement, and Webb was elected to it. Amid
the early fears of rising unemployment resulting from the dislocation of
war, Webb led the WEWNC to the policy of contra-cyclical public works
which Beatrice had championed before the Poor Law Commission. The
WEWNC also committed itself to the typically Webbian proposal of
municipal and central government control of food supply and prices.[5]
However, the most significant commitment for the WEWNC followed the
introduction of conscription. Webb, who had been greatly impressed by
wartime state control of the railways and mines, and by the development
of progressive taxation, persuaded the WEWNC to campaign for the
'conscription of riches' as a *quid pro quo* for the conscription of labour. In
effect, this brought the wartime labour movement to advocate nationalization and the Fabian model of collective state ownership of the means of
production.[6] This impressive unity of the whole labour movement behind
the socialist proposals took on real significance when in 1917 serious
thought was given to the future of the Labour Party.

Arthur Henderson, who as chairman of the WEWNC and later Cabinet
Minister in the Lloyd George coalition was Labour's leading parliamentary figure, shared Webb's moderate socialist views. Indeed, the two
cooperated closely between 1915 and the end of the war.[7] At a relatively
early stage in the war, both had decided that the Labour Party
organization needed overhaul, and Henderson's visit to Russia (in 1917,
between revolutions) convinced him that there must be a moderate
socialist party as an alternative to the 'big two' if revolutionary chaos were
to be avoided in Britain. So, in the aftermath of the WEWNC call for
conscription of riches, and amid the working-class optimism created by
the Russian revolution, Webb and Henderson strove to give the Labour
Party a socialist constitution and programme.[8]

The programme was contained in *Labour and the New Social Order*,
circulated in January 1918 and debated later in the year. In typically
Webbian terms, *Labour and the New Social Order* proclaimed the end of
the capitalist system and its replacement by a new, cooperative, planned,
equitable, democratic social order. It was an immensely wide-ranging
document, covering everything from the manufacture and retailing of

---

[5] J. M. Winter, *Socialism and the Challenge of War: Ideas and Politics in Britain, 1912–18*,
London, Routledge & Kegan Paul, 1974, ch. 7.

[6] For a pioneering account of the role of Webb in the WEWNC, see Royden Harrison,
'The War Emergency Workers' National Committee', in Asa Briggs and John Saville (eds),
Essays in Labour History, 1886–1923, London, Macmillan, 1971. Also, Winter, *Socialism and
the Challenge of War*, ch. 6.

[7] Margaret Cole, *The Story of Fabian Socialism*, London, Heinemann, 1961, p. 169.

[8] Winter, *Socialism and the Challenge of War*, ch. 8.

alcoholic drink to constitutional devolution. Webb gave the document a distinctly Fabian flavour; he wished not only to consolidate the favourable changes which had resulted from the massive wartime growth of the state bureaucracy but also to set longer-run socialist targets. The essence of his programme was to build the 'Four Pillars of the House of Tomorrow':

The Universal Enforcement of the National Minimum;
The Democratic Control of Industry;
The Revolution in National Finance; and
The Surplus Wealth for the Common Good.

The 'National Minimum' meant not only that a living wage should be paid but also that its real purchasing power should be kept in line with the inflation which had afflicted Britain since 1914. But governments would also have to *plan* (not only demobilization, but also peacetime economic development) to ensure that the demand for labour, and hence the living wage, was maintained.[9] In the transition to peace, government contracts would have to be phased out according to the state of trade in the major industries, and, in the longer term, public works would have to be used to offset any decline in private sector employment.[10] At this stage, public works were seen only as contra-cyclical stabilizers – the problem of mass, involuntary unemployment had yet to be faced.

Under the 'Democratic Control of Industry', we find Webb offering the same mixture of immediate objectives and longer-run socialist goals. The policy document repeated the WEWNC demands for continuing state control of the railways and mines, and nationalization of electricity generation, the extension of state controls over the individual firm, and the continuation of state importing and allocation of raw materials. *Labour and the New Social Order* hoped that these controls would be used in the longer term to build an economy in which production was geared to socially useful goods and services. Cheap power and transport would help keep costs low, and the powers of allocation could be used to favour efficient producers and to ensure that needs would be met in the order of and in proportion to their national importance.[11] At least, that was how planning should work in theory! Thus Webb was taking the Labour Party rather further than he had dared lead the WEWNC, towards a system which

[9] On the development of the concept of 'planning' in 1918, see Adrian Oldfield, 'The Labour Party and Planning – 1934 or 1918?', *Bulletin of the Society for the Study of Labour History*, 25, 1972.

[10] *Labour and the New Social Order*, London, The Labour Party, 1918, pp. 6–7.

[11] Ibid., p. 4.

implied moves towards the common ownership of the means of production.

The objectives of the Labour Party's first major programme seem explicitly socialist. Beyond the immediate proposals for postwar reconstruction, the socialist society was a hazy and ill-defined outline, but there is nothing in *Labour and the New Social Order* which could be realistically defined as 'convinced reformist', content merely to aim at a more decent capitalism. In a very large part, the optimism and sense of direction of the 1918 programme were founded upon a conviction that the wartime developments in collectivist control were not only capable of being made permanent, but were also 'socialist'. In this respect, the Labour Party was ill-served by the Fabians' tendency to equate state control with socialism and by the unwillingness throughout the labour movement to investigate the nature of the wartime state. To the Webbs, the state was an essentially friendly institution because it was staffed by bureaucrats who were fired by a vision of public service, and among whom the Fabian Society had recruited so successfully. But the wartime state had also sucked into Whitehall an enormous number of businessmen, especially in those areas controlling private industry. Not only were these businessmen still driven by the desire to maximise profits, they were also ideally placed to effect the rapid return of these publicly controlled industries to private ownership.[12] Thus the rapid dismemberment of the wartime state apparatus in 1918–19 not only undermined Labour's immediate proposals, it called into question, especially for the left of the party, the leadership's commitment to a moderate, constitutional path to socialism.

The 'Revolution in National Finance' was also a perplexing mixture of lessons learned from and complete misunderstandings of wartime developments. Webb had been much impressed by the extension of progressive income tax and the use of excess profits duty. Here lay the method of financing public works and the more expansive social services which had long been a favourite cause of both Sidney and Beatrice. However, wartime finance, with its heavy emphasis on borrowing, had also produced a massively increased national debt with high annual interest charges which threatened any constructive postwar policies. Webb's answer was a capital levy to wipe away, or at least reduce, the burden. As far as it goes, this programme is convincing. Unfortunately, it does not go very far. As Adrian Oldfield has pointed out, little attention was given to investment in the new social order, and, even in the reconstruction period, finance from the capital levy and new taxes on land

[12] See S. M. H. Armitage, *The Politics of the Decontrol of Industry: Britain and the United States*, London, Weidenfeld & Nicolson, 1969.

and capital was expected to stretch to pay for a wide range of new policies.[13] Indeed, none of the programmes was costed, and no estimates were given of the expected yield from the new taxes. The lack of detail is unfortunate because there is lack of economic understanding and woolliness of thought in this section of *Labour and the New Social Order*. Despite the extensive spending proposals, there is throughout no challenge to the orthodox view that budgets should balance. There is very little discussion of external finance or exchange rate policy despite the fact that Britain had *de facto* left the gold standard at the outbreak of war.[14]. Within 18 months of the publication of *Labour and the New Social Order*, the Lloyd George Cabinet was split between those who wanted to pursue the internal policy goals of reconstruction and full employment, and those who favoured the external goal of restoring the gold standard at the prewar parity. There is nothing in Labour's programme to indicate that it would have acted any differently from the government. In spite of its reconstruction pledges, there is every reason to suspect that even a Labour Cabinet would have been swayed by orthodox financial pressures into defending the exchange rate at the cost of higher domestic unemployment.

Of the 'Surplus for the Common Good', much less needs to be said. Revenue from taxation would be used to extend the social services, particularly education, housebuilding and unemployment insurance, to finance a better system of social and scientific research, and, in the longer term, to develop a society based upon cooperation. Of course, much of this anticipates the measures introduced by the post-*second*-world-war Attlee government.

On the whole, *Labour and the New Social Order* is a stirring, but finally unconvincing manifesto for reconstruction and the transition to socialism. Webb's main task had been to produce a draft behind which the whole Labour Party could unite. In many respects, therefore, the moderate, constitutional path was inevitable. But *Labour and the New Social Order* was not the best document to prepare the Labour Party even to identify the major issues in the achievement of socialism in postwar Britain. Above all, it was far too complacent. Party members could be forgiven for believing that the war had done most of their work for them and that socialism was just around the corner. Finance was almost totally absent from the draft and certainly did not equip Labour's politicians to see the threat which

[13] Oldfield, 'Labour Party and Planning', pp. 49–52.

[14] The one aspect which Labour did discuss was state control of agriculture to promote greater domestic production of foodstuffs and a lesser dependency upon imports. However, it is likely that the balance-of-payments aspects of this demand were much less powerful influences in pushing the party towards farming policy than the egalitarian desire to break up concentrations of wealth.

was mounting to reconstruction and intervention from vested interests. There might possibly have been some discussion of the constraints and dangers to Labour's goals if the concept of planning had been given a more prominent place and both the shorter- and longer-term plans had been specified in much greater detail. However, it has to be recognized that throughout the interwar period Labour's plans were always haziest when they discussed finance and the precise mechanisms and objectives of economic planning. As it was, *Labour and the New Social Order* did not even warn the party that it would have to *fight* for its most moderate objectives. The absence of 'fighting talk' reflected, above all, the structural divisions within the British labour movement. Webb had been a strong advocate of advance through the political system. To the proponents of parliamentary socialism, the vocabulary of confrontation was anathema. Confrontation smacked of extra-parliamentary action, and meant mobilizing the militant *industrial* wing of the labour movement. By 1918, however, this group had its own notion of how the transition to socialism should be effected, how economic planning should be organized, and how the socialist society should be ordered. The most surprising aspect of *Labour and the New Social Order* is the almost complete neglect of the analysis of the industrial militants.

GUILD SOCIALISM

In the first two decades of the present century, the strongest critique of parliamentary socialism from the left came from the adherents to the various workers' control doctrines, of which guild socialism was the most formidable. In this approach to socialism, the central problem was not maldistribution of income and wealth, but the system which made workpeople passive instruments of production, with no control over their working lives. In this respect, guild socialism in particular was the intellectual heir of Carlyle, Ruskin, Carpenter and Morris, a fusion of the cooperative movement and the English medievalist reaction against the nineteenth century.[15]

The medievalist strand is particularly evident in the work which did so much to inspire the development of guild socialism, A. J. Penty's *The Restoration of the Gild System*. An architect and disciple of Morris's arts and crafts movement, Penty despised capitalism's emphasis on quantity and cheapness, which alienated the worker from the production process.

[15] S. T. Glass, *The Responsible Society: The Ideas of the English Guild Socialist*, London, Longman, 1966, p. 6.

He looked back approvingly to the medieval guilds in which workers had controlled their crafts, determining both the quality and quantity of their products. To Penty, the trade unions could restore workers' control, taking over modern industries and transforming them into guilds based on workshop methods of production. National economic questions would be handled by an assembly elected from the individual guilds, and thus leaving Parliament free from concern with industrial questions.[16]

Such a backward-looking utopianism did not deserve serious consideration, but Penty had managed to strike a chord in Edwardian radical thought. Many shared Penty's view that the restoration of the workers' self-respect was the major problem for socialists at a time when mass production was spreading. More significant was the fact that Penty's volume appeared as one of the periodic explosions of British industrial unrest had just burst, and when American and Continental doctrines of workers' control were taking root. Luckily, Penty had like-minded friends who were able to make more effective use of his basic themes. The early development of guild socialism was undertaken by A. R. Orage, from 1907 editor of the journal *New Age* and an established friend of Penty, and by S. G. Hobson.

It was in the April 1912 edition of the *New Age* that Hobson began a series of articles (later collected into book form, *National Guilds: An Inquiry into the Wage System and the Way Out*[17]) which formed the first sustained statement of guild socialism. The basis of Hobson's position was that capitalism – the wage system – was undemocratic. In being forced to accept *wages*, the worker sold not only his labour power, but also the right to control his work. The parliamentary socialist objectives of nationalization and redistribution would not touch this problem; the bureaucrat would merely replace the capitalist as the *controller* of work. Like Penty, Hobson wanted a society which was divided vertically, into industries, each run by its own national guild and subject to a supreme council coordinating policies and resolving disputes in economic affairs. As in Penty's model Parliament would control non-industrial matters and the trade unions were to be the instruments of transition, first becoming all-inclusive industrial unions and gradually pressing for greater control over managerial functions.

The industrial unrest of the Edwardian period helped convince another, younger group – this time centred on Oxford and led by G. D. H. Cole –

[16] Penty's ideas are discussed by Glass in ibid., ch. 3.
[17] S. G. Hobson (edited by A. R. Orage), *The National Guilds: An Inquiry into the Wage System and the Way Out*, London, Bell, 1914. On Penty, Orage and Hobson, see Frank Matthews, 'The Ladder of Becoming: A. R. Orage, A. J. Penty and the Origins of Guild Socialism in England', in Martin and Rubinstein, *Ideology and the Labour Movement*.

that the tyrannies of capitalism could be cured only by achieving democracy at the workplace.[18] At this time, Cole was very active in the Fabian Research Department, which rapidly became the nerve centre of guild socialism, undertaking research on behalf of both the workers' control movement and of individual unions sympathetic to the cause.[19] Many members of the FRD were also involved in the National Guilds League, established in 1915 to conduct propaganda for guild socialism. This younger generation, therefore, gave the movement considerable vitality and *élan*, and provided, in Cole, the new intellectual leader. Though the output of the guild socialists was increasingly propagandist and polemical, Cole in particular offered more considered, reasoned statements of guild socialist doctrine which permit us to trace its development and to assess its relevance to the problems of the British economy following the first world war.

Cole's efforts went mainly into the development of the politics of guild socialism; its economics were badly underdeveloped even after the establishment of a pioneering guild in the building industry. The main problems to which Cole addressed himself and which took the analysis beyond S. G. Hobson were in two main areas: what to do about nationalization, which increasingly seemed to be a realizable demand for industries under wartime government control; and, how the consumer interest might best be represented under the guild system. In *Self-Government in Industry*, Cole first recognized that for the coal mines and the railways, nationalization was a real possibility. However, he argued that central control should not trouble guildsmen since the experience of the bureaucratic running of these industries would soon stimulate the demand for workers' control.[20] Thus Cole anticipated the formation of the first guilds in state-controlled enterprises such as the railways and the Post Office. Guild socialism seemed sufficiently flexible to accommodate developments in the real political world.

The problem of incorporating the consumer was not one which had troubled Penty or Hobson. Their willingness to make all decisions about quality, quantity and price the prerogative of the guild clearly opened the door to the abuse of monopoly powers, albeit by the entire guild rather than by profiteering entrepreneurs. Cole's first answer was a 'joint Congress, equally representative of the State, or the consumers, and the Guild

---

[18] Cole reached his position on workers' control independently of the articles in *New Age*. See L. P. Carpenter, *G. D. H. Cole: An Intellectual Biography*, Cambridge, CUP, 1975, p. 25.

[19] Margaret I. Cole, 'Guild Socialism and the Labour Research Department', in Briggs and Saville, *Essays in Labour History, 1886–1923*.

[20] G. D. H. Cole, *Self-Government in Industry*, London, Bell, 1917, pp. 217–19.

Congress, or the producers'.[21] But this did not satisfy him for long; at the root of Cole's political thought was a desire to devolve decision-making according to function, and this led him to propose the commune, a new body which would be composed of equal numbers of representatives from both the guilds and consumers' associations. There would be a hierarchy of communes, working upwards from the basic ward or village unit, through the regional to the national level. The object was a participatory democracy to encourage a far more active popular involvement in decision-taking.

The result for economic policy threatened chaos. The combination of decentralization, involvement and the consequent need for coordination at many levels pointed to *impasse*. As an illustration, the following represents Cole's blueprint of the way in which choices between consumption and investment would be made.

> Normally each Guild, economic or civic, will prepare a budget, showing its estimate of requirements both of goods or services for immediate use, and of extensions and improvements. In the preparation of these budgets, the Guilds will clearly consult one another. These Guild budgets will go before the various Councils of consumers or citizens, and the Councils will be able either to criticise and secure amendment, or to put in alternative requisitions of their own. In any case, all the budgets, with all the proposed amendments and requisitions, will go before the Commune, or probably in the first instance before its Finance Committee, which will have its staff of expert statisticians. The various budgets will there be brought into harmony with the estimated national production, and, after any further negotiations have taken place, the complete budget will come up before the Commune as a whole for ratification. In it will be included the estimated administrative and other charges of the Commune itself, which will be levied directly on the Guilds as a form of taxation at source.[22]

The utopian nature of such a scheme should scarcely need emphasizing, but perhaps can most easily be appreciated by trying to imagine how Cole's model would have coped with some of Britain's interwar economic problems. There were, of course, two rapidly unfolding economic slumps between the wars, and it is difficult to imagine how this system would have been able to respond to the speed of economic change. Indeed, the fact that both downswings were export-led indicates a further weakness in the guild socialist position. It is virtually impossible to subject quantities and especially prices of imports and exports to any process of democratic

---

[21] Ibid., p. 286.
[22] G. D. H. Cole, *Guild Socialism Restated*, London, Parsons, 1920, p. 145.

decision-making. The guild socialists were as guilty as Labour Party draftsmen of thinking purely in terms of production (excusable perhaps in a labour movement financially dominated by trade unions based in the manufacturing sector) and of ignoring foreign trade and finance in their pronouncements of economic policy.

The greatest achievement of guild socialism was, of course, the rejection of market forces and pioneering of 'planning' as the method of guiding economic development. Moreover, the model of planning favoured by guild socialists, that is by industry, with each industry regulating its own affairs subject to coordination and assessment by experts at the centre, was to prove immensely durable, and has been seen in much-watered-down forms in post-1945 policy. This model was not only lasting, it was attractive to groups outside the labour movement, especially to the Conservative planners of the 1930s.[23] 'Self-government for Industry' could, after all, be an enticing slogan for the capitalist class. Unfortunately, decentralized planning does not seem to be the best model to cope with Britain's interwar economic problems of structural rigidity compounded by the resistance to new technologies in the largest manufacturing industries. Indeed, Cole's socialist solutions to both problems were singularly unconvincing, and may even have made matters worse.[24]

Despite the attractiveness of the core of its ideas, guild socialism was a short-lived movement. It was a very flexible doctrine, appealing both to radical shop stewards and to Christian socialists. Such a broad, industrially based grouping was bound to suffer internecine feuding between its militant and moderate wings, especially after the Russian revolution had demonstrated to the militants the potential of the revolutionary seizure of political power. In fact, a breakaway faction from the National Guilds League played a leading part in the formation of the Communist Party of Great Britain.[25] Equally damaging was the slump of 1920–1 and the serious erosion of trade-union organization. The economic storm destroyed the first attempts to create local guilds in the building industry.[26] Even Cole's faith eventually weakened, in part because guild

[23] See below, pp. 58–63.

[24] Cole argued that the guilds would pay full income to their members, no matter what the state of trade. Every worker would be on the strength of his or her guild, and would receive social welfare benefits and services from the guild. This system would not help transfer workers out of industry facing secular contraction. See *Guild Socialism Restated*, p. 74.

[25] Glass, *The Responsible Society*, pp. 51–3; Carpenter, *G. D. H. Cole*, pp. 92–100; Margaret Cole, 'Guild Socialism and the LRD', pp. 280–2.

[26] Frank Matthews, 'The Building Guilds', in Briggs and Saville, *Essays in Labour History, 1886–1923*.

socialism had no practical policy to deal with the depression.[27] The lack of attention to the economics of guild socialism was exposed.

LABOUR IN OPPOSITION AND POWER, 1920–1924

While guild socialism was enjoying its brief but spectacular cycle of growth and crisis, the Labour Party's thinking on economic policy tended to be carried along by events, but events which did not conform to the pattern anticipated in *Labour and the New Social Order*. Government controls were rapidly dismantled, and even the coal mines, on which Labour had pinned such confident hopes, were eventually returned to private ownership. More seriously, mass unemployment engulfed the British economy in the spring of 1921 after a collapse in the demand for exports. Both developments set problems which the 1918 programme was ill-equipped to answer.

The party's initial response was to blame the Peace Treaty, which it heartily despised, and the government's failure to resume normal relations with Soviet Russia. This latter aspect was championed by the Council of Action, first established to prevent British military intervention in the Russo-Polish war. The Labour Party persistently called for an international economic conference to revise reparations, raise loans for the reconstruction of the devastated areas of Europe, and to persuade all nations to balance their budgets. Such sound finance would, in the Labour view, end inflation and stabilize exchange rates, so encouraging international trade and making possible a reconstruction of the gold standard, based to a large extent on a restoration of the prewar parities. Here was revealed the stunningly orthodox current of Labour Party economic thinking which was to remain so strong throughout the interwar period. However, at a time of inflationary unemployment, orthodox policies did have much to commend them, and the orthodox solution certainly commanded extensive popular support at this time.[28] Where Labour differed from other proponents of orthodox policies was to repeat its established socialist demand for a massive programme of loan-financed public works to reduce domestic unemployment.[29] Labour Party policymakers apparently could not see that deflation to balance the budget and

---

[27] Carpenter, *G. D. H. Cole*, p. 107.

[28] See Alan Booth, 'Corporatism, Capitalism and Depression in Twentieth Century Britain', *British Journal of Sociology*, 33, 1982, p. 217.

[29] See Labour Party, *Notes on Unemployment*, London, The Labour Party, 1921.

expanding credit to cut unemployment were mutually inconsistent. This speaks volumes for their lack of economic understanding.

The collapse of the export industries did have some beneficial effects on Labour's economic policy-makers. The party was now forced to recognize the importance of foreign trade, and the need to overcome unemployment brought the TUC closer to labour's political wing. The unions imported a 'wage consciousness' into Labour Party thinking, and helped prepare for the later interest in underconsumptionist ideas. A Joint Conference of January 1921 argued that wage cuts and short-time working should be resisted because both were damaging to domestic demand and irrelevant to the real problems of trade and currency dislocation.[30] Both the TUC and the party were asked to mobilize against cuts in wages or welfare benefits and for higher levels of public works expenditure. The object was to protect wages, but both organizations knew that the protection of wages implied raising the demand for labour by an expansionist budgetary policy and would lead, therefore, to certain conflict with powerful financial interests. In the event, the campaign was still-born as unemployment rose, wages fell, and the unions collapsed on 'Black Friday'. For those in the labour movement willing to see, here was an obvious demonstration that financial orthodoxy and expansion were not compatible, and that restrictive financial policies were the stronger.

However, the liberal orthodoxy of Labour's financial experts made it difficult for the party to see the economic problem in this light. Thus Philip Snowden, already Labour's potential Chancellor of the Exchequer, wrote in *Labour and the New World* in 1921 that capitalism had failed to supply satisfaction and contentment to the mass of the population and was therefore destined to fall to a careful, conscientious programme of reform developed by moderate socialists. Yet, when in 1920 the government was running a budget deficit, in part to support just such a programme of moderate social reform, Snowden criticized Lloyd George's financial policy as 'reckless prodigality' and proclaimed that 'sound finance is the basis of national and commercial prosperity'.[31] Although he had witnessed postwar decontrol and the defeat of the unions, Snowden and the vast majority of his colleagues still clung to the utopian belief that the transition to socialism was inevitable, within sight, and attainable by gentle persuasion.

This established Fabian perspective had served the party well, and had enabled it to emerge as the logical alternative government. But, even in the

[30] *Unemployment: A Labour Policy*, London, The Labour Party and the TUC, 1921, p. 10.

[31] The reference from *Labour and the New World* is cited by Colin Cross, *Philip Snowden*, London, Barrie & Rockliff, 1966, p. 176. The 1920 quotations are from *Labour and National Finance*, London, Parsons, 1920, pp. 8, 9.

early 1920s, there had surely been sufficiently obvious signs that the party would have to choose between socialism and bolstering capitalism. Unfortunately, there were equally pressing demands to avoid the splits and recriminations which would inevitably accompany any reconsideration of Labour's aims and philosophy. The prospect of office was looming large. To MacDonald and Snowden, this opportunity meant a programme which, above all, would not alienate electors; the existing mixture of orthodoxy for the centre and of slow, piecemeal progress to collectivism for the left seemed ideal. Thus the 1923 manifesto omitted all mention of nationalization as MacDonald tried to prove Labour's fitness to govern and its national, responsible perspective. To reduce unemployment, Labour proposed free trade, 'national schemes of productive work', improved social welfare benefits, the promotion of international peace, and a reduction of the burden of income tax. The tax proposals were a bolt from the blue, and, since most manual wage-earners were below the tax threshold, they were a clear bid for non-socialist votes. Up to 1923, the unmistakable message of Labour Party policy had been that reconstruction and redistribution would cost money which would have to be taken from the rich in new taxes and more steeply progressive income tax. The logic of this proposal to cut tax was that the party was now more interested in power than in building socialism or making socialists.

In the event, MacDonald's short-term tactics were magnificently vindicated. The party's share of votes increased and, in an election fought on tariff reform, Labour emerged in minority government as the larger of the free-trade parties. The ILP was pressing for a socialist King's Speech, quick defeat, and a new election campaign with an explicitly socialist programme.[32] MacDonald, with the support of almost the entire party leadership, decided to show that Labour could be trusted to govern in the national interest. The leadership looked, therefore, to implement those policies from its already moderated manifesto which would command Liberal or Conservative support. Thus the eight months of office were bound to be a disappointment to the socialists within the party's ranks.

Nevertheless, the government's record was not without achievement. Real progress was made on council housing and the establishment of the electricity-generating grid. Improvements were also made in the access to and levels of unemployment allowances, that other longstanding demand of the Labour Party. Yet unemployment remained obstinately high; indeed, Labour found that by easing benefit conditions more people

---

[32] See Ralph Miliband, *Parliamentary Socialism: A Study in the Politics of Labour*, London, Merlin Press, 1972, p. 97.

qualified for help and the statistics went up rather than down.[33] Even a period of office as short as eight months was enough to reveal that the programme Labour had developed since 1918 was little more than empty socialist rhetoric uneasily attached to a deeply orthodox economic analysis. Clearly, the latter would be the more powerful force. Sidney Webb, one of the main architects of the public works policy, was reduced to impotent irrelevance in government. Tom Jones, Assistant Secretary to the Cabinet, noted: 'It was really rather disappointing to find Sidney Webb, the author of pamphlets innumerable on the cure of unemployment regardless of cost, now, as Chairman of the Unemployment Committee, reduced to prescribing a revival of trade as the only remedy open to us.'[34] A similar, depressingly orthodox conclusion was reached in Labour's 1924 campaign document, *Work for the Workless:*

> It is not upon the programme of public works and relief schemes, useful as these may be in an emergency, that the Labour Government challenges comparison with anything that any Government has done in a similar period. It is not to its enormous improvements in the provision of necessary maintenance, necessary as these were, that the Labour Government points. So far as these eight months of office are concerned, it is on International Policy, which factor lies at the very root of the present unemployment problem, that it confidently asks for the continued support of the nation. The Russian Treaty itself was merely a step in the direction of trade and employment.[35]

Such orthodox views were not restricted to Webb, Snowden and MacDonald; they were shared by an overwhelming majority of the party. Labour's dilemma was obvious enough. The policies which promised short-term amelioration of the unemployment problem (and to which the party had been committed for many years) were unorthodox at a time when deflationary policies had become firmly entrenched.[36] To have adopted expansionist policies would have pushed the Labour Party in one of two directions. Public works and redistribution could have been presented either as the first step of the journey towards the socialist state or as the *only* alternative for a reformist party anxious to restore a prosperous capitalism. The former involved a timetable for the achievement of

---

[33] Labour Party, *Work for the Workless: How Labour has Handled Unemployment*, London, The Labour Party, 1924, p. 12.

[34] K. Middlemas (ed.), *Thomas Jones: Whitehall Diary*, vol. I: *1916–25*, Oxford, OUP, 1969, p. 269.

[35] *Work for the Workless*, pp. 12–13.

[36] Booth, 'Corporatism, Capitalism and Depression', p. 218.

socialism, and the latter implied a renunciation of all explicitly socialist commitments in order to convince mass opinion that the party really was attempting to save the existing system. But the doctrines of parliamentary socialism pretended that such choices need not be made, and, in the event, Labour preferred to avoid the difficult decision. Even the most moderate socialists comforted themselves with the belief that poverty, distress and unemployment were inevitable products of capitalism, and could be overcome, only in the long run, by changing the system. The party was not yet willing to devote its energies to finding ways of *managing* capitalism. Indeed, the efforts of the Labour Party moderates tended to be absorbed in the defensive task of countering the arguments of the left, which had now regained its self-confidence and its voice.

THE ILP: UNDERCONSUMPTION AND SOCIALIST ECONOMICS

After 1920, the ILP once more became the main forum for the discussion of new economic ideas. The driving force was Clifford Allen, the wartime pacifist leader, who wanted to reinvigorate the ILP's activities by attracting radical intellectuals into the party to help formulate a more coherent, attractive case for socialism. Initially, the ILP had no programme to compare with *Labour and the New Social Order*, and when it did secure agreement in 1922, it managed to unite (at least on fundamental questions, though not always on details)[37] behind a guild socialist position just in time to witness the collapse of guild socialism as an effective doctrine.

However, after 1923, the ILP's deliberations began to be dominated by the immediate problem of unemployment, and great contributions were made by the middle-class experts brought into the party by Allen.[38] The most influential were J. A. Hobson, E. F. Wise, H. N. Brailsford and E. M. H. Lloyd (who was not a member of the ILP, but was frequently consulted by Allen). Hobson's main contribution was the development of the underconsumptionist analysis which gave theoretical justification to the ILP's longstanding demand for the living wage.[39] Lloyd, through his

[37] Adrian Oldfield, 'The Independent Labour Party and Planning', *International Review of Social History*, 21, 1976, p. 9.

[38] Fenner Brockway, *Inside the Left: Thirty Years of Platform, Press, Prison and Parliament*, London, New Leader, 1942, p. 144; Arthur Marwick, *Clifford Allen: The Open Conspirator*, Edinburgh, Oliver & Boyd, 1964, p. 84.

book *Stabilisation*, brought the ILP to a better understanding of the role of financial policy and to a more workable model of planning than that of the guild socialists.[40] Finally, J. M. Keynes's articles for the *Manchester Guardian* and the *Nation* exerted great influence, though from a much greater distance.[41] Interestingly, none of these 'unorthodox' economists can legitimately be counted as 'socialists'; all were following the reformist path of building a stronger, more equitable capitalism. Yet their ideas, at least in the early 1920s, had their greatest impact on the explicitly socialist wing of the Labour Party.

However, before we consider the mature socialist mixture of Hobson, Keynes and Lloyd, we must take account of a reformist cocktail made from the same blend and which was fully compatible with the continuation of capitalism. This was Mosley's role in the ILP. He had joined both the Labour Party and the ILP in 1924, and almost immediately had switched his interests from foreign to domestic economic policy.[42] Like the Webbs, Mosley preferred an empirical, inductive approach to problems, and

[39] Hobson began his campaign within socialist circles for redistribution justified by an underconsumptionist analysis in the *Socialist Review*, Feb. 1922. At the core of his view was a belief that production would inevitably outrun consumption, causing a glut of commodities. This trend could be corrected only by periodic crises of the capitalist sytem; the trade cycle. Overproduction was caused by a maldistribution of income, with far too much going to rentiers and entrepreneurs. These groups were forced to choose between investing in new productive capacity or hoarding. If income were redistributed more equally among the whole population, consumption would be better sustained, less would be available for investment, and the tendency towards over-rapid growth of productive capacity would be overcome. *The Economics of Unemployment*, London, Allen & Unwin, 1922.

[40] Like Keynes, Lloyd argued that the function of monetary policy should be to stabilize internal prices rather than the exchanges (*Stabilisation: An Economic Policy for Producers and Consumers*, London, Allen & Unwin, 1923, pp. 49–50). This could be achieved if central banks cooperated in the regulation of credit not by reference to national stocks of gold, but according to trends in production and trade. The aggregate effect would be world price stabilization (p. 78). Stabilization of domestic prices was to be facilitated by centralized purchase of food and raw materials on long-term contracts; this reflected the lessons Lloyd had drawn from his wartime work in food control.

[41] The articles by Keynes in the *Manchester Guardian* of 1922 (which subsequently became *The Tract on Monetary Reform*) certainly influenced the ILP; see Oldfield, 'The ILP and Planning', p. 12. Mosley began reading Keynes in 1923, and was greatly taken by the arguments of the *Tract*: Robert Skidelsky, *Oswald Mosley*, London, Macmillan, 1975, pp. 125, 140. Later Brailsford explicitly acknowledged Keynes's connection between credit expansion and the growth of employment (*New Leader*, 28 Aug. 1923). At this stage, the left had not become thoroughly suspicious of Keynes, as was to be the case after collaboration between Keynes and Lloyd George in the mid-1920s. Relations between Keynes and the left were rather sour in the 1930s. See chapter 6.

[42] Skidelsky, *Oswald Mosley*, pp. 131, 133.

worshipped at the shrine of efficiency; unlike the Webbs, Mosley was not cluttered by the intellectual baggage of orthodox economics; he did not assume free trade, budgetary balance and the gold standard as fixtures of the institutional environment.

Mosley was greatly impressed by the arguments of Lloyd, Keynes, Mond and others that deliberate deflation was harmful and that monetary policy ought to provide internal price stability rather than stable exchange rates.[43] Both Mosley and his close collaborator, John Strachey, were greatly influenced by Keynes's *Tract on Monetary Reform* and his articles for the *Nation*. From this perspective, they began to criticize the ILP, somewhat unfairly, for its lack of a credit policy and ignorance about banking. The Mosley plan presented to the ILP conference in 1925 was to nationalize the banking system and, through it, to issue consumer credits to the unemployed and producer credits to manufacturers with the object of stimulating demand in the economy.

His most detailed statement of policy came later in the year with the publication of *Revolution by Reason*. Mosley accurately observed that deflation had reduced demand below the level which would guarantee full employment. He considered, but rejected as inadequate, redistribution — it was only a minor operation to be undertaken once the stimulation of demand, by credit expansion, had gathered momentum. In this way, the working class would receive greater benefit than by the mere redistribution of the existing national income.[44] Thus Mosley's analysis was not Hobsonian underconsumptionist, but Keynesian. The key to any solution was to expand credit, but, according to Mosley, this policy could take either a socialist or a capitalist path. Capitalist expansion would result in inflation; capitalism lacked a coordinating intelligence, and credit expansion would feed through into higher prices not higher production. The primary responsibility for planning a socialist credit expansion would fall upon an Economic Council, whose main task would be to 'estimate the difference between the actual and potential production of the country and to plan the steps by which that potential production can be evoked through the instrument of working class demand.'[45] To stimulate mass consumption, the wages paid by individual firms would be fixed at relatively generous levels, and firms would be forced to accept overdrafts from the nationalized banks, leaving private industry in the hands of the Economic Council. Producer credits would also be given to manufacturers in socially useful industries to raise output and lower prices. His most original

---

[43] For the views of Mond, see chapter 4.
[44] Oswald Mosley, *Revolution by Reason*, London, ILP Publications, 1935, pp. 16–17.
[45] Ibid., pp. 14–15.

contribution was on trade and payments. Mosley rejected the gold standard, preferring a floating exchange rate, and even criticized the preoccupation with the export industries. He hoped to replace some imports with domestic production and to keep down the aggregate import bill by the bulk purchase of food and raw materials on long contracts on favourable terms. In this way, Britain would need to export less to pay for her lower total imports.

By any standards, *Revolution by Reason* was an impressive pamphlet. Mosley identified the major constraints to expansionist policies – 'sound' money and the high exchange rate – and proposed the basis of workable policies on both counts.[46] Mosley's main problem was that he had chosen the wrong audience. *Revolution by Reason* was essentially reformist. True, nationalization of the banks was an essential ingredient and the document was sprinkled with socialist rhetoric, but Mosley's goal was a planned, *mixed* economy. But in the mid-1920s the ILP was deeply suspicious of reformism, and Mosley was denied the support and the close, sympathetic criticism his proposals undoubtedly merited.

At the same time, the ILP's own internal economic policy discussions were beginning to bear fruit. When he was elected chairman of the ILP in 1923, Allen established a number of expert inquiry commissions.[47] The most significant was that on the living wage, chaired by J. A. Hobson, and comprising H. N. Brailsford (Allen's nominee as editor of the ILP's journal, *New Leader*), E. F. Wise and Arthur Creech Jones. The commission produced an interim report, *Socialism in our Time*, which was debated at the 1926 ILP conference, and its final report, *The Living Wage*, was published in September of the same year.

The Living Wage was much closer to the mood of the ILP. Most ILPers wanted to dissociate themselves from the record of the MacDonald government and from the whole gradualistic strategy.[48] Although influenced by the same works as Mosley, the ILP proposals were very different in shape and direction. Not surprisingly, there was more Hobson than Keynes in *The Living Wage*, and the analysis of unemployment was explicitly underconsumptionist.[49] The commission thought that consumption could be sustained more effectively by redistribution than by

[46] Both programmes were workable, in the sense that they appear to have been reasonably internally consistent, to have identified most of the main problems involved in pursuing their chosen policies, and to have devised policies to meet these difficulties.

[47] Marwick, *Clifford Allen*, pp. 84–5.

[48] A substantial segment of ILP opinion went further and held that capitalism was in its death throes, and the days of gradualism had gone. Dowse, *Left in the Centre*, pp. 120–2.

[49] H. N. Brailsford, John A. Hobson, A. Creech Jones and E. F. Wise, *The Living Wage*, London, ILP Publications, 1926, pp. 8–12.

credit expansion (which would merely perpetuate the problems of mal-distribution and working-class underconsumption). Redistribution would be effected by more steeply progressive taxation and a system of family allowances to provide additional income for families with children. Secondly, there would be minimum wages fixed by law at a level sufficient for a couple. The authors did not specify their ideal target for the living income they proposed, but hinted at a figure twice the average annual working-class income.[50]

Hobson may have been the driving force behind the importance given to underconsumptionist analysis, but it was Brailsford who went on to use the living-wage idea as a foundation for a fully socialist policy.[51] Like Keynes, Lloyd and Mosley, Brailsford rejected the deflationary financial policies of the early 1920s, and wanted instead a policy which aimed at stability of internal prices rather than of the exchange rate. This meant bringing the Bank of England under political control – by nationalization (a policy favoured by Mosley). *The Living Wage* also called for a socialist industrial policy, since it was likely that some industries would not be able to pay full, living wages. First, 'key' sectors (such as banking, coal, electricity supply and the railways) would have to be nationalized to bring about price reductions.[52] Even with this benefit to their costs, some industries would still be weak and would have to submit to a thorough inquiry and compulsory reorganization in return for subsidies to pay the higher living wages. An Industrial Commission would be established for this work and would be empowered to create 'selling agencies' and to foster a 'genuine measure' of workers' control.[53]

On foreign trade, where Mosley had been so perceptive, *The Living Wage* was less convincing, but still ahead of any previous ILP or Labour Party programme. The authors recognized the threat of unbalanced trade, particularly from a drop in exports. Their remedy was to aim for greater self-sufficiency, using state control of investment to develop import substitutes. Essential imports would be subject to E. M. H. Lloyd's widely copied device of bulk purchase and the government would also become involved in international market-sharing agreements. In the longer term, Britain could protect its balance of payments only by fighting

[50] Ibid., p. 32.

[51] These arguments had been well to the fore in pieces written for the *New Leader* by Brailsford, and published later as *Socialism for Today*, London, ILP Publications, 1925. See especially pp. 120–1, which contain a glowing acknowledgement to E. M. H. Lloyd and J. M. Keynes.

[52] *The Living Wage*, pp. 37–8.

[53] The procedure of investigation, subsidy and reorganization was deliberately copied from the treatment of the coalmining industry in 1925–6 by the Baldwin government.

for living wages in competitor countries. Clearly, a little of Mosley's unorthodoxy would have greatly strengthened this aspect of the plan.

It is difficult to avoid the conclusion that neither *Revolution by Reason* nor *The Living Wage* have been accorded the attention they deserve. Both were incisive, coherent programmes with much greater realism than anything produced by contemporary academic economists.[54] They recognize that the economy of the 1920s was not a self-righting mechanism, both implicitly assume the multiplier, and both note the crucial importance of monetary demand in determining the level of employment. In both programmes, the major constraint against a more thorough examination of expansionist policies was adherence to a fairly crude quantity theory of money.[55] But both reached the conclusion that monetary expansion could only proceed *without* inflation if controls were used to prevent price rises and measures were taken to encourage production. It is hard to resist the conclusion that the ILP and the Labour Party suffered because it simply did not have enough trained expert economists to work on and improve these plans through discussion and research. At a more general level, both programmes reflect the widespread conviction, which extended beyond the labour movement, that economic problems would respond to a more vigorous application of science to industry. Within labour circles, it was thought that the vested interests within private capital were now blocking innovation and technology, so public ownership was increasingly seen as a means of exploiting British inventiveness. The other common feature was the re-emergence of centralized planning and *dirigisme* in socialist economic thinking. The brief flirtation with devolved decision-making and workers' control was effectively dead.

THE LABOUR PARTY IN THE LATE TWENTIES

Despite the coherence of the economic ideas circulating within the ILP, the impact on the Labour Party was marginal. The ILP had begun to disintegrate as a political force; membership had declined, factions become less tolerant, and less willing to unite behind a single pro-

[54] For the lack of 'realism' among university economists at this time, see K. J. Hancock, 'Unemployment and the Economists in the 1920s', *Economica*, 27, 1960, p. 319.

[55] For a brief period in 1925 Mosley defended the post-*General Theory* Keynesian position that, following monetary expansion, output would increase without inflation up to the point at which all factors of production were employed. Only monetary expansion beyond this point would produce inflation. However, he seems to have moved back quickly to his 'unorthodox' quantity position. See Skidelsky, *Oswald Mosley*, pp. 142–3.

gramme.[56] Powerful groups within the ILP refused to accept the programme in *The Living Wage*. Furthermore, *The Living Wage* antagonized the unions at a time of more cordial relations between the TUC and the Labour Party. Fundamentally, the ILP policy implied a fight for socialism across a broad front; accordingly, it was rejected by the leadership. Party moderates were once more becoming impatient with internal criticism, especially from the left; the prospect of office was looming once more. The strengths of *The Living Wage* were allowed to evaporate, or were channelled into harmless dead-ends. The 'living income' proposal was reduced to a joint Labour Party–TUC commission to examine family allowances. But the TUC regarded family allowances as a threat to union wage rates, and saw any ILP intervention into the wages question with the deepest suspicion. The commission took four years to report, and even then was divided. Other ILP proposals were defeated at Labour Party conferences. In fact, the Labour Party was moving steadily away from the ILP and towards the TUC as the organization upon which it relied for new policy ideas. The introduction of a strong and continuous trade-union contact at a time when the unions, following the debacle of the general strike, were determined to act with restraint and caution, injected a still more moderate strand into Labour Party thinking. In effect, the result of the general strike was to push all opposition groups into competition for the centre ground with similar proposals for expansion through a major public works programme and the introduction of more rigorous planning to improve the competitive performance of British industry.[57]

The first bid by the TUC–Labour alliance for the centre ground is evident in *On the Dole or Off!*, the first major collaborative enterprise since 1921. Trade-union consciousness revealed itself in the proposals for early retirement, raising the school-leaving age, and better training opportunities for the war generation.[58] More adventurously the document favoured increasing the public works effort, planned and promoted by a new Economic Development Board. The work would be financed from a fund which the government would create during prosperous times by setting aside annually £10 million to finance work during depressions. There were also hints that Labour was prepared to go further and embrace deliberate deficit finance if the programme were to begin during a depression. The Economic Development Board was also to 'promote the

---

[56] Dowse, *Left in the Centre*, ch. 11.

[57] For the Liberals, see chapter 2, and for the YMCA Tories, see chapter 3, pp. 56–8.

[58] *On the Dole or Off! What to do with Britain's Workless Workers: Report on the Prevention of Unemployment* by a Joint Committee representing the General Council of the Trades Union Congress, the National Executive Committee of the Labour Party, and the Executive of the Parliamentary Labour Party, London, 1926, pp. 6–8.

cooperative and scientific development of resources and economic possibilities', in part by helping industry with research and development. However, echoing Webb in 1924, the board was also to look to empire development and emigration.

The mixture was very similar to that of the Liberals at this time and, like the Liberals, Labour could not cast aside the strong orthodox element in its economic thought, especially when an election was imminent. Despite the more radical sections of *On the Dole or Off!* Labour needed a commitment to sound finance to demonstrate its moderation. The first shot in its election programme was *Labour and the Nation*, a vague, rambling document which, at MacDonald's insistence, indicated only the direction in which Labour hoped to move rather than offering any specific promises.[59] When it came for discussion before conference in 1928, *Labour and the Nation* had acquired an equally vague supplement on currency and finance. In fact, the main feature of the debate on economic and financial policy had little to do with anything in *Labour and the Nation* or its supplement, but concerned a statement by Snowden of the leadership's views on financial policy. He made it clear that there would be no deliberate attempt to use the budget as an instrument for creating jobs by a future Labour government:

> I have seen and I know something of the danger of the control of credit and the means of starting an inflation policy, and it might be highly dangerous in the hands of a Government that wanted to use this means in order to serve some purpose or to gain popular support. We know there is going to be a General Election in nine months' time. What would be the greatest cry for this election? In those nine months to have reduced the unemployed from 1¼ millions to a quarter of a million, and an unprincipled Government in the absolute control of currency and credit could do that, but they would do it at a terrible price which the country would have to pay sooner or later . . . That is a power I am not prepared to put without reserve and control into the hands of any political government.[60]

More depressing than Snowden's speech was the failure of the ILP to mount any criticism or to ask Snowden to specify what the terrible costs of the credit expansion to which both the ILP (in *The Living Wage*) and the Labour Party (in *On the Dole or Off!*) seem to have been committed. Instead, the ILPers were much more concerned with machinery – whether the central and joint-stock banks should be nationalized – than with policies or purposes. In the event, the supplement was accepted without

[59] *Labour Party Conference Reports*, 1928, p. 197.
[60] Ibid., pp. 231–2.

division and the commitment to deficit finance, which could have been used to scare voters away from Labour, was dropped.

The other main casualty of the 1928 conference was nationalization, as it had been in 1923 when the prospect of office had first appeared. *Labour and the Nation* proposed for 'the great foundation industries' that they 'shall be administered for the common advantage of the whole community' and promised an unhurried, piecemeal programme, listing the now familiar candidates. Efficiency, not socialism, was the touchstone. Moreover, by the time Labour had gained office in 1929, socialist nationalization seemed still further away as a result of agreements the TUC had reached in the Mond–Turner conferences. As we shall see, these talks between leading trade unionists and industrialists came to support the reorganization of industry into larger, more research-oriented units which would remain in private ownership.[61] Although the TUC moved on very quickly to link this proposal to state control, in 1929 simple rationalization seemed very attractive to a Labour Party trying to portray itself as a party of moderation, efficiency and a national perspective.

When it came to power, Labour confirmed the impression that radical policies would not be attempted and that its move to the centre since 1926 would not be reversed. Once more, MacDonald's strategy was to use his dependence upon Liberal votes to block his own left wing. The appointment of Snowden as Chancellor of the Exchequer again promised rigid financial orthodoxy. If there would be no new policies to counter Britain's economic problems, at least the machinery was different. MacDonald established a Cabinet team on unemployment, led by J. H. Thomas, with Lansbury, Mosley and Tom Johnson.[62] An innovative policy did seem possible, especially if Thomas could be prevailed upon to extract an expansionist policy from Snowden. However, Thomas and Snowden had agreed at the outset that 'inflation' (credit expansion), subsidies and protection were out.[63] Instead, Thomas began with a small, five-year programme of road-building, loan guarantees (rather than loans) for public authorities for developmental works, and help to colonial development. Indeed, the imperial slant was underlined by his visit to Canada and his involvement in the Colonial Development Act. Thomas also busied himself with rationalization, both in the Coal Act of 1930 and, less formally, by using his wide industrial and financial contacts to bring

---

[61] See below, pp. 85–7, 96–7.

[62] In many ways, this was an extremely promising group. Thomas was spoken of as a future Labour leader; despite his advanced age Lansbury had incomparable radical credentials; and both Mosley and Johnston were 'coming men' of the ILP. These appointments promised, initially at least, a radical innovative policy.

[63] Skidelsky, *Oswald Mosley*, p. 181.

bankers and industrialists together to support the re-equipment of industry.[64] But unemployment was rising and Labour's economic policy was in disarray. For new ideas, Labour turned to the experts; Snowden established the Macmillan Committee on Finance and Industry, and MacDonald called together the Economic Advisory Council, a 'think tank' of economists, trade unionists and businessmen.

It was against this background that Mosley produced new ideas to cure unemployment. Since *Revolution by Reason*, Mosley had visited America (in 1926) and had been greatly impressed by Ford's assembly line in Detroit. The fact that the producer of the cheapest car also paid the highest wages captured Mosley's imagination. After his return, he remained an active proponent of credit expansion, but with little impact on the party's programme. In office, he had endured a particularly frustrating period, having had his proposals for early retirement blocked, and having had no success in persuading Ministers and local authorities to spend more on public works. By Decmber 1929, Mosley was convinced that change was needed.

The memorandum Mosley circulated to his colleagues consisted of four sections: the first dealt with the machinery of government; the second with long-term planning of permanent reconstruction; the third with short-term relief of unemployment; and the last with credit policy.[65] Under long-term planning, Mosley supported Thomas's emphasis on rationalization and mergers to promote industrial efficiency. But Mosley wanted effort concentrated on industries supplying the home market. The analysis of *Revolution by Reason*, his glimpse of the American exploitation of its domestic market, and the problems for exporters all convinced Mosley that the imperial vision was misplaced. Mosley doubted whether the banks could secure this type of rationalization because they were so heavily involved with the export industries. No matter what direction rationalization took, Mosley recognized that there would be a short-term rise in unemployment. He considered a public works programme essential to absorb workers displaced by rationalization. To meet this need, he put forward again the ideas which had already been rejected: early retirement, raising the school-leaving age, and more generous grants for public works, particularly road-building. In the manner of the Liberal Yellow Book, the whole scheme would be financed by borrowing. Mosley also called for easier credit to give Britain a full-employment, high-wage economy based on a large home market and cheap money, similar to that which he had

[64] Ibid., p. 174.

[65] See the two studies by Robert Skidelsky, *Politicians and the Slump: The Labour Government, 1929–31*, Harmondsworth, Penguin Books, 1970, ch. 8; and *Oswald Mosley*, chs 9 and 10.

seen in America in 1926. Mosley recognized that to undertake this programme a new division of political responsibility would be needed. As Mosley knew only too well, the Thomas experiment had failed. He argued that since unemployment policy was the responsibility of several 'spending' Ministers, the only effective coordinator was the Prime Minister, who would be assisted by a secretariat of high permanent officials and advisory experts. This revolution in the machinery of government was the only really new element in the Mosley memorandum.

As a whole, this was an unexceptional programme, far less radical than *Revolution by Reason*. Socialization of banking and credit had disappeared along with all the other nationalization proposals; consumer and producer credits had been replaced by simple public works expansion as the main vehicle to increase credit. It was very much a reformist programme; the attempt of a junior Minister to persuade senior colleagues to redirect and expand existing policies. Even this was too much for the Cabinet. After consideration by Ministers, the Mosley Memorandum was rejected, as, subsequently, were modified versions by the PLP and the party conference.

Such a decisive repudiation by a party committed to parliamentary socialism is, at first, difficult to comprehend. Miliband has convincingly argued that the logic of British parliamentary socialism has been the progressive abandonment of socialist objectives for narrower, more opportunist aims and, in particular, for parliamentary careerism.[66] The Mosley Memorandum ought to have suited these tactics admirably. Yet the rejection was complete, and there is precious little evidence of Mosley and the PLP leadership sharing a common analysis of Britain's economic problems. What, then, were Labour's objections? The first was undoubtedly the threat to financial orthodoxy. Even the proponents of a radical credit policy gave little attention, beyond calling for the nationalization of the banking system, to the ways in which the policy was to be managed, especially under a gold standard. The best illustration of the orthodoxy of the Labour Party was the reaction to Snowden's appointment of the May Committee to propose 'economies' in public finance as the budgetary position began to deteriorate in 1931. There was an outcry over where the cuts might fall, especially over unemployment benefits, but relative silence about the principle of balancing the budget during depression. Secondly, the trade-union consciousness, which was becoming strong in the Labour Party in the late 1920s, made it difficult to cope with unemployment which was increasingly structural and intractable. The *raison d'être* of unions is to defend jobs, particularly in areas like

[66] *Parliamentary Socialism*, passim.

the export industries where the unions were powerful. Mosley's invitation to Ministers to consider a reorientation of the British economy away from these areas was bound to cause trouble with the unions and in many constituency strongholds. Similarly, Labour was reluctant to propose public works as a make-work expedient for expanding demand; hole-digging compromised proper union standards. Public works had to be for socially necessary schemes and provide satisfactory rates and conditions. The final obstacle was a continuing suspicion of a more interventionist state, especially in economic affairs. Popular opinion, and the vast majority of socialists, equated intervention with 'socialism'. This should have held no problems for a party pledged to achieving socialism by constitutional means, but, in practice, every new interventionist measure was a potential electoral liability as it could be portrayed as 'socialist', and hence 'immoderate' and 'unreasonable' by opposition parties.

The logical course would have been for the party to have renounced its socialist aspirations and to have concentrated more explicitly on efficiency and redistribution. Such have been the tactics of the Labour Party between 1950 and 1975, and they would have been consistent with the actual content of party programmes in the 1920s. Under these conditions, state intervention might have been less contentious. But, as we have noted, the socialist constitution of the party had been a triumph for even the moderate socialists of the Webbian efficiency school, and the doctrine of parliamentary socialism seemed to be an effective banner behind which moderates and militants could unite. The party declined both to try to overthrow capitalism and to follow the reformist tack of trying to understand capitalism better, to be able to correct its worst defects. Devoid of a commitment to either a socialist or a managed capitalist economy, the Labour Cabinet could only persist with its claims that unemployment was an inevitable part of capitalism, and watch as capitalist economic events unfolded to tear it apart.

Mosley, on the other hand, had a freer run to develop his ideas once he had resigned from the Cabinet. Although his picture of the political machinery necessary to manage unemployment policy took him eventually to a form of corporatism, his economic analysis of unemployment throughout remained that of the mid–1920s. The failure was essentially a lack of domestic demand, exacerbated by the 'export fetish'. Over-concentration on the staples encouraged demands for wage cuts, but, to Mosley, the result would be lower demand and higher unemployment. Expansion of the domestic market would reduce unemployment, and, to this end, monetary policies should favour industry rather than exchange stability. Further, since market forces could not effect a rapid structural change to a more domestically oriented economy, government would have to intervene much more in economic affairs.

Mosley's view on the form this intervention should take soon persuaded him to leave the Labour Party. After the Labour conference had rejected his ideas, Mosley prepared for his departure by gathering round him an all-party group of younger, impatient MPs. For them, Mosley produced the Manifesto, which was profoundly to influence centre radical opinion.[67] He urged the appointment of a super-Cabinet of five non-departmental Ministers, with emergency powers for a limited period to deal with the crisis. The home market was to be insulated by tariffs and other restrictive devices, to be managed by Commodity and Import Control Boards. The object was to build an imperial trading bloc. The Commodity Boards would grant protection only if standards of efficiency, prices and wages were maintained.[68] Here was the instrument to supervise long-term reconstruction. In the shorter term, public works, especially housing and slum clearance, were to be supervised by a state Public Utility Organization. Most importantly, economic development was to be *planned*, rather than left to market forces.

The next shot was fired by four socialist Mosleyites in *A National Policy*, published in February 1931, two months after the Manifesto.[69] A National Planning Council would coordinate the Commodity and Import Boards (on which consumers and workers would be represented) and the National Investment Board which was to mobilize and allocate capital. Significantly, reflecting the political sympathies of the authors, Anglo-Russian as well as inter-imperial trade was to be encouraged. Here was the policy of the New Party, formed by Mosley in March 1931.

Mosley's New Party enjoyed a brief, spectacular existence. It was split when the socialists defected, worried by the fascist direction of Mosley's ideas, and was routed at the 1931 election. From these ashes, Mosley built the British Union of Fascists. Here he developed his corporate theories. The machinery of Commodity Boards made up of representatives of employers and workers was now transformed into the Industrial Corporation, subject not to a Planning Council but to an industrial parliament, the National Council for Corporations. At this level, the national plan would be drawn up and, within its framework, each corporation would set its own prices, wages, conditions of employment, investment strategies, and so on. In this planned, united society, strikes would be abolished. The

[67] See, in particular, chapter 3.

[68] Mosley discusses his proposals in *My Life*, London, Nelson, 1968, ch. 15.

[69] Allen Young, John Strachey, W. J. Brown and Aneurin Bevan, *A National Policy*, London, Macmillan, 1931.

imperial trading bloc remained, but justified by racial as well as economic arguments. Mosley's long-standing antipathy towards financial interests was now vindicated by accusations that international financiers were conspiring to undermine national economies, and his bias towards undemocratic leadership was presented as a way to smash the vested interests of the 'Old Gang' in politics. Underlying everything was his fear that for western nations the apocalypse was at hand.

It was a tragedy for the Labour Party that it could not accommodate Mosley's perceptive analysis in 1930 to help it to the reformist path it had approached during the 1920s. In the event, the manner of Mosley's rejection seemed only to confirm his prejudices and encourage his later, wilder excesses which, justifiably, put him beyond the pale of British politics.

2

The Liberal Yellow Book

In the late 1920s, the Liberal Party issued two statements on economic policy which, despite their rather lukewarm initial reception, have come to be regarded as highly important stages on the road to modern economic policy. The massive 'Yellow Book', *Britain's Industrial Future*, is a detailed examination of the British economy in the mid-twenties, taking in industrial relations, the condition and structure of British industry, financial policy and the development of domestic resources.[1] Some months after the publication of the Yellow Book and with an eye on the 1929 general election, Lloyd George and Seebohm Rowntree took those sections which dealt with curing unemployment and public works, rewrote them in greater detail for a mass audience, added a specific commitment to cure unemployment and presented it as *We Can Conquer Unemployment*, the Liberal 'Orange Book'.[2]

The two documents have been highly praised, in large part because they were proto-Keynesian analyses; arguments for an expansionist monetary and fiscal policy. Keynes was, indeed, closely involved in the production of the Yellow Book, and, more generally, in the running of the Liberal Summer Schools which acted as a forcing ground for the party's new ideas. Thus the assessment of the Yellow and Orange Books rests largely on their contribution to economic theory, and has been made, in the main, by historians of economic thought.[3] The politics of the Liberal programme have been largely ignored, which is curious since both Books were overtly political; indeed, the Orange Book was an election manifesto. Now that Keynesian ideas have lost some of their former gloss and with the current developments in centre progressive politics, it is time to re-

[1] *Britain's Industrial Future: being the Report of the Liberal Industrial Inquiry*, London, Ernest Benn, 1928.

[2] *We Can Conquer Unemployment: Mr Lloyd George's Pledge*, London, Cassell, 1929.

[3] See, for example, Donald Winch, *Economics and Policy: A Historical Study*, London, Hodder & Stoughton, 1969, ch. 3; Jim Tomlinson, *Problems of British Economic Policy, 1870–1945*, London, Methuen, 1981, ch. 1.

examine these Books with a slightly different perspective, based more firmly upon the party political struggle in the years following the first world war.

LIBERALISM AND RADICALISM

The study of Liberal industrial policy must begin with the split in the party in 1916, when Lloyd George captured the premiership, and Asquith stubbornly refused to hold subordinate office. The radical nonconformists and the provincial businessmen in the Liberal ranks remained with Lloyd George whilst the rich metropolitan financiers joined Asquith in opposition. The radical reformers had finally separated from the orthodox anti-interventionists, and with this split the Liberals lost their foothold in the class politics of the twentieth century.[4] Thereafter, a Liberal revival was dependent upon either a realignment of centre parties or a *rapprochement* between the two wings of the party and their embittered leaders.

At first, Lloyd George appeared to have forged new alliances in the centre by drawing business and labour leaders into decision-making and securing parliamentary support from Labour and the Conservative back-benches. Decisions on economic policy were taken, not by Parliament, but by mediation between representatives of government, industry and the unions.[5] This system of tripartite bargaining is both pragmatic and opportunist; there is little room for ideological commitment. It is effective only for as long as consensus is possible, and subsequent experience has shown that as soon as deep social divisions emerge, the Lloyd George model cannot operate.[6] In 1918, these difficulties were still in the future, and Lloyd George was riding high, though more intent on consensus than radicalism.

The Asquithians, on the other hand, were in a miserable state. They were denied the support of the governing coalition at the 1918 general election, and lost all their leaders to leave a mere rump which considered disbanding altogether. Not surprisingly, they resented Lloyd George, and began to despise him as the scandal broke over the sale of honours and the accumulation of the Lloyd George private fund. More important in the longer run was their complete lack of a realistic political programme.

[4] The argument that the Liberals had managed to come to terms with the new electoral conditions of the twentieth century is put forward by P. F. Clarke in 'The Electoral Sociology of Modern Britain', *History*, 57, 1972, pp. 38–9.

[5] Keith Middlemas, *Politics in Industrial Society: The British Experience of the System Since 1911*, London, André Deutsch, 1979, ch. 5.

[6] Middlemas's analysis of the period since 1965 is most illuminating in this light. See ibid., ch. 15.

Their nineteenth-century concern with temperance and dissent was no longer of immediate interest, and their bias against government intervention in the economy seemed quaint when nationalization and social reconstruction were the crucial political issues. However, they did retain the considerable advantage of freedom from corruption, and they remained the vigorous defenders of free trade, a doctrine which continued to exert a great hold over working-class voters. These virtues were enough to retain the allegiance of a large number of radical intellectuals who remained unsympathetic to socialism and the Labour Party. This group was of vital importance in overcoming the political bankruptcy of orthodox Liberalism at the end of the first world war.

Immediately after the war, conditions could not have been worse for a Liberal revival, whether by a Lloyd George-led realignment or by reconciliation between the two leaders. Britain was torn by severe class conflict which polarized society and presented the Liberals with few opportunities to find a centre path.[7] Lloyd George's attempt to restructure the centre of British politics came to a swift and disastrous conclusion. As we have seen, the Labour Party had moved towards socialism during the war, and withdrew from the coalition to fight the 1918 election with its own policies to further working-class political and economic interests.[8] The new programme and constitution, with Sidney Webb's careful blend of socialist and reformist proposals, helped cut the radical ground from beneath Lloyd George at the same time as the Conservative majority in the coalition and economic circumstances drove the Lloyd George Liberals inexorably to the right. The coalition did have opportunities to cultivate the centre ground with social reconstruction, but the measures were inadequately prepared and fundamental problems were ignored.[9] The arrival in 1920 of a full-scale international economic downturn unleashed a broadly based demand for retrenchment and orthodoxy, which took Lloyd George still further from his radical roots.

Conditions were also difficult for the orthodox Liberal Party, but a group of Manchester Liberals including Ramsay Muir, Ernest Simon and E. T. Scott had met in 1920 to formulate a modern, progressive industrial policy for their party at a time when industrial unrest had reached record levels and the intense class conflict was also evident in controversy over the nationalization of industry. The result was Muir's book *Liberalism and Industry*, in which he recommended, *inter alia*, governing councils for each industry to fix wages and conditions and establish profit-sharing schemes,

[7] B. A. Waites, 'The Effect of the First World War on Class and Status in England, 1910–1920', *Journal of Contemporary History*, 11, 1976.

[8] See above, pp. 7–12.

[9] Philip Abrams, 'The Failure of Social Reform, 1918–20', *Past and Present*, 24, 1963.

nationalization of the railways and the mines, housing provided by public finance and regulated by town planners, free education to university level, yet 'the most rigid economy in national expenditure' was to be pursued with the equally orthodox policy of debt redemption, albeit by a levy on wartime increases in wealth.[10] Although the enormous shift in political power soon after the publication of *Liberalism and Industry* prompted the disappearance of the nationalization proposals, the questions of the joint control of industry and profit-sharing remained central to progressive Liberals throughout the 1920s, because they appeared to offer a way of overcoming the deep divisions in British society after the war.[11] Less creditable, but equally persistent, was the failure to face the contradiction between a preference for expanding public spending and extremely orthodox views on financial policy.

Informed help, however, was at hand, with the offer of assistance from three Cambridge economists, Walter Layton, Hubert Henderson and Maynard Keynes. Together Manchester and Cambridge combined to establish the Liberal Summer Schools, which were conceived as a method of passing new ideas to the party faithful, to the more thoughtful politicians and to sympathetic administrators and intellectuals. The Liberal intelligentsia gave the Summer Schools its firm support, with contributions from Professors Henry Clay and L. T. Hobhouse, Dennis Robertson, Sir William Beveridge and H. A. L. Fisher in addition to the founder members. *The Daily News* published the more interesting lectures in a series of pamphlets (The 'New Way' Series), so the size of the potential audience was greatly increased. The subjects ranged from Beveridge on Insurance to Lord Astor on Temperance and Politics, but with the main emphasis on economic questions. In fact, the progressive Liberals were well equipped to publicize the new way, with the acquisition of *The Nation* in 1923 by a group chaired by Keynes. Throughout the twenties, in these and other publications, it is possible to see further development in the ideas which were to come together in the Yellow Book.

Ramsay Muir gave a more concise version of his vision of the direction for new Liberalism to the first Summer School,[12] but the focus of progressive thought soon shifted from ideological questions to the nature and causes of unemployment. The first contribution came from a group of Liberals chaired by Walter Layton and including J. J. Astor, A. L.

[10] Ramsay Muir, *Liberalism and Industry: Towards a Better Social Order*, London, Constable, 1920, p. 172.

[11] Seebohm Rowntree at this time of intense social upheaval also publicly advocated selective nationalization and the restructuring of the ownership of industry: 'Prospects and Tasks of Social Reconstruction', *Contemporary Review*, Jan. 1919.

[12] Ramsay Muir, *The New Liberalism*, London, The Daily News, 1923.

Bowley and Seebohm Rowntree, and was an empirical survey, *The Third Winter of Unemployment*.[13] The bulk of the book was taken up with reports from the main towns and cities with persistently high unemployment, but the authors did contribute an introduction in which they pointed to the severe social and psychological effects of unemployment. They suggested that the piecemeal measures which had grown since 1920 should be rationalized and coordinated. They did not find 'relief works' a satisfactory solution, but recommended instead that the government should encourage both larger-scale public works in Britain and the economic development of the colonies during depressions. These investigations were continued in the group's second publication, *Is Unemployment Inevitable?*[14] Once again the authors contributed an introductory survey focusing this time on the trade cycle and the prospects of longer-term trade expansion. The section on the trade cycle is a good indicator of the indecisiveness of progressive economic ideas at this time. Keynes's proposal that monetary policy should aim for price stability rather than a stable exchange rate was noted but considered administratively difficult and likely to create international suspicions. Nor were the authors prepared to accept that the return to the gold standard and stability of the exchanges was the correct policy. They opted instead for a further inquiry into monetary policy to examine whether it would be possible under the gold standard to use changes in Bank rate to give greater stability to the price level.[15] They repeated the earlier call for the use of public investment to smooth the trade cycle, but in the longer run they hoped that industry would revive and the economy return to full employment. On the whole, they were surprisingly optimistic about the economic future:

These figures point to certain conclusions, which may be reassuring to those holding alarmist views of the difficulty of finding employment for the increasing population. They are:

1. The problem of the increasing working population is one of the next few years only.

2. Normal emigration would reduce this problem to comparatively small dimensions.

3. If emigration became normal, the immediate problem could be entirely removed by raising the school leaving age to 16, which would withdraw from the labour market some 700,000 lads.

[13] *The Third Winter of Unemployment: A Report of an Inquiry Undertaken in the Autumn of 1922*, London, King, 1923.

[14] *Is Unemployment Inevitable? An Analysis and a Forecast. A Continuation of the Investigations Embodied in 'The Third Winter of Unemployment'*, published in 1923, London, Macmillan, 1924.

[15] Ibid., pp. 41-7.

Thus, while the increasing working population is an important element in the situation, an analysis of the figures shows that it is not in any case so serious as is sometimes supposed, and may in fact presently be found to be non-existent. *If no change occurs in the birth rate, the problem fifteen years hence may be an insufficiency of labour.*[16]

This attitude was possible only because Layton and his colleagues believed the economy to be essentially sound and, like their Manchester partners, they retained their faith that orthodox policies, albeit with minor improvements, could solve the unemployment problem.

A slightly different view was taken in *The Nation*. Henderson had been appointed editor with full independence, but he and Keynes cooperated closely during the twenties and shared the view that the modifications required to orthodox policies were rather more substantial. We have noted that Keynes wanted a monetary policy which helped domestic industry by providing stable prices, even at the cost of abandoning the objective of returning to the gold standard. He was disturbed that British financial institutions favoured the export of capital at the expense of sound domestic projects, and he wanted the state to continue to hold the responsibility for financial policy which it had been forced to accept during the war.[17] Henderson was rather more orthodox in that he hoped for restoration of the gold standard, but only after the state had experimented with an expansionist monetary policy to finance a large programme of capital development as a cure for unemployment.[18]

The final important strand in Liberal economic ideas during the early twenties came from Lloyd George himself. Abandoned by his coalition partners in 1922, Lloyd George had been forced to reassess his political strategy and look once more to the Liberal Party as his home. Spurred by Philip Kerr, his former secretary, he began to make economic policy the focus of his attentions. He, too, argued that government should start a public works programme because he was afraid that recovery might be slow. He called for public works on a massive scale to modernize the nation's social capital and, indirectly, to make Britain's industries more efficient.[19] Keynes endorsed this programme in *The Nation* and began to cooperate with Lloyd George,[20] but the internecine squabbles of the Liberal Party and the tendency of the Summer School to be hostile to

[16] Ibid., p. 9. Emphasis added.
[17] See below, pp. 166–9.
[18] H. D. Henderson, 'Will Unemployment Increase?' *The Nation*, 4 April 1925.
[19] D. Lloyd George, 'The Statesman's Task', *The Nation*, 12 April 1924.
[20] John Campbell, *Lloyd George: The Goat in the Wilderness*, London, Cape, 1977, p. 194.

Lloyd George temporarily prevented further development and full integration into the growing radical expansionist movement.

It would be wrong to present the Liberals striving hopefully forward towards progressive policies and awaiting only a release from the grip of financial orthodoxy. The early twenties saw a strengthening of one of the traditional planks of Liberal economic policy when, in 1923, Baldwin proposed a snap general election on tariff reform. The threat of general protection brought a temporary reconciliation between Asquith and Lloyd George in defence of free trade. Free trade was an indispensable part of Liberal thinking throughout the twenties even though it did not sit well with domestic expansion at a time of relative weakness in the balance of payments. Free trade was more than a traditional Liberal policy, it was one of the foundations upon which orthodoxy had been built. Free trade left very little room for government intervention to protect the balance of payments, and none if it was combined with the gold standard. It implied a continuing emphasis on the export industries as the main sources of employment and suggested only a limited effort to restructure the economy. In the early 1920s, therefore, Liberal economic thinking mirrored the state of the party – confused, divided, and unable to recognize clearly its own strengths.

THE YELLOW BOOK

Happily for the Liberals, there were forces in the mid-1920s which inevitably brought to the fore the progressive strands of the earlier proposals. First, mass unemployment, which had prompted suggestions for experimental policies, persisted and continued to provoke deep concern within the party. Secondly, radical ideas were known to be gaining currency within the Labour Party and were threatening to pre-empt a Liberal revival. But the most important stimulus to action for the Liberals, and indeed for other shades of centre progressive opinion, was the general strike. Just as the intense class conflict and industrial warfare in the years immediately after the first world war had galvanized the progressives into discussion and print, the general strike brought a new burst of activity on many fronts. The effect on the Liberals can be judged from Philip Kerr's lecture to the 1926 Summer School.

> The truth is that the General Strike revealed to the whole world that . . . there are in Britain to-day 'two Nations warring within the bosom of a single State'. On the one side there are the Trade Unions, whose members, almost

to a man, thought it their duty to obey the call of the Trade Union Congress, when it ordered them to stop the railways, close the docks, suspend road transport, silence the Press, and cut off light and power, as the means of coercing the community to yield to the miners' demands. On the other side is the rest of the community which responded with equal unanimity to the call of the lawfully constituted representatives of the nation, to come forward and maintain these vital services in being, in order to save Parliament from being compelled to yield to *force majeure*.[21]

Kerr was adamant that economic and social ruin lay ahead unless some method could be found of reuniting the nation. As Kerr was Lloyd George's confidant, we may assume that these thoughts were uppermost in the leader's mind when in 1926 he invited the Summer School to examine the industrial question in detail. He promised money from his private fund to meet the costs, and he conceded that he would have no right of veto over any proposals. Industrial relations and unemployment provided an excellent political opportunity for Lloyd George, but he needed to unite the Liberal Party behind him. The Liberal intellectuals needed Lloyd George's mass appeal and political leadership if their ideas were to have any influence over policy. Thus, despite the mutual suspicions, the Liberal Industrial Inquiry was established in 1926.

Walter Layton was appointed chairman and Ernest Simon vice-chairman. With an impressive assembly of talent at the inquiry's disposal, it divided into five main sub-committees which were led by Keynes (Industrial and Financial Organisation), Simon (Labour and Trade Unions), E. H. Gilpin (Worker Remuneration and Status), Ramsay Muir (the State and Industry), and Lloyd George (Unemployment). Direction was supplied by an executive committee which comprised the six leaders plus Hubert Henderson, C. F. G. Masterman, Seebohm Rowntree, Philip Kerr, H. L. Nathan, Sir Herbert Samuel and Sir John Simon. The team had its own 'economic adviser' in Hubert Phillips, and secured the services of Ralph Brand, L. T. Hobhouse, Dennis Robertson and Sir Josiah Stamp. It was not without expertise.

The inquiry worked through most of 1927. Each sub-committee prepared material for submission to the executive committee, which then considered the material as a whole and brought the report to its final shape. Henderson undertook much of the drafting.

As a whole, the Yellow Book gives a fascinating insight into Liberal economic thinking in the twenties. Setting themselves apart from the Labour Party progressives, the Liberals thought private ownership and enterprise superior to any alternative economic system, but that the

---

[21] Philip Kerr, *The Industrial Dilemma*, London, The Daily News, 1926.

benign use of state power, directed by impartial experts, could remedy any failures of private initiative.[22] The Liberals, in common with most inter-war radical groups, claimed to be steering a middle course between rigid *laissez-faire* and an equally stylized socialism. They saw themselves in the broad-based, radical tradition of Edwardian 'New Liberalism', but mass unemployment, the changing structure of British industry and the growth of the public sector all made enlightened state intervention inevitable and desirable in economic affairs as well as social policy. The middle way sought by the Liberals claimed to guarantee liberty against the compulsion of the socialists and the equally undemocratic forces of unrestrained private enterprise.[23]

The greatest strength of the Yellow Book was its commitment to the new ideas of the 1920s. These policies were justified by the analysis in Book One, on the problems facing British industry. Central to the whole exercise was a recognition that the export industries had suffered a permanent loss of markets and had to reduce their operations. Resources had to be transferred to the home market and this would be facilitated by channelling a large proportion of the funds destined for capital export into domestic schemes of national development. Thus the Liberals had recognized the existence of structural unemployment and were prepared to use Keynes's ideas on financial policy as a basis of their remedial measures.

The machinery of transferring resources was outlined in Book Two, 'The Organisation of Business', which was Keynes's most important contribution. He pushed forward the ideas which had seized Muir in 1920, and which Keynes himself had also explored in his Summer School lectures, 'Am I a Liberal?' and 'The End of *Laissez-Faire*'.[24] It was clear from changes taking place within business organization that there was considerable scope for the proper development of the 'public concern' within a basically free-enterprise economy. The public concern could legitimately become the major form of organization in three areas: first, where capital requirements were heavy and the gestation period was long (in these circumstances, private investment, looking for a more rapid return, would be unwilling to supply funds); secondly, where monopoly was inevitable; and, finally, where the private shareholder 'had ceased to perform a useful function'.[25] Much of this could have been taken from Adam Smith, and was being used to justify a programme very similar to

[22] The Yellow Book, ch. 10.
[23] Ibid., pp. xvii–xxi.
[24] *The Collected Writings of John Maynard Keynes*, vol. IX: *Essays in Persuasion*, London, Macmillan, 1972, Part IV, chs 2–3.
[25] The Yellow Book, p. 75.

that of the ILP which claimed a socialist paternity for its proposals!

The Liberals could not follow the ILP's recommendations that the state *direct* funds into domestic projects; it would have been totally contrary to Liberal ideas on the nature of economic freedom. The inquiry hoped that the publication of more informative business accounts would lead share-holders to restructure their portfolios in a rational way towards domestic projects where returns would be high. To encourage domestic industry, a National Investment Board would raise money in the City to finance a programme of national development. All requests to export capital would have to go through the NIB, and permission would be granted only if domestic claims on capital had been satisfied. In this key area, advice would be tendered by 'impartial' experts; an Economic General Staff would supply Ministers with coherent advice and forecasts of economic trends. By these means, the Liberals intended to include a separate capital account in the budget, leaving the cash account to cope with the more orthodox categories of public expenditure. In fact, the inquiry proposed both an expansionist investment policy and an orthodox policy of economy in the cash account, with especially severe cuts in armament spending. But, on social services, the Liberals remained true to their Edwardian initiatives; there could be no cuts under this heading, and social welfare financed out of local rates should become a charge to central government.

Of course, the whole approach implied a supply of projects of national development ready to be implemented. In part, the answer was found in the earlier Layton proposal to concentrate public spending when private industry was slack. However, the real effort to create jobs to take up the contraction of employment in the export industries would come, following Lloyd George's 1924 proposals, from the modernization of Britain's social capital by road-building, transport improvement, electrification, new housing and slum clearance. The programme was to be financed by the NIB and from levying a 'betterment tax' on the increase of land values resulting from transport improvements. Lloyd George had been searching for an effective land tax since before the first world war.

Improvement in national social capital would be backed by an agricultural policy designed to increase Britain's self-sufficiency both by settling more people on the land, particularly in small holdings, and by allowing tenant farmers greater security of tenure, and thereby encouraging them to improve their lands. In effect, Lloyd George had inserted his 'Green Book' on Liberal agricultural policy, complete with afforestation and the development of rural industries, into the Yellow Book.[26] He also managed to incorporate much of the argument of his

[26] *Land and the Nation: Rural Report of the Liberal Land Committee*, London, Hodder & Stoughton, 1925.

earlier inquiry into the coal industry, *Coal and Power*,[27] with recommendations for amalgamations, concentration of production, and the nationalization of mining royalties. This part of the Yellow Book shows very clear indications of having been written by Lloyd George himself. The prose style is much more urgent than elsewhere, there are numerous references to Lloyd George's own achievements in social welfare policy during previous periods of office, and only in this section of the report are there examples of the trademark of the party politician – denouncing the policies of opponents and setting new proposals within a framework of existing party commitments.

If the Yellow Book had contained only these progressive suggestions, it woud have merited much of the high regard shown to it by historians. These proposals were not without their weaknesses, but they had undoubtedly been very carefully considered, and could have made a positive contribution to the reduction of unemployment. The major problem for the Liberal Industrial Inquiry was that these ideas were not dissimilar from those of the ILP and the progressive wing of the Conservative Party.[28] The Liberals had to differentiate their radical plans from radical plans elsewhere; they had to make their separate anti-socialist bid for working-class allegiance and had to give a distinctly 'Liberal flavour' to measures which had wide circulation among those impatient with government economic policy. In this exercise, the inquiry imported irrelevant and utopian strands from the ideas of the early 1920s and tended to accentuate the weaknesses and contradictions of the programme in Books Two, Four and Five.

Book Three, on industrial relations, revealed once more the difficulties faced by radical Liberals in finding practical proposals to overcome the class antagonisms which had so undermined their party's political status. The essence of the policy in the Yellow Book was that greater industrial efficiency and harmony in workplace relations could be achieved by a high-wage policy. The proposals bore the stamp of Ramsay Muir, Philip Kerr and Seebohm Rowntree. Rowntree had long been an advocate of high wages and family allowances,[29] and Kerr had been greatly impressed by the American high-wage economy.[30] The inquiry maintained that wages should be negotiated rather than be imposed by employers, and should consist of three elements: a basic living wage; an addition in the

---

[27] *Coal and Power: The Report of an Inquiry Presided over by the Rt. Hon. D. Lloyd George*, London, Hodder & Stoughton, 1924.

[28] See above, pp. 21–6 and below, pp. 56–8.

[29] Asa Briggs, *Social Thought and Social Action: A Study of the Work of Seebohm Rowntree, 1871–1954*, London, Longmans, 1961, pp. 105–7.

[30] *The Industrial Dilemma*, pp. 44–8.

form of a family allowance for dependants; and a final element which would represent the proceeds of profit-sharing schemes, for long a favourite idea of Muir. This final portion would not be large; it was intended to foster the spread of capital ownership and of the sort of cooperation at all levels of industry which had featured so strongly in the writings of the early twenties. Under this system, workers would also be given shareholdings in any profits reinvested in the business. By these measures, cooperation in industry would lead to self-government by each industry. Guidance would be given by a separate Ministry of Industry and a tripartite Council of Industry. Though this section represents a strong and essential trend in interwar radical Liberal thought, it gravely weakened the whole of the Yellow Book. Its proposals appeared totally divorced from the realities of industrial relations in the twenties. Although the Liberals were meeting within twelve months of the general strike, there were very few references to trade unions and still fewer to ways of resolving the conflict of interest within industry. It is impossible to understand how the Liberals imagined that they could win the support of industrialists and investors for high wages and worker participation in the government of industry. The Liberals made no attempt to examine industrial relations in the mining industry, for example, where disputes over these same issues had been marked by fierce antagonisms and resistance to compromise. Trade unions and class conflict were entrenched in British industry; the Liberals could offer only pious hopes that both sides would endorse what amounted to a utopian, impractical course. The Liberals did need an industrial relations policy, but this was not it. Moreover, there were great dangers to the standing of the whole report by the inclusion of such a large dose of naive wishful thinking. In the mid-1920s, expansionist policies were still thought of as impossibly unrealistic by orthodox opinion. The Liberals could not afford to have the radical programme undermined by the flights of fancy of Kerr and Muir.

The second main weakness came from the radicals' inability to cast off the bonds of entrenched Liberal Party dogma. The case is most clearly seen in relation to the balance of payments. In the later 1920s, the British balance of payments came under increasing pressure and the Bank of England was forced to experiment with new methods of controlling the export of capital.[31] Against this background, there needed to be in the report clear methods of defending the external account because, under the gold standard, the first effect of a balance of payments deficit was a rise in interest rates which threatened employment levels. Moreover, the Liberal

[31] Donald Moggridge, *British Monetary Policy: The Norman Conquest of $4.86*, Cambridge, CUP, 1972, ch. 7.

proposal to restructure the economy to favour domestic production meant higher levels of imported raw materials, and full employment meant higher imports of food. Protection had to be ruled out on principle, but even if it had been considered on economic grounds, there were sound political reasons for the Liberal Party unreservedly to support free trade – it was one of the few unifying factors for a deeply divided party. Devaluation was another possibility to ease pressure on the balance of payments, but, once the gold standard had been restored, the Liberals gave it their blessing and dropped their earlier more progressive ideas. The Yellow Book urged: 'it ought to become part of the recognised duties of the Bank of England to regulate the volume of credit, so far as is possible, with a view to the maintenance of steady trade conditions',[32] but the inevitable conclusion is that the needs of the gold standard would have precedence over the expansionist policies. There were measures to protect the balance of payments – control over exports of capital, greater agricultural self-sufficiency, and increasing industrial efficiency – but it is difficult to believe that any would be sufficient to meet the pressure which would have undoubtedly followed higher levels of domestic economic activity.[33] The radical Liberals had not yet grasped that they were dealing with something more than a problem of slow transition from an export to a home market economy, but, even if they had, the need to maintain party unity and to distinguish the Liberal proposals from those emerging from other parts of the political spectrum made it inevitable that the party would cling to free trade and the gold standard. To a significant extent, political demands had constricted the economic thinking of the radicals.

The press comment on the Yellow Book was also far from favourable. *The Times* thought it little more than 'an incorporation of recent facts and current ideas in compendious form', whilst others criticized it as being too close to socialism or to Conservative Party ideology.[34] John Campbell, in his major study of Lloyd George between 1922 and 1931, argues that these reactions were unfair, and were prompted by a fear that the Liberals would seize the middle ground with the Yellow Book.[35] However, it is difficult to support this view. The Liberal group had produced few concrete proposals. There were, indeed, many suggestions for action, but many were simply unworkable in Britain in the late 1920s. The Yellow Book was a flawed document: an expansionist limb grafted onto a body of deep economic orthodoxy, combining perceptive economic analysis with

---

[32] The Yellow Book, p. 414.
[33] This conclusion is based on the econometric work cited above, p. 2.
[34] Campbell, *The Goat in the Wilderness*, p. 201.
[35] Ibid., pp. 200–1.

ill-judged hankering for a world free of class conflict. The economic analysis was undermined by the political requirements of a centre party which lacked a secure foothold in class politics. But the Yellow Book did raise a tantalizing question: could Lloyd George, whose political reputation had been founded on his ability to recognize what was necessary and to get things done, take the Yellow Book and fashion its more promising sections into a workable policy to reduce unemployment? But even Lloyd George was a mixed blessing for the radicals; his reputation for trickery and deceit meant that any proposals with which he was associated would attract popular suspicion and intense opposition from Conservatives and Labour.

THE ORANGE BOOK

The onus to make something politically attractive out of the Yellow Book was thrust even more squarely upon the shoulders of Lloyd George in February 1928 when the Liberal Council, the remnants of Asquith's faction, rejected the Yellow Book, preferring to remain committed to the traditional Liberal aims of retrenchment and free trade. This was undoubtedly a severe blow for the radicals who had consistently taken Asquith's side, but this rejection by Liberal orthodoxy was not without its opportunities. In theory, the radical sections of the Yellow Book could now be given greater emphasis and some of the inconsistencies could be ironed out. Yet the radicals were as committed to these true Liberal principles as was the Liberal Council. Even among the radical Liberal economists, there was no one with sufficient economic understanding or political detachment to recommend measures to strengthen the proposals of the Yellow Book.

Lloyd George was not likely to give the lead on such technical matters. Moreover, he seemed curiously ambivalent towards the report of the inquiry which he had established and in which he had participated. In his political speeches of 1928, he was very reluctant to use anything from the Yellow Book, even the public works proposals which he had championed some years earlier. Knowing that a general election had to be called before the end of 1929, he preferred to pursue informal discussions with Churchill to investigate the basis for a Liberal–Conservative pact should the election be inconclusive.[36] Significantly, free trade and a Cabinet reshuffle were higher up Lloyd George's list of priorities than an unemployment programme.[37] It was Rowntree, not Lloyd George, who

---

[36] Ibid., pp. 222–3.
[37] Ibid., p. 222.

proposed to make an expansionist programme the basis of the Liberal appeal in 1929. The experts were called in once more as Lloyd George called another series of conferences at Churt to turn his own chapter of the Yellow Book into one of the most famous of all political manifestos, *We Can Conquer Unemployment*, the Liberal Orange Book.[38]

At Churt, the 'National Development' sections of the Yellow Book were reworked to produce a number of costed public works schemes, to which were added plans to extend the telephone network and modernize London's railways. The whole programme claimed to offer work for 600,000 for two years at a cost of £250 million, which would be found in the ways indicated in the Yellow Book. Road-building would be financed out of a Road Loan and a new betterment tax on the increase in site values caused by the new roads. Much of the remaining work would be financed out of the National Development Loan suggested in the Yellow Book, and any additional calls on the Exchequer would be found from savings in expenditure on unemployment benefits and from increasing tax revenue as incomes rose. The Orange Book has long been thought an outstanding document, if only for its expansionist commitment and its practical determination to put the unemployed to work.

Despite Lloyd George's pledge,

> If the nation entrusts the Liberal Party at the next General Election with the responsibilities of Government, we are ready with schemes of work which we can put immediately into operation, work of a kind which is not merely useful in itself but essential to the well-being of the nation. The work put in hand will reduce the terrible figures of the workless in the course of a single year to normal proportions, and will, when completed, enrich the nation and equip it for competing successfully with all its rivals in the business world,[39]

there are very grave doubts whether the Liberals could conquer unemployment with the Orange Book because it contained most of the weaknesses of its predecessor and added some of its own. The public works schemes were to take up the short-term slack in the labour market and reduce costs for British industry. Beyond this, the longer-run solution to the unemployment problem lay in international cooperation to stabilize prices, freer trade, cheaper money for industry, greater industrial efficiency, new industries and labour mobility. It was crucial, therefore, that the public works should be under way quickly both to reduce the scale of the immediate problem and to begin to ease the competitive position of industry. In a very thorough survey of the Orange Book,

[38] *Social Thought and Social Action*, pp. 207–8.
[39] The Orange Book, p. 4.

Tomlinson has recently argued that a battery of administrative and technical difficulties faced any government wishing to implement at speed a major expansionist programme.[40] In fact, he endorses the practical objections raised by government officials in the White Paper issued by Baldwin as a riposte to the Liberals.[41] The administrative machine needed to carry out the Orange Book schemes within two years would have required enormous compulsory powers for central government over local authorities and suppliers of materials, and possibly even over the labour market.

The financial arrangements were taken entirely from the Yellow Book, but were now specified in much greater detail. The Liberals aimed to:

1 lower interest rates to give industry cheaper money;
2 mobilize existing idle savings, whose existence was demonstrated by a rise in the proportion of time deposits to demand deposits;
3 redirect foreign investment;
4 retain free trade, the gold standard and the commitment to internationalism.

These objectives would be compatible only if the external account were strong and the idle-balances argument were correct. However, we have already noted that the balance of payments implications had not been fully considered at the time of the Yellow Book, and it is interesting to see that Keynes quickly changed his mind about the existence of idle balances and showed that the analysis of bank deposits had given mistaken conclusions.[42] Tomlinson is quite right in asserting that behind the Orange Book there is an analysis of unemployment which is every bit as orthodox as that of the Treasury, which so vehemently criticized the Lloyd George plans.[43] Both believed that the supply of savings for investment was fixed; whereas the Liberals believed that part of the 'investment fund' lay frozen, waiting for suitable schemes to 'thaw' them out, the Treasury held that existing capital resources were fully utilized so that higher interest rates would inevitably follow if government entered the market for new funds. Thus the Orange Book claimed: 'If capital is not available for the absorption of the unemployed on a policy of national development, then it is not available for their absorption at all.'[44]

[40] Tomlinson, *Problems of British Economic Policy*, pp. 82–5.
[41] *Memoranda on Certain Proposals Relating to Unemployment*, Cmd 3331, London, HMSO, 1929.
[42] *Problems of British Economic Policy*, p. 90.
[43] Ibid., p. 88.
[44] The Orange Book, p. 57.

In fact, the Liberal analysis seems to have become rather more orthodox between the Yellow and Orange Books. In the latter greater government involvement in the economy is seen as a purely temporary development. The pamphlet claimed:

> Unemployment is industrial dislocation. It is brought to an end by new enterprise, using capital to employ labour. In the present stagnation the Government must supply the initiative which will help to set going a great progressive movement.[45]

But the government initiative was to last only two years, after which 'industrial dislocation' would be corrected. The Liberals recognized that public works expenditure had linkage effects on some of the depressed industries, and that an unspecified multiplier would operate,[46] but there was no question of continuing the public works programme beyond that outlined in the Orange Book. Annual national savings were adequate to meet the total demand from investors, and the programme of national development would stimulate new investment opportunities. The orthodox belief that the economy would return to its normal state of full employment once transitional problems had been solved had certainly not been rejected by the radical Liberals at this stage.

Nor is it surprising that the Liberals should have been so fundamentally orthodox. Despite the war and despite the postwar currency upheavals, there was little to cause even progressives to question the orthodox basis of their beliefs. The severity of the slump of 1920–3 could be attributed to special wartime and postwar influences. Thereafter, unemployment had gradually fallen, except when progress had been interrupted by further 'special influences', such as the general strike. Despite the heavy unemployment in the export industries, there were also hopeful signs on the international front; the volume of world trade was rising and the prospects for international finance were improving after Britain's restoration of the gold standard. Even the general strike, which had so shaken the Liberals, seemed to have passed without permanent damage to the social fabric,and seemed to have brought a resolution from both sides of industry that a more responsible approach was needed in the conduct of their affairs. On the other hand, to have admitted that the capitalist system could not provide full employment without permanent state support of the capital and employment markets came far too close to the socialist contention that the capitalist system was showing signs of breakdown in the 1920s. It needed the slump and the collapse of the international system to induce

[45] Ibid., p. 53.
[46] Ibid., pp. 52–3.

centre progressives to abandon their orthodox assumptions and seek new models.

THE DECAY OF PROGRESSIVE LIBERALISM

Despite the trumpetings of the Orange Book, Lloyd George was never fully committed to the Liberal programme. The reluctance to use the Yellow Book was repeated with the Orange. Although the Orange Book's pledge attempted to make the 1929 general election a vote of confidence in Lloyd George, astonishingly he took very little part in the campaign, and even left the eve of poll broadcast to Sir John Simon.[47]

After MacDonald's administration began to lose its way in domestic affairs, Lloyd George did begin to campaign for a more active policy. When, in 1930, MacDonald invited both Baldwin and Lloyd George to consider emergency measures, another Liberal working party was formed (of Lloyd George, Rowntree and Kerr – now Lord Lothian) to rework the national development proposals once more. But Lloyd George's concern for the unemployed had not reawakened. G. C. Allen, in 1930 a young economic adviser to the Liberal Party, observed that only agricultural reform aroused Lloyd George's interest. Beyond this narrow field, he seemed prepared to agree to whatever economic arguments were expedient – expansion if he wanted to cooperate with Labour but wage cuts if he was looking towards the Conservatives.[48] Indeed, Lloyd George's need to keep all his options open was evident in the working party's pamphlet, *How to Tackle Unemployment*.[49] It called for a development plan, for agriculture in particular, but also for road-building, regional planning and electricity. But retrenchment in public spending was assuming ever greater import- ance and the Liberals proposed a 'new Geddes–Axe Committee'. With the economy collapsing, the Liberals were as devoid of practical suggestions as either of the main parties, with Lloyd George anxiously waiting for an opportunity to influence events. Ironically, when the chance came, he was prevented by illness from realizing his ambitions. He should have been a member of the National Government, but was prevented from attending the vital discussions by ill-health. When he had recovered, free trade, the one economic policy about which he cared deeply, had been abandoned, and Lloyd George felt he could no longer support the coalition.

[47] *The Goat in the Wilderness*, pp. 236–7.

[48] G. C. Allen, 'Advice from Economists – Forty-Five Years Ago', *The Three Banks Review*, 106, 1975, p. 49.

[49] *How to Tackle Unemployment: The Liberal Plans as Laid Before the Government and the Nation*, London, Press Printers, 1930.

At a broader level, rising unemployment, the collapse of the international economy and the vigorous retrenchment of the early 1930s sounded the death knell of radical Liberalism as a force in British politics. Keynes, realizing that the restructuring of the British economy could not be undertaken under free trade, became convinced early in 1930 of the need for protection, albeit as a temporary expedient.[50] When he made these views public in the following year, with the support of Henderson, there was a rift with Lloyd George and with formal Liberal politics. Henderson became a civil servant, part of the secretariat of the Economic Advisory Council, and, though he remained a supporter of a contra-cyclical public works programme, he bitterly disagreed with Keynes over *The General Theory*. Seebohm Rowntree also left the Liberal Party after a violent disagreement with Lloyd George in 1935 over agricultural policy.[51] Others began to drift away from Lloyd George to find refuge with the radical Conservatives or in the centre groupings which appeared in the mid-1930s.

However, the combination of orthodox analysis and radical proposals which lay at the heart of progressive Liberalism did have its final fling. Lloyd George produced the programme yet again in 1935, his 'New Deal for Britain'. He did manage to create a sufficiently large stir to win discussions with Ministers, and at one stage he was almost taken into the Cabinet, but the official records of these talks reveal that by this time Lloyd George was very much a spent force (the New Deal was launched on his seventy-second birthday). He talked not about policies, but about the weaknesses of cowards and blunderers who would not attempt a daring policy.[52] He was still reliving the glories of his wartime achievements. The government merely played for time; while they were talking to Lloyd George economic forces were bringing recovery and lower unemployment. Having missed his opportunity in 1929, Lloyd George could not conjure another.

If the Liberal Party was persistently unsuccessful with the Yellow Book proposals, it has been suggested that the programme had its greatest influence outside the party – on the British Labour Party, the Swedish socialists, and the British progressive Conservatives of the thirties. However, the British Labour Party, as we have seen, possessed, long before the publication of the Yellow Book, both the orthodox view of the working of the economy and a radical, expansionist, pro-planning strand evident in the ILP programme. In fact, there was fruitful contact between

[50] R. F. Harrod, *The Life of John Maynard Keynes*, Harmondsworth, Pelican Books, 1972, p. 500.
[51] *Social Thought and Social Action*, p. 215.
[52] PRO CAB 27/583 and 584.

both sets of radicals and both groups appear to have been responding to the same economic and political stimuli.[53] In the Swedish case, it has been argued that the economic policy of the Social Democratic Party, which came to power in 1932 with a programme of loan-financed public works, owed much to Ernst Wigforss's reading of the Yellow and Orange Books.[54] More recently, it has become clear that the Liberals (and the ILP) merely reinforced the views which Wigforss had formulated before the first world war.[55] Clearly, it would be much more accurate to say that the Liberals tended to clarify and extend some of the radical ideas of the labour movement. When we come to the progressive Conservatives, as we shall see in the following chapter, the position is rather less clear.[56] In the 1930s, British progressive opinion was far more fragmented and far more volatile than it had been under Liberal leadership during the 1920s. The Yellow and Orange Books were undoubtedly very significant, especially in the preparation of the economic programme of the Next Five Years Group, but they were scarcely the sole or even the most important forces shaping radical economic thought in the 1930s.

Thus it is impossible to believe some of the more enthusiastic claims for the Yellow and Orange Books. The thinking of the progressive Liberals during the 1920s was firmly rooted in the orthodox view of the economy, to which was added an array of practical and utopian reformist ideas. The involvement of Keynes has given the Liberal proposals a lustre they do not merit. The economics of the Liberal programme faithfully reflected the Liberal Party's own need to combine radical working-class appeal with its orthodox traditions. Ultimately, the Liberals depended entirely upon Lloyd George's ability to resolve the contradictions in the manifesto and to get things done. The mass electorate did not have sufficient confidence (in the 1929 election, the Liberals found it impossible to shake off the 'third party' tag) and even Lloyd George had little trust in his advisers' proposals. It is tempting to believe that the electorate gave the Orange Book the judgement it and the Liberal Party deserved.

[53] For example, Mosley and Strachey were particularly impressed by the articles in *The Nation* by Lloyd George, on public works, and Keynes, on currency matters. Robert Skidelsky, *Oswald Mosley*, London, Macmillan, 1975, pp. 131–41.

[54] See Donald Winch, 'The Keynesian Revolution in Sweden', *Journal of Political Economy*, 74, 1966, p. 170.

[55] Carl G. Uhr, 'The Emergence of the "New Economics" in Sweden: A Review of a Study by Otto Steiger', *History of Political Economy*, 5, 1973, p. 248.

[56] See below, pp. 58–67.

3

Macmillan and the Conservative Planners

After 1931, the leadership of the opposition radicals moved rapidly away from the Liberal Party. The Liberals suffered badly at the 1931 general election and their central economic policy, free trade, seemed increasingly inappropriate to the problems of British industry in the 1930s; they were leaderless when Lloyd George withdrew from politics to write his war memoirs; and, finally, there was a widespread revival of conservatism as Britain craved stability when the slump began to wreak havoc. Small wonder therefore, that the 'left' wing of the Conservative Party should become the focal point for the non-socialist radicals.

The shift brought a great change in the style of the presentation of radical ideas on economic policy. There was no longer a unified 'party line', but rather a series of programmes advocated by rebels who were out of step with their own party. The renegades within the Conservative Party also stretched out to embrace others working in the non-socialist, progressive tradition. There were attempts to build a popular opposition front to government policy during the mid-1930s. As we shall see, they achieved little and their unity was short-lived. One could, therefore, discuss the ideas of the progressive Conservatives either by devoting a little space to each of a large number of individuals, or by concentrating on one man who is deemed to be representative of the group. We have chosen the latter course and will focus, for the most part, on Harold Macmillan. He was one of the most able of the progressive MPs of the late 1930s, and made economic policy his particular concern. Convinced that his own party's policy was damaging the economy, Macmillan undertook an extensive search for a practical alternative and came into contact with many of the leading theorists of the decade. His great quality of being open to new ideas makes Macmillan the perfect weathervane of progressive conservative opinion in the 1930s, and he was closely involved in some of the more ambitious attempts to unite radical opposition to the policies of the government. He can, therefore, legitimately be considered a leading and representative dissident Conservative of the decade.

INDUSTRY AND THE STATE

In the Conservative Party, more than in any other part of the interwar political spectrum, radicalism was an occupation of the younger generation and, particularly, a badge of those who had seen active service during the war. Macmillan, though of undeniably bourgeois background, had a profound respect for the ordinary British workman, which was reinforced both by his experiences in the the trenches and by the waste and misery which he saw in his parliamentary constituency of Stockton-on-Tees.[1] Shortly after his entry into Parliament in 1924, he duly allied himself with the YMCA, the group of younger Tories many of whom had served in the army during the war. These young bucks became increasingly impatient with their party's leaders, being especially critical of the failure to reduce unemployment. Just as the general strike seems to have prompted the Liberals to establish the Industrial Inquiry, in late 1926 and 1927 the progressive members of the Conservative Party also felt the need to reconsider 'the industrial question' in all its aspects. The result was *Industry and the State: A Conservative View*, published in the names of Macmillan and three other members of the YMCA, Robert Boothby, Oliver Stanley and John Loder.[2]

Industry and the State has much in common with the Yellow Book. Both plead for a middle course between socialism and *laissez-faire* in an attempt to define a 'national interest' above the sectarian strife of industrial relations in the 1920s, and for both the obvious engine of reform was the economic power of the state. For the YMCA, the highest priority was the building of new attitudes in industry. They wanted statutory authority to be given to some forms of collective bargaining, and an extension of the trade-boards system to fix wages, hours and conditions of work. If these boards were to give legally binding decisions, the trade unions would be encouraged to drop their militant, negative character, and industrial relations would gradually assume a more responsible air. Under these conditions, it would be easier to apply modern scientific discoveries to British industry and unemployment would fall. Industry could also become more competitive if the local rating system were reformed and if monetary policy aimed at price rather than exchange stability. The authors

---

[1] Harold Macmillan, *Winds of Change, 1914–1939*, London, Macmillan, 1966, chs 2–6.
[2] London, Macmillan, 1927.

rejected deliberate 'inflation', but their definition was much more elastic since they appear to have grasped that monetary expansion could produce changes in the real economy, and not just on the price level.

> Inflation may be regarded as a creation of money in anticipation of an increase in production *which the increase in money itself helps to bring about.* Everything, however, depends upon the anticipation being realised.[3]

If this was a tantalizing glimpse of an expansionist monetary policy, most of the book was more orthodox. The convention of the annually balanced budget was accepted without question, and so, too, was the *principle* of retrenchment, though further reductions of public spending were considered impossible in the prevailing economic climate. In the light of these confused ideas on monetary policy, it is fortunate that they did not hope to reduce unemployment by financial measures!

The most significant proposal was a policy of encouraging industry to form amalgamations and cartels to help control production, eliminate waste and stabilize prices. The cartel, run with more regard to the interests of its workers than had been the case hitherto, would become highly efficient, participate in major international combines, and help bring more rationality to British industry. If the YMCA shared with the Liberals and the Mond-Turner Unemployment Committee an enthusiasm for concentration of British industry, they went further in their recommendations for new legislation to foster this growth.[4] Government should take powers to enable a majority of industrialists in any industry to force an unwilling minority into amalgamations. Here we have the first discussion in Conservative circles of the corporatist idea of self-governing industries; although the implications had not been considered in any detail, it is interesting to note that even at this early stage, progressive Conservative opinion had great faith in the ability of businessmen to conduct their own affairs and, by extension, the industrial life of the whole nation, with rationality and without seeking personal advantage. The government was also expected to conduct its own business with greater efficiency with the formation of an economic general staff to advise on home and foreign economic policy. Foreign trade could also be rationalized if Britain were to form a trading bloc with the empire countries, but the authors could not agree whether such a system necessitated protection.

In a country which had seen the chaos of a war, massive social unrest

---

[3] *Industry and the State*, p. 95.

[4] The Liberal proposals are considered in chapter 2, and the Mond–Turner talks in chapters 4 and 5.

and a general strike, a call for rationality and an appeal to the national interest were understandable. But the whole programme offered much less than the Yellow Book or the Mond–Turner *Unemployment Report*. Amalgamation of industry could do little for unemployment in the short term, an area in which, we have seen, the authors were imprecise and confused. Their enthusiasm for monopoly could look suspiciously like an invitation to mulct the consumer, and anyway there was no mechanism to ensure that the plans of one cartelized industry would be compatible with the plans of other such industries. The empire offered no solution to Britain's economic problems, and, in 1927, a redirection of trade might have made those problems worse.[5] Finally, instead of providing convincing new economic policies, the authors reveal a tendency to abdicate responsibility for proposing initiatives to the experts, be they scientists, economists or businessmen. The real significance of the book is that it raised the main themes which dominated progressive thought in the 1930s: the quest for expansionary finance; the faith in corporatist structures to invigorate the economy; the search for the national interest in economic policy; and the belief in the ability of the impartial expert to solve problems. Macmillan developed each of these themes throughout the 1930s and, although the relative importance of each changed over time, they remained the main ingredients of the plans of the dissident conservatives before the war.

THE CORPORATIST PHASE: RECONSTRUCTION

As economic dislocation increased with the unfolding of the slump, so the prospects of expansion became increasingly remote, and stability became the great aim of all opposition groups. Market forces appeared to bring only chaos; if men could combine and, with the aid of expert advice, control that which had previously been regulated by the invisible hand of competition working through free markets, they would regain command over individual and national economic destiny. Thus the planning movement of the early 1930s represented a loss of faith in the market mechanism and a belief in the ability of agreement and expert knowledge to manage the economy more effectively. 'Planning' became the dominant theme in the discussions of the early 1930s, just as the 'industrial question' had prevailed after the general strike. Mussolini's Italian corporatism won

---

[5] A recent study of the depression has indicated that Australia and Canada were amongst the first countries to experience rising unemployment: Peter Fearon, *The Origins and Nature of the Great Slump*, London, Macmillan, 1979, p. 31.

many admirers, though his fascist politics did not;[6] Soviet planning was beginning to attract rose-tinted attention, particularly from the intellectual left.[7] However, domestic influences were equally important, as planning had been entrenched in Labour Party thinking since the end of the first world war, and British industry was turning increasingly to planning in the 1920s as cartels and amalgamations began to spread.

The first indication that wholesale planning had gripped the progressives came in the *Week-End Review*, which had been created to expose 'the "Old Gang" and their out-of-date, ineffectual ways of running the country'.[8] One of the editorial staff, Max Nicholson, drew up a 'kite-flying' 'National Plan for Great Britain', which was published in February 1931.[9] Following the example of Mosley some months earlier, Nicholson poured scorn on the political establishment and doubted whether existing institutions could cope with the instability in the British economy and society. He proposed to remove from ministerial responsibility into autonomous public utilities health, education and transport. Self-government would be extended to industry with the formation of a planning council for each industry. At the top of the whole structure would be a National Planning Commission of eminent economists, Ministers and industrialists from each planning council, with the task of producing a master plan for British economic development, incorporating a series of annual targets, much as in the Orange Book. The deterioration in the world economy since the late 1920s had greatly lowered even the radicals' expectations of economic policy.

The Plan is not offered specifically as a cure for unemployment because that approach is considered fundamentally unsound. Unemployment, in its present economic excess, is a symptom of economic illness which will disappear with the revival of economic health. It is anticipated that the scale of the proposed 'spring cleaning' will remove for the time being all 'abnormal' unemployment, while the provision for raising output and adjusting wide discrepancies between industry and markets is the only soberly probable method of eventually disposing of it for good. Reduced unit costs, better competitive power, elimination of waste and incompetence, great increase of reconstruction work, disappearance of incessant labour troubles through dissolving the employer-trade union deadlock, and

[6] Luther Carpenter, 'Corporatism in Britain, 1930–45', *Journal of Contemporary History*, 11, 1976, p. 4.

[7] See below, pp. 150–1.

[8] Max Nicholson, 'The Proposal for a National Plan', in John Pinder (ed.), *Fifty Years of Political and Economic Planning: Looking Forward 1931–1981*, Heinemann, London, 1981, p. 6.

[9] 'A National Plan for Great Britain', Supplement to the *Week-End Review*, 14 Feb. 1931.

control over the home market offer a fairly definite prospect of rapid absorption of the entire employable labour force.[10]

Stability and control were the first objectives; once these had been secured, unemployment could be reduced as a by-product of the modernization of British society. Unfortunately for the progressives, stability and control were far more difficult to secure than Nicholson had imagined. At a more general level, Nicholson reveals the complete loss of faith in the ability of politicians to cope with economic problems, which increased the tendency for progressive opinion in the 1930s to cultivate the expert, and in particular the economist and the businessman, to fill the vacuum in economic policy-making.

The publication of the plan led directly to the formation of Political and Economic Planning (PEP), a group of academics, professional people and progressive leaders of finance and industry. The first chairman was Sir Basil Blackett, formerly a Treasury official and a director of the Bank of England, and himself a leading propagandist for 'planning'. To Blackett, planning involved both the defensive combination by industry to control output to match demand and the establishment of a National Industrial Council to coordinate the plans of the individual industries. Less of an expansionist than Nicholson, he nevertheless shared the view, which was common to all the conservative planners, that all groups should make sacrifices to promote an atmosphere of harmony.[11] Progressive conservative planning, just like Liberal expansionism in the 1920s, could operate successfully only in an environment in which the national interest was more important than class conflict.

Under Blackett's leadership, PEP began a programme of work to revise and improve on Nicholson's pioneering plan.[12] Unfortunately, relationships within PEP were far from harmonious. Blackett's conviction that Britain should look to much closer economic links with the empire were not shared by other members of the directorate and he relinquished his chairmanship.[13] Moreover, the closeness of the corporatist themes in the work of Nicholson and Blackett to those of the totalitarian planners disturbed many of PEP's supporters, with the result that PEP's earliest years were marked, ironically, by confusion, chaos and dissent.[14]

[10] 'A National Plan', p. ix.

[11] Carpenter, 'Corporatism in Britain', p. 15.

[12] The objectives of PEP are set out in the minutes of the first meeting of the directorate, held at Dartington Hall on 18–19 April 1931. Box M1, PEP Archive, British Library of Political and Economic Science.

[13] Minutes of the 23rd Meeting, 18 July, 1932, Box M1, PEP Archive.

[14] *Fifty Years of PEP*, pp. 16–19.

Macmillan was less inhibited. His concern about unemployment and the paralysis in government, and his willingness to investigate new ideas, led him rapidly forward from the position taken by *Industry and the State*. He had been greatly impressed by the Liberal Orange Book,[15] and found it very hard to resist Mosley's combination of charismatic charm and unorthodox, expansionist approach to economic policy.[16] But it was the slump which forced Macmillan to reappraise his position and actively search for a more radical, imaginative approach to policy-making.[17] Mosley remained the great influence, and Macmillan agonized at length before deciding against joining the Mosley-Strachey New Party. The Mosleyite influence endured, not least because Macmillan acquired as his secretary Allan Young, until 1931 Mosley's economic adviser. Under the twin influences of Mosleyite economic ideas and the climacteric of the slump, Macmillan accentuated the corporatist strands in his own ideas, which culminated in the publication in December 1933 of his first main work, *Reconstruction: A Plea for National Policy*.[18]

Like other conservative planners, Macmillan saw over-production as the immediate economic problem. The competitive ethos of capitalism did not allow producers to regulate the supply of goods coming onto the market, and, whilst the misallocation of resources was masked during phases of rapid national and international growth, the recent increase of productivity and spread of industrialization had made a crucial difference. It was now easy for supply to outrun demand since savings could exceed investment opportunities when prices were being forced down by excessive competition. Whereas Mosley had reached this position from a Hobsonian underconsumptionist analysis and had recommended redistribution of income to swell demand, Macmillan followed the other conservative planners in looking to industry to check supply. Like Blackett (and Lord Melchett, Sir Arthur Salter and Roy Glenday),[19] Macmillan favoured a national industrial council to regulate prices and production for each industry behind a protective tariff. At the national level, these individual plans were to be coordinated by a Central Economic Council, consisting of representatives of government and finance, economists to make forecasts and assessments of policy, and industrialists from each national industrial council. Thus the corporatist, technocratic and nationalistic threads in Macmillan's economic thought had been enhanced to produce machinery similar to that of Melchett, Blackett and

---

[15] *Winds of Change*, p. 246.
[16] Ibid., p. 263.
[17] Ibid., pp. 284–5.
[18] London, Macmillan, 1933.
[19] Carpenter, 'Corporatism in Britain', pp. 6–7.

Salter. But Macmillan, like Nicholson before him, took from Mosley a supreme confidence in the ability of planners to control economic variables; his planning went beyond that of most progressive conservatives.

He saw further applications for planning in foreign trade. The Central Economic Council would use all manner of restrictive devices such as bulk purchase of imports, tariffs, quotas and bilateral agreements to achieve balance of payments stability, while the export industries would be subsidized by the duties collected on imports. Whereas Blackett saw planning operating on an empire scale and Salter wanted a much less ambitious version to aid international recovery,[20] Macmillan focused mainly on the domestic economy, where the possibilities of coordination and the scope for control seemed greater. Thus Macmillan's *Reconstruction* is one of the most comprehensive of the planning manifestos of the 1930s.

Macmillan did share the view that there was no room in the planned economy for class conflict; the national interest must come first. Like the other conservative planners, he assumed that self-government for industry meant planning by industrialists, but Macmillan was emotionally and intellectually incapable of omitting all reference to the working class (as had been the case with Nicholson, Blackett and Salter).[21] For the unions, Macmillan proposed an ineffectual system of councils shadowing those of the employers, and to win working-class support and minimize conflict, he offered reduction of working hours, statutory contracts of employment, and holidays with pay. But, in addition to these minor concessions, Macmillan's version of the planned economy promised not just stability but full employment if sectional differences could be buried and the national interest pursued. Here Macmillan followed Mosley rather than the conservatives. At this stage, he could not accept the ILP proposals for a minimum wage and redistribution through extensions of the social services, but he did strongly endorse cheap money, and in his parliamentary speeches of the early 1930s, he followed Mosley in advocating an Investment and Development Board to encourage investment in industry and national resources.[22] Alone of the conservative planners, Macmillan recognized that overproduction would inevitably lead to low investment, and, as his ideas developed during 1933, he came to doubt whether cheap money and the Development Board would be enough. Only government could raise investment levels in these conditions, and Macmillan was

[20] Sir Arthur Salter, *Recovery: The Second Effort*, London, Bell, 1933.

[21] The emphasis in Salter's *The Framework of an Ordered Society*, Cambridge, CUP, 1933, and in *Recovery* is quite firmly on the businessman to bring economic revival by industrial planning at the national and international levels.

[22] *Winds of Change*, pp. 266–8.

drawn in his speeches to Mosley's idea of balancing the budget over a three-year period; in year one the government would undertake a massive injection of credit, to be followed by a smaller deficit in year two, and yielding an overall balance in year three.[23] Unfortunately, monetary policy was not Macmillan's strength, and he was quite clearly in some confusion in the early 1930s,[24] so we must accept that his commitment to expansion was ruled by his heart rather than his head, and accordingly it finds little place in *Reconstruction*.

In many ways, it is impossible to assess the *economic* validity of many of the works of the conservative planners of this period, because their principal objective was to devise systems in which the ordinary laws of economics ceased to function. Since the operation of market forces at this time seemed to promise only disruption and misery, the objective is understandable. None of the conservative planners managed to shed all their orthodox intellectual baggage, particularly in monetary matters. Macmillan's confusion mirrored that of Nicholson, who had explicitly rejected monetary expansion, the unbalanced budget and any failure to meet the targets of debt redemption.[25] But, even on political and administrative grounds there are enormous weaknesses in the plans of the early 1930s. Above all, these conservatives overestimated the potential of planning. In the much simpler economy of the second world war, it was possible to plan only at the very crude level of manpower allocations, and even in aircraft production, where planning achieved its greatest successes, production patterns continued to display massive instability and remained dogged by bottlenecks and shortages.[26] Under no circumstances could planners deliver what was being asked of them. The conservative planners were also open to criticism of the undemocratic nature of their plans. Although many were openly hostile to fascist politics, and they had the best of intentions, a number were strongly influenced by corporatist ideas, and their proposals resembled fascist institutions and methods. Even in 1933, these parallels were unwelcome to many progressive conservatives, and the more overtly corporatist schemes began to lose favour.

---

[23] *Hansard*, 276, HC Deb, 5s, col. 349, 22 March 1933.

[24] The clearest example of his 'flexibility' on monetary policy is the footnote on p. 59 of *Reconstruction*, which directs readers to the writings on monetary policy of 'Keynes, Hobson, Hayek and others'.

[25] 'A National Plan', p. x.

[26] See the essays by E. A. G. Robinson and Ely Devons, in D. N. Chester (ed.) *Lessons of the British War Economy*, Cambridge, CUP, 1951.

EXPANSION AND THE CULT OF THE EXPERT – THE NEXT FIVE
YEARS GROUP

The swing away from corporatist institutions began where these methods
may have appeared most firmly entrenched, in PEP. The suspicion of
totalitarian methods which was growing both inside and outside the
organization during the summer of 1932 led PEP to abandon its work on
the revised national plan and to concentrate instead on exposing the lack of
coordination and integration in various aspects of British economic and
social life.[27]

Macmillan, who had been more committed to corporatist machinery,
was slower to adapt, but his search for political allies pushed him in the
same direction. In March 1935, he added his signature to *Planning for
Employment*,[28] together with 13 other dissident government MPs
including Lord Eustace Percy, who had earlier published his own vision of
a corporatist system for Britain.[29] The pamphlet is interesting on two
counts; there is some weakening of the corporatist machinery and a return
to parliamentary control of economic policy; more importantly, the
argument was much more expansionist than had been the rule in programmes drafted during the depths of the depression. Falling unemployment and signs of recovery in the British economy were clearly raising
expectations.

The most striking evidence of a new direction in non-socialist
progressive thought came with the formation of the Next Five Years
(NFY) Group, in which Macmillan and other conservative planners took
leading roles. Significantly, the NFY Group began life as an attempt to
build a broad movement to draw attention to the evils of totalitarianism;[30]
from the outset, the conservative planners would have to adopt more
democratic institutions in economic policy. The Group began in earnest
with a meeting at All Souls College, Oxford, in the summer of 1934 and
started work on a programme which could be implemented within the
lifetime of a single Parliament, five years. It was led by an executive
committee chaired by Clifford Allen, who had moved successively from
the ILP to the centre of the Labour Party and had followed MacDonald in

---

[27] *Fifty Years of PEP*, pp. 34–6.

[28] *Planning for Employment: A Preliminary Study by Some Members of Parliament*, London,
Macmillan, 1934.

[29] Percy believed that the Italian example would have to be followed if national unity
broke down: Lord Eustace Percy, *Government in Transition*, London, Methuen, 1934,
p. 122.

[30] *The Next Five Years: An Essay in Political Agreement*, London, Macmillan, 1935, p. 2.

1931. The Group concentrated its attentions on economic policy and international relations and appointed two small drafting committees to prepare reports. Those responsible for the report on economic policy were Macmillan, Salter, Geoffrey Crowther (editor of *The Economist*), and Hugh Molson, one of Macmillan's closest allies in Parliament.

In the NFY report Macmillan finally renounced the undemocratic elements of the Mosleyite programme. Responsibility for economic policy was located firmly within the political system, with supreme authority being given to a Cabinet Planning Committee, comprising senior Ministers without departmental responsibilities and echoing, in many respects, the Lloyd George War Cabinet. Advising this committee would be an economic general staff, staffed by both economists and representatives of various interest groups, including the trade unions. It was intended as rather more than an Economic Advisory Council with greater access to policy-makers; it was a significant step towards policy-formulation by consensus and tripartite mediation which has proved indispensable since 1945. With the need to build a broad movement, the conservative planners had been forced to recognize for the first time the political potential of the trade unions and had at last found a realistic method of negotiating the 'national interest', and one which has been turned to on frequent occasions in the postwar period.[31]

Having recognized the power of the labour movement, there was no longer any justification for the earlier model of self-governing industrialists, and planning could no longer be regarded as the automatic panacea. The NFY report stated:

> We do not envisage here that the Government should aim at a planned economy which would, throughout every sphere of economic activity, replace the adjustments of the competitive price system by deliberate direction. Such planning as we have in mind would be essential even if the responsibilities assumed by the State were to remain only of the same kind as at present, and will be all the more necessary if the State accepts such extensions of its responsibilities as we consider both inevitable and desirable.[32]

Planning was no longer considered a prerequisite for all industries. The NFY report (and the Industrial Reorganization League, in which Macmillan was also active) called for an enabling Act, to allow combination where a majority in any industry wanted it. The Act would

---

[31] See Keith Middlemas, *Politics in Industrial Society: The British Experience of the System Since 1911*, London, André Deutsch, 1979, Parts Two and Three.

[32] *The Next Five Years*, p. 13.

also establish an Industrial Advisory Committee to vet any proposed combination to ensure that the interests of consumers and workers would be safeguarded. The main objective was to help the depressed industries cope with excess capacity by following the model of the Coal Act of 1930. The lesson that the wholesale manipulation of prices, wages and production was incompatible with political freedom had been learned, and the drift of conservative planning towards totalitarian methods was reversed. In keeping with the hope for a wider political base, there was now a much expanded role for public corporations and nationalized industries under direct political control.

Although the NFY Group improved the administrative and political machinery of economic policy, it merely exposed the lack of economic understanding of Macmillan and the conservative planners. Their efforts since 1931 had been directed towards devising new *structures* rather than new *policies*, and these structures had been shown to be fundamentally unsound by developments in Germany and Italy. They wanted to cure unemployment because it was the obvious threat to democracy, but they had no workable expansionist policies of their own because they had not yet faced the problem of how to reduce unemployment *within the existing political and administrative framework*. They were fortunate, however, in that there was a ready-made expansionist tradition for them to exploit. Since the whole object of the NFY Group was to build a broad, workable alliance, the conservative planners had to turn to the labour movement for some, at least, of its policies. The Labour Party had produced in 1934 a major policy statement, *For Socialism and Peace*, which combined a major public works programme of electrification, housing, land drainage, road-building and agricultural development with the nationalization of key industries and extensions of the social services to permit socialist planning across a broad front of British economic and social life. Clearly, the NFY Group could take the expansionist elements without the strong socialist overtones. This policy had further advantages because it brought the NFY Group firmly into contact with the Liberal expansionist tradition, as Lloyd George was about to launch similar proposals in his New Deal for Britain. Unfortunately, the financial arrangements were a horrible compromise of inadequate measures from both sources. The NFY report suggested that a nationalized Bank of England, reorganization of the capital market and the creation of a National Development Board would be sufficient to mobilize finance for the public works programme. It is worth remembering that Macmillan had considered a similar programme inadequate only two years earlier when he had been drawn to the idea of balancing the budget over three years instead of one. The report also called for a monetary policy to achieve price stability, but the budgetary implications were ignored. The search for an expansionist monetary policy was quickening, but further development was needed.

The NFY movement helped extricate the radical conservatives from their *cul-de-sac* of planning, and the contact with other strands of unorthodox thought, particularly those developed in the labour movement, helped enrich their economic thought, as we shall see from Macmillan's later development. But the NFY report, as befits a political manifesto, was intended primarily to win support. Issues were fudged, inconsistencies were allowed to creep in, and difficult areas were avoided to minimize opposition. For example, following Crowther's campaign in *The Economist* for greater liberalization of world trade and Salter's expansionist bias, the report pronounced in favour of a variety of measures to increase world trade. But these proposals did not sit easily beside a scheme to shore up British agriculture by import quotas and subsidies to domestic production. The most disappointing aspect of the report was the quality of the economic thought. None of the participants had an intellectually satisfying solution to unemployment, which the report claimed to be the greatest threat to democracy. Instead, the NFY policy resembles a collection of sectional shibboleths – some planning for the Conservatives, land reform for the Liberals, nationalization for the unions – with no clear sense of direction. There was a heavy responsibility on the experts in the economic general staff to make the parts into a coherent whole and to make expansion work. The conservative planners had not yet lost the habit of thinking in terms of structures rather than policies. With these shortcomings, it is scarcely surprising that the NFY movement achieved little, as we shall see below.

THE MATURE PROGRAMME: *THE MIDDLE WAY*

The publication of *The Middle Way* in 1938 marks the final chapter in Macmillan's search for a convincing ecomomic policy.[33] The book is the most impressive of all the radical programmes of the 1930s. While the skilful blend of policies owed everything to Macmillan, the most important analytical contribution came from Keynes's *General Theory*. There are many references to Keynes's work and several lengthy passages are quoted verbatim. In no way is this meant to devalue *The Middle Way*; Macmillan grasped the validity of Keynesian ideas when others lacked intellectual flexibility and the courage to consider policies outside their own narrow ideological preconceptions. Lloyd George was by now too old and too suspicious of Keynes; the Labour Party was too firmly committed

[33] *The Middle Way*, London, Macmillan, 1938.

to socialism even to heed the younger Keynesians within its own ranks; and the unions had long been much more interested in the wages of those in work than in a cure for unemployment. Macmillan's openness to new ideas had at last brought him to managed capitalism – the middle way between socialism and *laissez-faire* capitalism which he had been seeking since the mid-1920s.

It would be wrong to assume that Macmillan completely understood *The General Theory* – economic theory was never his strong suit. It is more likely that he saw in Keynes what he had earlier seen in Mosley; obvious intellectual ability, independence from the suffocating bonds of orthodoxy, great self-confidence and ample personal charm. Macmillan was Keynes's publisher, but the links between them grew stronger during the thirties. The pamphlets which had formed the basis of *Reconstruction* had been sent to Keynes, who provided constructive criticism; Macmillan was so impressed by *The General Theory* that he quickly offered his services as a propogandist of Keynesian theory.[34]

His experience with the NFY movement had an equally large, if less direct, effect. The Macmillan of *The Middle Way* is a much more sophisticated thinker, aware of the economic divisions within British society, and prepared to tailor policies to meet those needs. In general, he seems much more mature than earlier in the 1930s and much more successful at weaving together the main strands in the economic thinking of the progressive conservatives. The NFY Group, for example, had prodded Macmillan towards accepting the labour movement's demands for more secure arrangements for collective bargaining, reduction of the length of the working week, earlier retirement and the raising of the school-leaving age. But the Keynesian analysis that unemployment resulted from deficiencies in aggregate demand enabled him to go further than the NFY report on redistribution, and with much greater conviction. *The Middle Way* proposed a national minimum wage, a living 'wage' for the unemployed, nationally distributed basic foods such as milk, butter, cheese, eggs, sugar and bread with free supplies for those most in need, and proposals for national regulation of the cost of fuel, light and housing. All these measures had been advocated by other radicals, but the combination of Macmillan's expansionist bias guided by Keynesian analysis, his determination to act on the findings of the specialists such as nutritionist Boyd Orr and the social investigator Seebohm Rowntree (both are cited in *The Middle Way*), and his preference for efficiently planned production and, in this case, distribution gave an outstanding social policy in the tradition of Tory paternalism.

[34] *Winds of Change*, p. 490.

Although he had travelled much further to the left, especially in his attitude to expansion and trade-union rights, than most other progressive Conservatives of the period, Macmillan had not been converted to socialism. He wanted to ensure the survival of democracy and the capitalist system; unemployment was the main threat to both, and unemployment could be eradicated by the policies he had outlined. His commitment to the private ownership of property can be seen in his proposals on industrial policy, which again owed much to the better points of the NFY report. For industries in phases of vigorous growth, Macmillan felt that private ownership should prevail, and that they should operate within an environment of uncontrolled competition. This sector would comprise the largest part of the economy. For more mature industries, there should be, as outlined in the NFY programme, the opportunity to combine under the Industrial Reorganization (Enabling) Act. Although there would be close public supervision of these monopolistic concerns, private ownership and direction were to remain. Finally,

> certain industries and services which are of key important to the vigorous economic life of the community, and which have reached a stage of development when their conduct requires to be governed by much wider social considerations than the profit-making incentive alone will provide, should be brought under either some suitable form of public ownership and management or, in certain cases, a form of statutory control or supervision which may not involve public ownership.[35]

Of course, the railways, public utilities and coalmines were already subject to considerable public control yet remained in private ownership, so Macmillan may have retreated somewhat from the position of the NFY report. On the other hand, he did make explicit reference to the virtues of the public corporation to complete the modernization of the coalmines and to rationalize the transport services.[36]

On finance, however, Macmillan was much more specific than the NFY Group. In many ways, the finance markets would function as before; he wanted to prohibit speculation and the holding of idle money balances, but offered no suggestions about the ways of achieving these aims. Like many before him, Macmillan suspected that the money markets and the banking system were neglecting the small, often high-risk business, and proposed that the National Investment Board should help nurture new industries, in the manner of the various institutions operating in the

[35] *The Middle Way*, pp. 237–8.
[36] Ibid., pp. 230–4.

Special Areas of the 1930s.[37] The main change in financial policy was the proposal that henceforward it should be conducted following Keynesian principles according to the needs of industry and employment. To facilitate this new direction, the Bank of England was to be nationalized to bring monetary policy securely under government control. The expansionist monetary policy would underscore the increase of aggregate demand via the improved social services noted above and stronger collective bargaining. The final boost to growth would come from the type of expansionist trade policy proposed by the NFY Group, though without the contradictory arrangements for British agriculture.

The programme outlined in *The Middle Way* is an impressive statement of the positive aspects of interwar non-socialist, radical thought. The book made no attempt to win popular political appeal in the fashion of the NFY manifesto, but it did try to confront unemployment, the most urgent domestic problem of the day, with a coherent and promising set of policies. Macmillan, with the assistance of Keynes, had improved on the economics of the NFY Group. Having identified the deficiency of aggregate demand as the cause of unemployment, Macmillan could demonstrate that much of what was desirable on grounds of social justice also served a sound economic purpose. Expansion and growth pervaded *The Middle Way* more than any other work of the conservative planners during the 1930s. Consequently, planning could become much more growth-oriented. In *The Middle Way*, planning is concerned with promoting best practices in industry and society, coordinating the expanding industries, and managing the level of demand. The use of planning as a restrictive device to reduce capacity and extract monopoly profits had been quietly dropped.

In the same way, the national interest was no longer seen as synonymous with the interests of business. Macmillan retained his belief that it was possible to produce a consensus on economic policy and to produce measures which were seen as being in the national interest by all strata of society. The key was economic growth and to ensure that the benefits were transmitted to all. Sectional differences would arise, but these would be resolved by tripartite bargaining or by appeal to the 'impartial expert'. However, subsequent experience has shown that economics is not a value-free science capable of giving such precise, unequivocal answers. More generally, in this search for the national interest there is an assumption by many non-socialist progressives (including Keynes and his colleagues at

---

[37] This shortcoming in the coverage of financial institutions was first identified by the (Lord) Macmillan Committee on Finance and Industry, and was known thereafter as the 'Macmillan Gap'.

this time)[38] that workers and their unions would 'behave responsibly' and not 'abuse' their economic power once full employment had been achieved. The radicals misunderstood the psychology of the individual worker and the *raison d'être* of their industrial and political organizations. Even today, 50 years later, in economic policy the national interest seems as elusive as ever.[39] Nevertheless, Macmillan's book did provide a firm basis for a sound, expansionist policy. If somewhat optimistic about the prospects of expanding trade and winning acceptance for higher, more progressive taxation, for the most part his programme avoids the utopian pipe-dreaming which characterized so much of progressive thought throughout the whole interwar period. Macmillan's major misfortune was to publish *The Middle Way* at a time when questions of economic policy had faded into the background once the focus of political debate had switched to defence and foreign policy. Before the war, his arguments did not receive the attention they deserved.

CONCLUSIONS: PLANNING AND THE PROGRESSIVES

The basic premise which united the progressive conservatives was that the 'Old Guard' could not cope with the problems caused by the depression. They were afraid that economic collapse might provoke the sort of revolutionary political developments which would overturn the existing system of private ownership of property and democratic politics; in this sense they were truly conservative. However, they were in a curious party-political position because the 'Old Guard' was at the head of a very popular, anti-socialist government which also claimed to be preserving the capitalist system, and, if electoral results are to be interpreted at all realisticallly, had firmly grasped for itself the centre ground of interwar British politics. In fact, the National Government was surprisingly resilient, and, within its own limited horizons, innovative in economic policy.

The progressive conservatives did, however, possess one potent advantage; they were the most forceful proponents of 'planning' at a time when faith in the efficacy of market forces was at a very low ebb.

[38] The Henderson Papers at Nuffield College, Oxford, contain comments on a paper given to the Marshall Society by Henderson during 1936, at which these opinions on the unions were attributed to Keynes's colleagues. Henderson Papers, Box 10, Henderson to Keynes, 4 June 1936.

[39] The continuing postwar discussions on the control of inflation have invariably failed to balance the wage-earners' interest in higher incomes with the national interest of lower rates of inflation. The persistent breakdown of incomes policies suggest that it is virtually impossible to reconcile the two in British political conditions.

Competition was 'destructive' and one of the causes of the malaise of the depressed industries.[40] 'Planning' was in vogue, but it was also deliciously vague; planning could mean anything from the dismantling of excess capacity in a single depressed industry to the central direction of the national economy which implied extensive bureaucratic control of prices, distribution, foreign trade and investment. Planning could be applied equally to socialist and capitalist sytems. The only common factor was that all planners wanted to interfere with the forces of free competition.

Thus, for the progressives, planning was initially a device to enable industry to restrict production in order to raise prices and hence profits and, subsequently, employment. In so doing, primary responsibility for the making of economic policy was given to industrialists. To be sure, the planners conceived a system of coordination, control and expert advice to prevent this from becoming a licence to extract monopoly profits, but their proposals were wide open to the criticism that they encouraged exploitation by industrialists.

To some extent, the planners were following the corporatist models of Mosley and Mussolini, but they were also driven by what seemed to be the logic of British social and political conditions. Excess capacity was rising and prices falling; the trade unions were weak (organizing about one-quarter of the total workforce) and were losing members steadily as unemployment rose; the government was unwilling to assume greater responsibility for running the economy and had shown itself to be incapable of finding a solution to unemployment. The expert businessman guided by the expert economist seemed the last hope. This was the high spot of corporatist influence on British progressive thought, and has been ably documented by Trevor Smith and Luther Carpenter.[41] Both authors stress continuity in the ideas of the Conservative planners and the persistence of corporatist themes throughout the 1930s. However, both the model of Conservative planning and the nature of British corporatism underwent significant changes in the mid-1930s. British economic recovery made restrictive planning inappropriate, and the perception of the threat of fascist dictatorships made the more overt corporatism unacceptable.

Under these circumstances, the Conservative planners, as we have seen, reached out to other radical groups to try to build a broad anti-fascist coalition. With the government securely holding the centre and right of the political spectrum, the Conservative planners had little option but to

---

[40] Leslie Hannah, *The Rise of the Corporate Economy*, London, Methuen, 1976, p. 33.

[41] 'Corporatism in Britain'; and Trevor Smith, *The Politics of the Corporate Economy*, Oxford, Martin Robertson, 1979, ch. 2.

forge alliances with the left. In many respects, the new direction had much to commend it as the organized labour movement had also become strongly attracted to planning, albeit with a very different ideological slant. The two groups did manage, in *The Next Five Years* programme, to weld together a set of proposals which emphasized planning in the sense of introducing modern methods to industry and pruning the inefficient, aiming at greater coordination and efficiency to raise output, and controlling the distribution of the national product to ensure higher average living standards. These aspects were not alien to the Conservative planners; Macmillan and PEP, in particular, but also Salter and Blackett had seen these possibilities though all tended to give far more weight to the restrictive defensive potential of planning.[42] This willingness of the progressive conservatives to sink their differences and to broaden their policies has been seen by Marwick, in a highly influential article, as evidence that they were one of the groups promoting political agreement during the 1930s.[43] Accordingly, he presents the NFY movement and its report in a very favourable light, referring to:

> *The Next Five Years*, which, if it is not to be included in the same shelf as the Webbs' *Minority Report*, Keynes's *Economic Consequences of the Peace* and the Beveridge Report, must certainly be put in the same bookcase.[44]

However, we have argued above that the NFY report scarcely deserves such acclaim on the basis of its economic ideas, and there are good grounds for believing that the political aspects have been exaggerated; the economic programme of the NFY report was not an heroic compromise. The Conservative planners who drafted it had very little to offer from their own earlier work. For maximum political effect, they needed to embrace the Labour Party with its mass membership, and the charisma of Lloyd George. The NFY leadership almost managed to win both, but eventually 'agreement' was possible with neither. In large part, the problem was caused by the uncertain status of the NFY Group itself. Some of its leaders wanted to take their programme into party politics, but Allen resisted, and with some justification.[45] He could not count on the complete support of all the signatories to the report, the movement lacked inspirational leadership, and the programme itself did not look remarkable beside the Liberal and Labour manifestos. Moreover, when Lloyd George launched the *third*

[42] *Fifty Years of PEP*, ch. 3; *Reconstruction*, p. 19; *Recovery*, p. 288.

[43] Arthur Marwick, 'Middle Opinion in the Thirties: Planning, Progress, and Political "Agreement"', *English Historical Review*, 79, 1964.

[44] 'Middle Opinion', p. 293.

[45] *Winds of Change*, pp. 376–7.

version of the Orange Book in 1935, he attracted far more attention and
interest than anything mounted by the NFY Group. Marwick's claim for
the Conservative planners as 'apostles of political agreement' is far from
secure *on economic policy*. Agreement and temporary alliances on anti-
fascist themes were far more acceptable, but on economic questions
mutual suspicions and fundamental divisions remained.

Finally, we must consider whether the progressives were heralds of the
mixed economy, Keynesian management and the welfare state, all
established in Britain after 1945. Marwick argues of 'these advocates of
political agreement':

> But the future was with them. Almost all of their proposals were
> implemented in the nineteen-forties; and beyond that they opened the way
> to the social and economic attitudes of the nineteen-fifties.[46]

Again, it is difficult to believe so much of the pre-Keynesian economics of
the NFY Group. To suggest that it opened the way to the crude
Keynesianism of postwar Butskellism is patently absurd. Marwick is
obviously thinking of nationalization and improved social services which
were foreshadowed in *The Next Five Years*. But, even here, the picture is
more complicated than he allows. None of the draftsmen of the NFY
economic programme had given much weight to either policy in their own
earlier work. However, these policies, albeit with strong socialist
overtones, had been forcefully advocated by the labour movement and
were brought to the centre radicals through the Liberty and Democratic
Leadership Group, the predecessor of the NFY, and in which labour
leaders were involved. The NFY report was based in large part on the
earlier, broader-based discussions.[47] Although the proposals which finally
appeared had been purged of their socialism, it is difficult to attribute
their development unequivocally to the progressives of the NFY Group.

A similar criticism can be made of Paul Addison's *The Road to 1945*.[48]
Addison argues that the plans implemented by Labour after 1945 had
been fashioned by the wartime coalition to a considerable extent from the
interwar ideas of Liberal intellectuals. Whilst Addison accounts, in a way
Marwick cannot, for the appearance of Keynesian policies, he also raises
many questions. Why, for example, did the economic ideas of Hubert
Henderson, a noted interwar Liberal intellectual, not prevail after 1940,
whilst those on insurance of Sir William Beveridge, who during the 1930s
was very indecisive and certainly was not firmly committed to the liberal

[46] 'Middle Opinion', p. 297.
[47] Ibid., p. 293.
[48] Paul Addison, *The Road to 1945*, London, Quartet, 1975.

collectivist tradition, were successful? Addison notes that Labour acted as a wartime filter of reconstruction plans and a great promoter of reform during the war. Might it not be that wartime Labour leaders championed, not the ideas of the centre, but variations of the policies they themselves had fought for in the 1930s?

Thus we suggest that, in many respects, the importance of the interwar, non-socialists has been greatly exaggerated.

4

Progressive Paternalism and Orthodox Reaction: The Economic Ideas of British Industrialists

It is essential to begin by recognizing that the economic ideas of interwar British businessmen covered a far wider range than those in any other party or functional grouping under consideration in this volume. The term 'businessman' or 'industrialist' covers everything from the director of a large international company to the owner-manager of the smallest firm. The specific economic policy needs of industry will clearly differ between not only large and small concerns, but also those concentrating on the domestic market and the exporters, the capital- and labour-intensive sectors, monopolistic and competitive enterprise, and so on. Industrialists also seem to have had many avenues to pursue these diverse economic-policy objectives. The heads of the largest companies have rarely found it difficult to find a public platform for their views and the politically ambitious have reached the highest level of Cabinet office. On the other hand, British industry also possessed an extraordinarily large 'silent majority' whose opinions very rarely came to public attention. The task of exploring all these avenues is clearly beyond our scope, but we are fortunate in that there was one occasion in the late 1920s when the whole of British industry seems to have been galvanized into thought and discussion about economic policy. The stimulus was the Conference on Industrial Reorganization and Industrial Relations, more popularly remembered as the Mond–Turner talks, in which industrialists and trade-union leaders sought a *rapprochement* in the aftermath of the general strike.[1] The programme which industrialists put to the conference and the reactions of ordinary businessmen to the issues raised offer a unique insight into the thinking of interwar businessmen. However, in order to understand why the episode unfolded in the way it did, we must begin with the first world war and the founding of the central industrial organizations.

[1] The popular name of the talks derives from Sir Alfred Mond, the leader of the industrialists' side, and Ben Turner, the TUC President, who led the union team. The chair alternated between Mond and Turner.

WAR AND BRITISH BUSINESS

During the first world war, there was an enormous increase in state involvement in the economy and a consequent blurring of the boundaries between industry and the state. Government regulated industrial production by controls over prices, materials and labour and even produced munitions. Businessmen entered Whitehall to help supply the skills of organizing and directing economic activity. Not surprisingly, Whitehall preferred to deal wherever possible with collective representative bodies rather than on a firm-by-firm basis and began to encourage business combination. Two important groups were formed, the British Manufacturers Association (BMA), based in Birmingham and largely devoted to protection, and the Employers' Parliamentary Association (EPA), based on cotton textiles in Manchester and staunchly supporting free trade.[2] These groups were, however, too small and localized to satisfy those who wanted to ensure that industry would have a say in shaping the postwar world. Almost by definition, these were radical industrialists seeking a major shift in economic policy. One such was Dudley Docker, a member of the BMA and chairman of the Metropolitan Carriage, Wagon and Finance Co. In 1916, Docker formed the Federation of British Industries (FBI) as an all-embracing industrial pressure group with an aim of corporatist and imperial postwar economic policy.[3] Docker's vision was of a new form of society in which each industry would have its own formal organizations of workers and of managers, with each side headed by a peak federation which would send representatives to a great national forum on economic policy. His major economic policy objective was the formation of an imperial economic bloc behind a common tariff.[4] Whitehall certainly supported the FBI during the war and membership began to expand rapidly.[5] The EPA joined in late 1916, and, by 1917, 337 firms and trade associations had joined.[6]

The effectiveness of the FBI as a pressure group did not, however, rise in proportion. This mixing of strongly protectionist and free-trading groups quickly brought not consensus but impotence, threats of splits and

[2] Stephen Blank, *Industry and Government in Britain: The Federation of British Industries in Politics, 1945–65*, Farnborough, Saxon House, 1973, p. 14.

[3] Blank, *The FBI in Politics*, pp. 14–15.

[4] Ibid., p. 15.

[5] The FBI deliberately aimed to recruit as broadly as possible to establish a balanced, representative body for industry. Keith Middlemas, *Politics in Industrial Society: The British Experience of the System Since 1911*, London, André Deutsch, 1979, p. 112.

[6] Blank, *The FBI in Politics*, p. 15.

a consequent inability to pronounce on the one topic about which industrialists had firm opinions.[7] Moreover, the fact that the FBI was led by the employer equivalent of the guild socialists created immense suspicion among the employers' associations, the organizations which had traditionally handled direct negotiations with trade unions. The employers' associations, and particularly the very conservative Engineering Employers' Federation, had no time at all for the lofty ideal of co-partnership or union participation in decision-making. The employers' associations flexed their muscles and in 1917 managed to force the FBI to keep out of questions 'affecting working conditions or rates of pay except at the request of employers' associations established to deal with such questions'.[8] These divisions between free traders and protectionists and between corporatists and the defenders of managerial prerogatives were to recur throughout the interwar period whenever industrialists turned to economic policy.

The FBI was able to contain dissent over protection by avoiding the subject, but the 'labour' question was a persistent source of friction. It flared up in December 1917, when the first (and last) report of the FBI's Labour Committee urged that employers and employees cooperate to remove restrictive practices, contribute together to schemes of sickness, unemployment and superannuation benefit, and work together to establish minimum-wage schemes. The employers' associations almost withdrew from the FBI.[9] The report was dropped and with it went all prospects of the FBI acting as a lobby for corporatist arrangements. The conservative employers' associations had now won absolute control over the labour question. This proved decisive in the government initiative to quell postwar industrial unrest.

The rapidly deteriorating climate of industrial relations after the Armistice and fears of 'political' strikes in 1919 induced the government to call representatives of management and unions to a National Industrial Conference in February 1919. Ministers hoped for a 'Peace Conference for Industry' to parallel efforts at international conciliation at Versailles. Although the government had initially not been fully committed to the idea of the NIC, when the delegates assembled Lloyd George took a strong lead, setting out an ambitious programme for discussion, embracing unemployment, housing, hours of work, minimum wages and reform of industrial relations. Unfortunately, this agenda cut right across the division of function which industry had worked out (the FBI taking

[7] Ibid., p. 16.

[8] CBI Papers, NCEO/C4/11/N.C. 0115/5 Dec. 1919.

[9] Blank, *The FBI in Politics*, p. 17.

general economic questions and leaving labour matters to the employers' associations) and left the employers in some disarray. Sir Allan Smith of the Engineering Employers' Federation took the lead and established the National Confederation of Employers' Organizations (NCEO) to lead the employers' side and to try to prevent them from conceding too much.[10] He argued at the first meeting that the industrial relations problems of early 1919 were merely a temporary response to transitory conditions and would best be overcome by leaving industry to put its own house in order in the traditional manner. The 'traditional manner' was for management to insist on managerial prerogatives, a position which the EEF repeated constantly.[11] Smith's plea for a return to normalcy fell on deaf ears. The NIC established a Provisional Joint Committee (PJC) to look at three separate areas (wages, hours and conditions; unemployment and its prevention; cooperation between capital and labour) which were dear to the progressive corporatists among industrialists who were disorganized but still powerful. The PJC recommended and the full NIC accepted two measures which encroached upon the territory of the employers' associations: the legal enforcement of minimum time rates in each industry and a statutory maximum working week of 48 hours. On less important matters, the PJC could agree that organized short-time working, the contra-cyclical planning of public works, a government housing drive and state support of new industries should all go ahead. Faced with this common ground between capital and labour, the government had little choice but to begin legislative action.

On the face of it, it is astonishing that the employers' side should have conceded so much when the purpose of Smith and the NCEO had been to prevent deals of this type.[12] Smith has been described by Walter Citrine of the TUC as a master of procrastination, and the wider purposes of the NCEO have been described as to unite employer opinion against reform.[13] The conclusion must be that the progressives were in the ascendant among employers at this time. Certainly, political conditions did not favour any sort of vigorous campaign for the exclusion of the state from areas which had before the war been the preserves of management. Ministers had been heard to favour nationalization,[14] and in the interim report of the Sankey

[10] Roger Charles, *The Development of Industrial Relations in Britain, 1911-1939*, London, Hutchinson, 1973, p. 252.

[11] Rodney Lowe, 'The Failure of Consensus in Britain: The National Industrial Conference, 1919–21', *Historical Journal*, 21, 1978, pp. 668–9.

[12] Charles, *The Development of Industrial Relations*, p. 252.

[13] Lowe, 'The Failure of Consensus', p. 669.

[14] S. M. H. Armitage, *The Politics of Decontrol of Industry: Britain and the United States*, London, Weidenfeld & Nicolson, 1969, pp. 64–5.

Commission on the coal industry, not even the industrialist members could be induced to pronounce in favour of continuing private ownership.[15] In this climate, the conservative NCEO had to salvage what it could, principally by buying time. This crisis for the hawkish employers soon passed. Ground had been given in April 1919, but by the summer it was clear that the basis for a corporatist consensus did not exist, and that the future direction of economic policy and even of the form of social organization would have to be settled by conflict.[16] Meetings of the PJC became deadlocked. The NCEO took a leading part in ensuring that nothing positive came of the final Sankey report on the long-term future of the coal industry.[17]. Ministers and employers appeared to be conspiring to destroy the working-class movement, especially its better-organized, more radical elements.[18] The conservatives within industry were now clearly in the ascendant, and their hold was strengthened by the economic collapse in 1920. Markets slumped, especially for exports; margins were squeezed; the need to cut costs was paramount. The burden of taxation was a frequent target, and industry welcomed retrenchment, deflation, the Geddes Axe, and the more orthodox complexion to policy in the early 1920s.[19] This was probably the closest industry came to unity in its demands of economic policy in the whole interwar period.

MOND AND THE REVIVAL OF PROGRESSIVE PATERNALISM

After 1919, industry's national organizations were incapable of giving a lead in economic policy. The FBI could not pronounce on wages and hours, even though it knew that most employers firmly believed that wages were too high. Nor could it enter the debate on tariff reform even though both sides came to see their own cause as the panacea for Britain's economic problems in the 1920s. The FBI drew in its horns to become principally a service and defence organization for its members.[20] The NCEO did little better. It shunned publicity, in part because of its heavy involvement in strike-breaking. At the same time, it was being sucked into

[15] Ibid., pp. 120.

[16] Middlemas speaks of 'power bargaining' in this period; *Politics in Industrial Society*, p. 141.

[17] Ibid., p. 147n.

[18] Ibid., pp. 146–7.

[19] Alan Booth, 'Corporatism, Capitalism and Depression in Twentieth Century Britain, *British Journal of Sociology*, 33, 1982, pp. 210–14.

[20] Blank, *The FBI in Politics*, p. 21.

a continuing relationship with government in the preparation of labour legislation. Its freedom to campaign was being eroded.[21]

New ideas in economic policy came instead from individual industrialists, frequently from the larger companies. Although they might be members, and even leading lights, of the FBI or NCEO, they tended to use these organizations as but one vehicle of advancing their ideas. The most important was undoubtedly Sir Alfred Mond, the chairman of the chemicals firm Brunner-Mond, and one of the driving forces behind the creation of ICI. In many areas of economic policy, Mond was rigidly orthodox and an extreme individualist. He called again and again for the utmost financial stringency to reduce debt and ease taxation, and was not above equating state intervention in industry with socialism and bureaucratic tyranny.[22] When he held ministerial office in the 1918–22 Lloyd George coalition, he took satisfaction in slashing the 'homes fit for heroes' postwar housing programme, and was the only Minister to be praised by the Geddes Committee for his efforts to curtail public expenditure.[23] These were not promising foundations upon which to build a critique of orthodox economic policies, but Mond, like many other leaders of large-scale, modern British industry in the early twentieth century, saw distinct limits to the realm of market forces. Like Docker, he was a protectionist, favouring a strategy of empire development behind a common external, imperial tariff.[24] He came to these ideas as a member of the wartime Balfour Committee, appointed to consider the postwar reconstruction of British trade and industry. Mond continued to be impressed by the raw material and population resources of the empire and wished to see it forged into a coherent economic unit. While in office, he submitted to the Cabinet plans for closer imperial economic integration and followed this with a proposal to relieve unemployment by assisted empire settlement.[25] The imperial vision derived from his identification of trends towards the formation of trading blocs, both in North America and in Europe. The options for Britain were either to join one of these units or to form its own bloc based on the empire. Both Europe and the USA were, or could be, balanced economic units containing strong primary producing

[21] Middlemas, *Politics in Industrial Society*, pp. 161–2.

[22] See Sir Alfred Mond, *Industry and Politics*, London, Macmillan, 1927, pp. 36, 308–37, and Hector Bolitho, *Alfred Mond: First Lord Melchett*, London, Martin Secker, 1933, pp. 223–5.

[23] Bolitho, *Alfred Mond*, pp. 223–4.

[24] Mond, *Industry and Politics*, pp. 274–90. His most cogently argued case came in *Imperial Economic Unity*, London, Harrap, 1930.

[25] Bolitho, *Alfred Mond*, pp. 321–2.

and manufacturing sectors, and as such were potential threats, especially to British manufacturing industry. Mond thus regarded imperial unity as an essential strategy and urged British manufacturers to follow his lead and pursue imperial mergers of the major industrial combinations in order to hasten the process of integration. Within this protected unit, British capital could provide the major stimulus to development and growth with the promise that guaranteed markets would promote continuing efficiency and productivity improvements. He recognized the immense political difficulties of this strategy, but offered a very flexible and pragmatic path beginning with reciprocal trade deals between Britain and empire countries.[26] Mond was not an effective propagandist. Public opinion took very little notice of his arguments until his ideas were taken up by Beaverbrook in 1929, with the start of the Empire Free Trade campaign and the formation of the Empire Economic Union. However, it was not until 1932 and the Ottawa imperial economic talks that the real weaknesses of the strategy became apparent. In a nutshell, the leaders of empire governments were much more concerned with their domestic economic and political problems to act as saviours to the British economy. Empire countries had their own industrial workers. They did not intend to become dumping grounds for the British goods which had been priced out of world markets.

Mond also had more direct and short-term plans to reduce British unemployment. The first had been developed during his period as Minister of Health in 1921–2, and involved the use of the unemployment insurance fund to subsidize new jobs rather than to maintain the unemployed. The original scheme had fallen with the Lloyd George coalition, but Mond returned to the plan in 1925 and tried to win support for it in the FBI Grand Council. He proposed to concentrate subsidies upon the most depressed industries and so arrange the scheme that support would go only to jobs which would not otherwise have been created. How this difficult feat might have been arranged was never fully explained. The FBI could not accept the plan as it stood, but did propose a more broadly spread subsidy to industries in severe depression which were both internally well organized and dependent on a small number of large contracts. The FBI's discussions coincided with the 1925 coal dispute, and the FBI warmly welcomed the government's decision to subsidize the industry for a limited period, provided that industry as a whole was not asked to pay higher taxes. The aim was greater competitiveness for coal without burdening the rest of British industry. Radical and orthodox ideas could intertwine.

[26] Mond, *Imperial Economic Unity*, pp. 81–3.

A similar mixture is evident in the FBI position in the 1920s on monetary policy and the exchange rate. During the brief postwar inflationary crisis, the FBI had asked for any return to the gold standard to await more normal economic and financial conditions.[27] Although the FBI's policy stance soon became very orthodox, suspicion of monetary policy remained, especially among the leadership. Mond, with support from Sir Peter Rylands, wanted monetary policy to be more mindful of the needs of industry.[28] He argued that the decision to aim for a return to gold had been taken very rashly and prematurely in 1919, and that the subsequent deflationary policy had depressed business and the rising sterling–dollar exchange rate had caused lost markets and strained industrial relations. Mond also drew attention to the determination of the monetary authorities to reduce the national debt. The great expansion of the debt had occurred during wartime and had been engineered in *depreciating* pounds. By trying to redeem these debts while *appreciating* the currency, the authorities were, in Mond's view, attempting the impossible and sacrificing industry for financial stability. Practical experience had driven some of Britain's top industrialists to a position similar to that of Keynes.

The FBI leadership was unable to take a very strong line against the monetary policies of the mid-1920s because most of the FBI membership were either ignorant of the problems or willing to leave decisions in this area to the government's experts. The FBI did, however, enter the debate at the time of the Chamberlain–Bradbury Committee.[29] The federation pointed to the short-term problem that British prices were 10 per cent above those ruling in America, but also recognized that long-term benefits would accrue from greater international financial stability and increased confidence. However, the FBI, like Keynes, were not convinced that the benefits outweighed the costs of a quick return. The dangers of overvaluation included serious temporary dislocation with higher unemployment, losses for all those who traded on borrowed money, a threat to industrial relations from the need to cut wages, a loss of competitiveness in

---

[27] L. J. Hume, 'The Gold Standard and Deflation: Issues and Attitudes in the 1920s', in Sidney Pollard (ed.), *The Gold Standard and Employment Policies between the Wars*, London, Methuen, 1970, p. 140.

[28] Mond's ideas are most conveniently approached through his speeches, 'The Napoleonic Era' and 'Trade, Currency and Unemployment', collected in *Industry and Politics*, pp. 13–34, 52–70.

[29] The Chamberlain–Bradbury Committee, more formally the Committee on the Currency and Bank of England Note Issues, was convened to consider the amalagamation of the Treasury note issue (a wartime expedient) with that of the Bank of England. However, this was merely a technical device on the road to restoring the gold standard. The discussions are surveyed by Donald Moggridge, *British Monetary Policy: The Norman Conquest of $4.86*, Cambridge, CUP, 1972, pp. 38–50.

export industries, and a rising real burden of the national debt.[30] The FBI, again echoing Keynes, doubted whether US prices would be allowed to rise to ease Britain's adjustment process and accordingly judged that a return to gold at an early date would be premature and inadvisable.[31] Indeed, in internal memoranda the case against the gold standard was much stronger, pointing to the need to rectify the enormous structural changes in international trade and finance since 1914 before a restored gold standard could provide national advantage. In many respects, this gloomy analysis is more perspicacious even than that of Keynes, and the despair about the prospects of ever restoring the conditions under which the international economy might retain its dynamism led Mond and others more resolutely to empire economic union.[32]

The final area in which Mond led FBI thinking was in 'rationalization'. Industrialists as a whole had become increasingly concerned about foreign competition since 1921, but many were inclined to blame any loss of markets on external factors, such as the unions, taxes or rates. Mond tried to get British industrialists to see that all was not well with British methods of production. He was a strong advocate of increasing the scale of British enterprise, since his own capital-intensive and science-based chemicals sector showed that large production units were a precondition of deploying both capital and research effort. Mond firmly believed in the existence of an evolutionary process to larger economic units, but he wanted wise industrialists to accelerate it as a major weapon to frustrate a tendency to overproduction caused by increasing technical efficiency. Monopolistic firms were in a position to adjust production to anticipated consumption. The drive to larger, more efficient but less competitive industries which relied heavily upon scientific reasearch to find new and better products was termed the 'rationalization movement' and was particularly associated with Mond.[33] The formation of ICI in 1926 under the guidance of Mond and Sir Harry MacGowan was the high point of its influence. In many ways, this programme was not especially inventive, little more than might be expected from any major industrialist in any capital-intensive sector. The remarkable element in Mond's version of rationalization was the way it was to be achieved, by winning the confidence of and cooperating closely with the labour force. Mond was a progressive paternalist. He abhorred socialism but this did not conflict with a very conciliatory attitude to organized labour, as long as workers kept out of ideological

[30] CBI Papers, MSS 200/F/4/45/1.
[31] Hume, 'The Gold Standard and Deflation', p. 143.
[32] CBI Papers, MSS 200/F/3/E1/411, Memorandum dated 5 Feb. 1925.
[33] *Industry and Politics*, pp. 35–51, 210–21.

territories. From these presuppositions grew his concept of the 'Industrial Trinity' – capital, management and labour.[34] Only if all three worked together would industry prosper. Mond understood that labour would be most cooperative if it could be made to see an identity of interest with capital and management. He advocated, and introduced into his own firms, co-partnership through profit-sharing and close cooperation with unions over factory-level decisions. He favoured a high-wage economy, and openly rejected longer hours and wage cuts as a solution to the unemployment problem.[35] To prevent industrial disputes Mond advocated an extensive network of arbitration culminating in a League of Industry to prevent industrial warfare as the League of Nations was designed to contain international conflict.[36] The strong corporatist elements in Mond's thinking and the closeness to the views of wartime industrial progressives such as Docker are very clear.

With this approach to industrial relations, it is hardly surprising that Mond should have been involved in industrial reconciliation after 1926. The general strike had demonstrated that the unions had immense disruptive power and that conflict was extremely costly. The time was ripe for cooperation, a mood which government Ministers sought to foster. The institutional divisions on the employers' side made an 'official', representative conference unlikely, but Mond could not pass up an offer from the TUC of talks.[37] Accordingly, he invited TUC leaders and a number of prominent industrialists to talks which were to cover rationalization, the security and status of employment, trade-disputes procedure, the disclosure of information to unions, and schemes for worker participation. In short, the conference was to cover the full range of industrial relations and economic policy topics in which a 'producer alliance' might have been constructed, and on which Mond was known to hold progressive views.

Most of the employers invited by Mond did take part, though the high office holders in both the FBI and the NCEO remained aloof. Alongside Mond were the 'statesmen of industry', drawn from all industries but with an overrepresentation of the largest firms, especially from those with dominant market positions and which were better able to cooperate with labour. A significant number came from firms supplying a rapidly expanding consumer market, though staple industries were represented.

---

[34] The phrase recurs throughout the speeches collected in *Industry and Politics*, especially at pp. 36–9.

[35] Ibid., p. 48.

[36] Ibid., pp. 127–46.

[37] One of his reasons for seizing this opportunity (initially suggested by Baldwin) was his need to demonstrate his loyalty to the Conservative Party, which he had joined after breaking with Lloyd George over Liberal land policy.

The position of the Mond group in the Mond–Turner talks should therefore offer an insight into the economic ideas of the least conservative of British employers.

The full conference met for the first time in January 1928 and immediately established a small sub-committee to discuss the main areas. Much of the ground was covered in a Joint Interim Statement, approved by the second full conference in July 1928, and the remaining issues dealing with broader aspects of economic policy were outlined in a Joint Interim Report on Unemployment, approved by the third and final full meeting in March 1929. Although the conference and its first interim report have received much attention from historians of industrial relations,[38] the employers' economic programme has been comparatively neglected. The Mond side was willing to move away from the rigidly orthodox position that wages should be forced down to increase competitiveness. Employers accepted the right of unions to represent their members and urged full cooperation between management and unions on *all* matters of joint interest. A new National Industrial Council was proposed to strengthen conciliation of disputes, though compulsory arbitration was rejected. This was not the machinery through which to force down wages, and in return for 'moderation' on this issue, the employers sought union support for a joint initiative to the government to protest about monetary policy. The Mond side feared that domestic deflation had made British industry unattractive to investors, resulting in high foreign lending and a loss of momentum in the domestic economy.[39]

Willingness to compromise was also evident in the unemployment programme. Despite their strong doubts about existing levels of public spending, the employers supported higher state relief to the unemployed in coal-mining, contra-cyclical timing of public works and government contracts, the expansion of the Development Fund, earlier pensions, and the raising of the school-leaving age.[40] Both employers and the TUC were happy to press for greater state aid to imperial development and assisted migration. In return, the employers gained unequivocal union support for rationalization, provided the unions were included in any talks on the

---

[38] The best sources for the talks are: Charles, *The Development of Industrial Relations*, pp. 261–306; Howard F. Gospel, 'Employers' Labour Policy: A Study of the Mond–Turner Talks, 1927–33', *Business History*, 21, 1979; G. W. McDonald and H. F. Gospel, 'The Mond-Turner Talks, 1927–33; A Study in Industrial Co-operation', *Historical Journal*, 16, 1973.

[39] The Mond side persuaded the TUC to address a memorandum on this subject to the Chancellor of the Exchequer in April 1928; Gospel, 'Employers' Labour Policy', p. 187.

[40] Conference on Industrial Reorganisation and Industrial Relations (hereafter CIRIR), *Interim Joint Report on Unemployment*, London, CIRIR, 1929, p. 16.

rationalization of a particular industry, especially when labour-force reduction was an issue. Even more important was a proposal to levy firms during 'normal' times to establish a labour fund to help sustain or create jobs for displaced workers. A more favourable monetary policy was required to supplement the programme, and the conference called for an inquiry into currency and banking policy in which the producer interest would be given a sympathetic ear. This was the origin of the Macmillan Committee on Finance and Industry.

The programme was impressive, and the reports won praise for their good sense and advocacy of practical solutions. The economics were simple but sound; shift the direction of the economy more decisively towards the empire, make industry more technically efficient, and create jobs for those displaced in the process. The similarity with Mond's pre-conference position is scarcely coincidental. There were, however, unanswered questions, not least on monetary and budgetary policies (which the proposed inquiry might solve), the efficacy of rationalization, and the economic possibilities of empire development. The prospects of ultimate success depended upon the ability of employers and unions to unite to shift the government. The TUC's position was clear, but the views on economic policy of the majority of employers were unknown and the representativeness of the Mond group was untested.

EMPLOYER REACTION

The initial responses of the FBI and NCEO were not promising. The two organizations established a special committee to consider tactics, and it was clear imediately that the Mond–Turner exercise had aroused great suspicion. This committee did not want the Mond–Turner talks to terminate because it feared that the FBI and NCEO would be drawn into the vacuum.[41] Employer thinking was dominated not by economic questions but by the knowledge that a general election was imminent and that the Labour Party was strengthening its position in public opinion. Employers were afraid that their actions or inaction might be exploited by a 'highly political' TUC for Labour's electoral advantage.[42] The most important tactical decision was to retain the separate identities of the FBI and NCEO. This was more than a restatement of the division of responsibility established in 1917. In many industries, the body dealing with wages and hours and affiliated to the NCEO had a considerable overlap of member-

---

[41] CBI Papers, MSS 200/F/1/1/160, Meetings 28 and 29 Sept. 1928.
[42] CBI Papers, MSS 200/F/3/S1/18/2, Memorandum dated 21 Feb. 1929.

ship with a parallel organization dealing with more general economic questions and a member of the FBI. There was some support on the committee for a quick breakdown between the TUC and NCEO over wages while trying to use more constructive TUC–FBI talks to exert some leverage over a potential Labour government upon issues of broader economic policy.[43] Whether by accident or design, the actual outcome was similar to this pattern.

Both the FBI and NCEO did nothing until the views of their members had been taken. Gospel has used the replies to show that a minority of the NCEO, representing approximately one-quarter of its membership, approved of the suggestions in the first Mond–Turner interim report.[44] The vast majority were deeply suspicious (above all, of trade union recognition and the establishment of a new NIC) but wanted to pursue further meetings with the TUC. A substantial minority, including the powerful engineers and shipowners, wanted nothing to do with the unions. Opposition was accompanied by a vigorous defence of managerial prerogatives, especially over wages. The FBI received similar responses, with vigorous rejections of the Mond group's programme. The British Engineers' Association, for example, could see no prospect of cooperation between 'two parties whose policies are fundamentally opposed to one another'.[45] Even rationalization ran into intense opposition from staple industries, with the Wool Textile Employers' Association severe in its condemnation both of rationalization and 'the economy of high wages'.[46] The orthodox view, which had been noticeably absent from the Mond group, was clearly still strong in the circles of British management.

However, when Labour emerged from the 1929 general election as the biggest party, the employers were forced to agree to talks with the unions. The agenda for discussion included unemployment, industry and finance, taxation of industry, and foreign trade. The TUC talked to either the FBI or the NCEO as appropriate. The NCEO, which conducted the employer side of the unemployment talks, was from the outset reluctant and half-hearted.[47] As economic conditions began to deteriorate in late 1929, the NCEO began to sense a strengthening of the employers' position against labour, and it increasingly emphasized the primacy of managerial prerogatives. Talks did, however, drag on until 1931 when the NCEO issued *The Industrial Situation*, which called for a one-third reduction in unemployment insurance benefits, reduction of all wages to the levels set

[43] Gospel, 'Employers' Labour Policy', p. 191.

[44] Ibid., pp. 189–90.

[45] CBI Papers, MSS 200/F/3/S1/18/3, letter from BEA, 16 Jan. 1929.

[46] CBI Papers, MSS 200/F/3/S1/18/3, undated memorandum by WTEA.

[47] McDonald and Gospel, 'The Mond–Turner' Talks', p. 827.

by the export industries, and an all-round lowering of British costs. In the crisis, such orthodox sentiment was hardly surprising. But there is no indication that the NCEO was ever anything other than highly orthodox. The employers had kept the unemployment talks going only for as long as was politically expedient.

The TUC–FBI talks progressed further, but the FBI did have positive objectives; protection, empire preference and cheap money. It hoped to use the TUC to exert additional pressure on the Labour government.[48] As economic conditions deteriorated, the free traders within the FBI were weakened, and a full protective programme was adopted in 1930. The TUC could not be swung behind the campaign for tariff reform because of its own internal divisions, and industry was left to pursue this objective without TUC assistance. Prospects were initially more favourable over a joint initiative on interest rates. The establishment of the Macmillan Committee brought the suggestion of a joint FBI–TUC submission, but the plans fell through and separate memoranda were presented. The approach of both sides was, however, very similar, so a further attempt was made to construct a joint submission. As we shall see, the FBI was badly split over certain aspects of monetary policy, with the result that the joint initiative collapsed for a second time. The record on empire development was happier, with both organizations calling for the establishment of an inter-imperial economic secretariat leading to a joint representation to MacDonald in September 1930. Although TUC–FBI cooperation wilted during the depths of the crisis, both sides sent representatives to the Ottawa conferences to act as observers and advisers, and joint discussions were taken up once more.

As the economic crisis began to worsen, the direction of industrial thinking was governed less by these hesitant feelers towards a producer alliance and much more by indications of increasing uncompetitiveness. The strategy seems to have been that the FBI should concentrate on a campaign for a tariff with the NCEO fighting for lower wages.[49] The FBI had at last been freed to campaign openly for protection by the results of a survey conducted in the summer of 1930 which showed almost unanimous opinion in favour of tariff reform. The Grand Council adopted the policy in October, and in March of the following year a major policy statement was published. By this time, however, there was already a sizeable groundswell of opinion behind tariff reform, and the FBI tended to concentrate its attentions much more on the need for retrenchment in

---

[48] Ibid., pp. 826–7.
[49] CBI Papers, MSS 200/F/3/51/13/1, Memorandum by J. B. Bibby, n.d., and Rylands to Locock, 9 Feb. 1931.

public spending. In *Industry and the Nation*, for example, the FBI matched its calls for protection with a vigorous demand for cuts in both central and local government spending.[50] Its post-devaluation programme, *Public Expenditure*, was more extreme, noting that central government spending had risen in real terms by 400 per cent since 1913, and implied that *all* state expenditure was a diversion of resources away from industrial investment.[51] The FBI had no compunction in campaigning for a sharp pruning of public spending which was 'defensible on purely social grounds', but was 'beyond what the nation could afford', with housing, education, health expenditure and social insurance identified as targets. The number of government departments should be cut with corresponding losses in civil service employment, and local authority services 'should be reduced to a minimum'.

It is, of course, scarcely surprising that the collapse of national and international demand between 1930 and 1932 should have produced severe intensification of competitive pressures and a violent thrust by industrialists to lower costs and decrease the forces of destructive competition. The NCEO and the FBI had little alternative in 1931 but to press vociferously for lower wages, lower public spending and hence lower taxes, and protection. But there is little doubt also that industrialists were attempting to shift as much of the burden of economic adjustment away from their own shoulders as they possibly could. This rather unattractive trait is clearly evident in the extracts from *Public Expenditure* cited in the previous paragraph, but it was by no means confined to the FBI's stand on retrenchment. The FBI's position on protection and empire economic union was riddled with the same approach. Whereas Ministers and late converts to protectionism like Keynes tended to see the tariff as a means of offering industry a *temporary* respite during which it would re-equip and regain competitiveness, tariff reformers in industry always saw the policy in a rather more permanent light. The progressives such as Docker and Mond linked protection, as we have seen, with a permanent restructuring of the British economy towards the empire. To others, protection seems to have been seen as a panacea, a cure for all the problems of lack of competitiveness and poor profitability. However, when the results of protection in the early 1930s were very disappointing, the FBI concluded neither that its faith in the tariff had been misplaced nor that British industry had fundamental problems in efficiency and technique, but

[50] The pamphlet was published by the FBI in 1931.

[51] It was argued that all taxation 'dissipated' capital: FBI, *Public Expenditure*, London, FBI, Oct. 1932, p. 5.

rather that the system of protection needed revision. There was a continuing demand for the dropping or restriction of the 'Most Favoured Nation' clause in commercial treaties, much more extensive use of bilateralism including the use of economic force in bilateral trade deals, and action to prevent empire countries from protecting their domestic manufactures against British goods.[52] This is more than a response to autarkic policies by other nations; it is an attempt to force other nations to accept uncompetitive British goods. The FBI's hope to use the empire as a dumping ground or a 'soft' market for British manufactures was particularly unfortunate and a crude betrayal of the ideals of men such as Docker and Mond. In the 1930s, empire countries tended to have higher average levels of unemployment than the UK and were desperately attempting to diversify vulnerable, narrow economies ravaged by the fall of agricultural prices.

Beneath the FBI's determination to have others bear as much of the burden of economic adjustment as possible in the difficult years of the early 1930s lay a conviction that industrialists were not at all responsible for Britain's economic problems since the end of the war. Trade unions and high-spending governments came in for much blame, but particular importance was attached to monetary policy and the gold standard. The FBI's submission to the Macmillan Committee blamed many of industry's difficulties in the 1920s on the efforts first to restore and then maintain the gold standard. The memorandum was, in fact, an attempt to show that the FBI's predictions to the Chamberlain–Bradbury Committee had been proved correct. A feature of the analysis was a belief that every country except the UK had manipulated the gold standard for national advantage.[53] Britain's signal failure to subjugate the needs of finance to the needs of industry and employment had produced specific problems of poor competitiveness in the export industries and a general weakening of industry by continuing monetary stringency. The FBI made the valuable point that an effective gold standard needed genuine international agreement, but its picture of the hard-done-by British industrialist facing unfair competition from every corner of the globe and bearing the burdens of a domestic monetary policy which was totally unfavourable to business interests was scarcely realistic. The FBI Industrial Policy Committee which had prepared the submission was convinced that the decision in 1925 to restore the gold standard had been wrong and that gold would

[52] FBI, *British Commercial Policy*, London, FBI, Feb. 1934, pp. 4–5; FBI, *British Tariff Policy*, London, FBI, June 1936, pp. 3–5.

[53] CBI Papers, MSS 200/F/4/45/1, Evidence of the Federation of British Industries to the Committee on Finance and Industry, 26 Feb. 1930, p. 5.

have to be abandoned. However, the members could not agree whether it was practical politics to urge abandonment, and failed to submit a second memorandum on domestic monetary policy.[54]

The FBI leadership was less divided after the abandonment of gold in 1931. The demands for a new orientation in monetary policy reveal some of the selfishness and self-rightousness evident in the post-1931 position on tariffs and empire preference. The key to the FBI's position was to make finance the servant of industry.[55] The primary objective of a post-gold monetary policy was to give stable prices, but at a level which permitted reasonable profit. The first priority on the national savings should be new investment calculated to secure the maximum advantage for British industry, and that which remained for foreign investment should be confined within the sterling area and go only to countries which were complementary trading partners; in short, foreign investment should not go to competing manufacturing enterprise, but should be concentrated in food and raw material projects. British industry was clearly demanding feather-bedding. The inability to compete with industry in other nations was admitted, albeit implicitly. British industrialists no longer wanted to face the chill winds of external competition, but sought instead to create permanent 'soft' markets both at home and abroad. That much of the programme implied the creation of an enormous bureaucracy in the Italian or Nazi German manner (for example, to control imports and operate bilateral trade agreements, and to supervise investment policy) completely escaped the FBI's policy-makers. The proposals on trade and monetary policy sat very uneasily with demands for retrenchment and withdrawal of the government from industrial affairs. Above all, one is struck by the sheer complacency which emerged after 1931.

In sum, the alternative economic ideas of British industrialists in the years up to 1932 were striking for containing both highly progressive and highly orthodox wings. There can be little doubt that the programme associated with the Mond groups was among the most impressive of either decade. Perhaps aided by their remoteness from the day-to-day problems of industry, the Mond group could take a broad and intelligent view of Britain's economic problems. Their conviction that the return to gold was harming British economic performance, while commonplace today, was both brave and perceptive by the standards of the time. Their intensely practical scheme was, of course, much more clearly within the grasp of governments and business leaders than were the ideologically more pure

---

[54] CBI Papers, MSS 200/F/1/1/76, Minutes of the Industrial Policy Committee, Nov. 1930.

[55] FBI, *A New Financial Policy: Industry's Plan*, London, FBI, April 1933, p. 20.

schemes of, say, the ILP or the Liberals. However, the Mond scheme did have its weaknesses. The political obstacles to empire economic union were only partially appreciated, and the whole programme betrayed many of the shortcomings on monetary policy which were common to most expansionist programmes of this period; the finance of public works and of the rationalization 'labour fund' were both sketchy and the Mond group also shared the general haziness about the precise route to lower interest rates under a gold standard. These were, however, common failings and were certainly shared by parties with impressive lists of economic advisers.

The worst aspects of employer economic thinking occurred between 1929 and 1932. There are strong hints that the employers orchestrated their reactions to the Mond–Turner proposals with a cynicism and even duplicity which would have embarrassed the major political parties. It is clear that the majority of employers had no faith in any state-organized attempt to expand the economy but pinned their faith on efforts to reduce wages and restrict competition by protection. The FBI, in particular, used the division of responsibility between the FBI and the NCEO to maximize pressure for protection, empire preference and cheap money, while dodging the wages question, on which the majority of its members had a hawkish attitude. The TUC was outflanked and manipulated. The second and even less endearing aspect of employer economic thinking was the pathological unwillingness of either main business organization to admit that there was anything wrong with British management or to shoulder its share of the burden of unemployment. In a capitalist society, the owners and managers of capital bear ultimate responsibility for ensuring that capital is utilized efficiently and profitably. However, both the FBI and NCEO were ready to produce long lists of those culpable for Britain's economic problems but neither admitted entrepreneurial weaknesses as a cause. With such an exaggerated view of their own qualities, British industrialists turned increasingly to special pleading and self-protection rather than continue in the Mond tradition of careful study of the dynamics of national and international economic forces.[56]

---

[56] Those industrialists who retained a commitment to progressive or radical ideas tended to work during the 1930s not through business organizations but through the loose, informal groupings in the radical centre. See chapter 3.

5

The TUC and Economic Policy in the 1930s

During the 1930s, the TUC's record, as an organization representative of the interests of labour, was marred by two significant failures. The first of these was the failure to re-establish the Labour Party, after the debacle of 1931, as a viable alternative to the National Government, in spite of the controlling influence the TUC exercised over party affairs and policy. The second was the failure to develop and campaign for a comprehensive counter-cyclical strategy with deficit-financed public works as a central feature. On this issue, it will be demonstrated that, contrary to the assertions of Pollard and Bullock[1] that the TUC had within its grasp only the *possibility* of developing a coherent expansionist programme it had, in fact, a concrete and theoretical set of alternative economic policies readily *available*. These alternatives were produced by the International Federation of Trade Unions (IFTU) and its affiliated national centres among which the TUC itself was numbered. The TUC chose to ignore these alternatives, in part through a self-induced myopia based upon Bevin and Citrine's notion of 'realism' but also because of the caution and rightward shift evident in many aspects of the General Council's orientation during the 1930s.

A major precept of this orientation was the desire on the part of the Bevin–Citrine duumvirate to secure the trade-union movement's assimilation into the power structure of the state[2] – a process that had been embarked upon initially in the shape of the Mond–Turner talks, accelerated by the 'moderation' of the TUC in the 1930s and perhaps not

[1] A. Bullock, *The Life and Times of Ernest Bevin*, vol. I: *1881–1940*, London, Heinemann, 1960; S. Pollard, 'Trade Union Reactions to the Economic Crisis', *Journal of Contemporary History*, 4, 1969, pp. 101–15. See also D. I. MacKay, D. J. C. Forsyth and D. M. Kelly, 'The Discussion of Public Works Programmes, 1917–1935: Some Remarks on the Labour Movement's Contribution', *International Review of Social History*, 11, 1966.

[2] *The Life and Times of Ernest Bevin*, vol. I, pp. 347–8, and W. Citrine, *Men and Work*, London, Hutchinson, 1964, pp. 238–9.

fully consummated until the extensive collaboration between the unions and government in the second world war. One example of this tendency was the acceptance by Citrine and Pugh of knighthoods from MacDonald in his 1935 resignation honours list, but the following developments were of more significance: the systematic assault mounted by the trade-union leadership upon the notion of a Popular Front with the Communist Party; the displacement of communist militants from trade-union organizations; the opprobrium poured on the NUWM and its attempts to mobilize the unemployed; the suppression of rank-and-file movements; and finally, the virtual abandonment of the nationwide industrial strike. It is arguable that the pursuit of assimilation was entirely justifiable in terms of the end results. Unlike most other European trade-union movements, the TUC actually registered an increase in membership between 1929 and 1939.[3] It was gradually accepted by government and slowly drawn into the decision-making process.[4] All these 'gains' were, however, purchased at a cost to the British labour movement. Part of the cost was the refusal of the TUC to embrace and actively campaign for an expansionist programme. It is on this issue that the remainder of this chapter will concentrate.

TUC ECONOMIC POLICY

After the debacle of the general strike in 1926, the right-wing elements in the General Council (led by Citrine, Pugh and Bevin in particular) emerged as the dominant force which determined the direction of TUC policy for the remainder of the interwar period. The lessons of the strike's failure had indicated at least to Bevin and Citrine that confrontation in general and the use of the political strike weapon in particular were inappropriate means for securing the best interests of labour.[5] From 1927 onwards the accent of TUC policy in both the industrial and economic spheres was on cooperation with and conciliation of the employers and government, although relations with the Baldwin administration were strained immediately after the general strike because of the passage of the

[3] The membership of trade unions affiliated to the TUC increased from 4,858,000 in 1929 to 6,298,000 (rounded off to the nearest 1000) in 1939, although the latter figure never reached anywhere near the peak of the interwar period of nearly eight and a half millions established in 1921. J. E. Cronin, *Industrial Conflict in Modern Britain*, London, Croom Helm, 1979, p. 237.

[4] Between 1931 and 1932 the TUC was represented on only one government committee but by 1938–9 this had risen to twelve. V. L. Allen, *Trade Unions and the Government*, London, Longmans, 1960, pp. 32–3.

[5] H. A. Clegg, 'Some Consequences of the General Strike', *Transactions of the Manchester Statistical Society*, 1953–4, pp. 2–3, 16–17.

Trade Disputes Act through Parliament. A firm indication of the nature of the shift in the TUC's approach was given in September 1927 when in his presidential address to Congress George Hicks inserted a passage at the behest of Citrine[6] decrying the lack of 'effective machinery of joint consultation between the representative organisations entitled to speak for industry as a whole'. He went on to call for a direct exchange of practical views between the two sides of industry on how cooperation could be achieved to secure the mutual goal of improved industrial efficiency and a higher standard of living for labour.[7] Within two months an unofficial group of major industrial employers led by Alfred Mond (later Lord Melchett) responded to Hicks's plea and after preliminary negotiations a course of talks was readily agreed to by both sides.

The content of the Mond–Turner talks and their subsequent history have been sufficiently chronicled elsewhere for them not to detain us here.[8] Briefly, the talks reached their high-water mark in 1928–9 with the publication of two joint interim reports. They faltered thereafter because of the depth of opposition within the ranks of the employers' organizations and the increased difficulties caused by the onset of the slump. Collaboration did continue between the TUC and FBI on a piecemeal basis up to 1933 but without achieving much in the way of concrete results. Although the talks failed to provide any immediate and lasting benefits to the participants, they were highly significant in terms of the maturation of the TUC's approach to economic questions. Both interim reports contained a policy orientation that was to prefigure much of the British trade-union movement's response to the subsequent period of economic slump and rising mass unemployment. In particular, major elements of the TUC's programme of recovery measures were already outlined in terms of monetary policy, international trade, relief, redistribution of work, purchasing power and public works. All that remained was to adapt the policies to prevailing circumstances.

In the field of monetary policy and currency management, the TUC had developed a clear position in the course of the Mond–Turner deliberations.[9] Under Bevin's influence the General Council had been gradually won over to the view that the policy of deflation required by the operation of the gold standard had seriously hindered the recovery of British industry. It identified the reduction of export competitiveness by an

[6] *Men and Work*, pp. 243–4.

[7] *Trade Union Congress, 59th Annual Report*, 1927, p. 67.

[8] See chapter 4.

[9] *Interim Joint Report adopted by the Full Joint Conference on 4th July, 1928*, London, CIRIR, 1928 and *Interim Joint Report adopted by the Full Joint Conference on 12th March, 1929*, London, CIRIR, 1929, pp. 5–6, 12–13.

artificially high exchange rate and the restriction in the supply of credit for industrial investment purposes by a concomitant domestic monetary policy as direct causes of unemployment. Thus the demand made by Ben Tillet in his presidential address to Congress in 1929 for a fundamental reconsideration of the gold standard 'as a basic fact of trade and exchange' and a financial policy 'framed to serve the best interests of industry' reflected accurately the line of TUC thought at this stage.[10] At the same Congress a resolution was also passed calling upon the government to establish a royal commission to investigate the relationship between finance and industry. The pressure from the TUC, combined with other factors, eventually compelled the Labour Chancellor, Snowden, to establish the Macmillan Committee a few months later with Bevin as a serving member.[11]

In a two-part memorandum submitted to the Macmillan Committee during 1930, the TUC confirmed its antipathy towards the gold standard. The first section of the General Council's evidence recorded in detail the disruptive effect which deflation, contrived in preparation for an eventual return to gold, had had on both the economy and industrial relations throughout the 1920s. The second section contained an evaluation of policy options concerned with the raising of adequate funding for industrial investment and the management of the currency. In the case of the latter, maintaining the existing exchange rate by competitive wage cuts or import controls was condemned as inadvisable and as a strategy more likely to hinder than enhance economic recovery. As an alternative, the TUC recommended that the four leading industrial nations should jointly revise the statutes of their central banks in order to reduce the legal minima of the ratio of gold reserves to liabilities. The resultant stabilization of world prices and the continued functioning of the international system of exchange would, it was argued, stimulate economic recovery.[12]

The TUC acknowledged that although such concerted action was desirable it was likely to be extremely difficult to achieve in practice. The Macmillan Committee was urged, therefore, to consider seriously the option of devaluation if circumstances became pressing before international measures could take effect. From the labour movement's point of view, devaluation 'would reverse the ill-effects of raising the exchange rate

---

[10] *TUC, 61st Annual Report, 1929*, pp. 64–6.

[11] Ibid., pp. 423–4. The resolution reiterated a demand already advanced in the interim reports of the Mond–Turner group. *Interim Joint Report adopted by the Full Joint Conference on 12th March, 1929*, p.13.

[12] *TUC, 63rd Annual Report, 1931*, pp. 265–86.

in 1925 to restore the gold standard'[13] and avoid in particular the need for
a deflationary policy of wage reductions. The much-vaunted reservations
concerning the desirability of devaluation and necessity of contingency
planning for the eventuality made by Bevin,[14] published as an appendage
to the main body of the Macmillan Report, were thus largely a
reformulation of the TUC's submission which he had helped to draw up.
In commenting upon the findings of the Macmillan Committee published
in May 1931, the General Council expressed its full support for Bevin's
reservations and condemned the report's rejection of devaluation as 'ill-
advised'.[15]

Although the TUC had supported the policy of devaluation, its attitude
during the sterling crisis of August–September 1931 was remarkably
ambiguous. When representatives of the General Council met the Cabinet
Economy Committee in August, only four days before the second Labour
government fell, devaluation was not counselled as a possible solution to
the crisis. To counter Snowden's policy of financial retrenchment by cuts
in unemployment benefits, the trade-union leaders, including Bevin,
argued for a threefold alternative strategy of a graduated levy on profits,
incomes and earnings to finance unemployment insurance; new taxation
upon fixed-interest securities and other unearned income; and the temporary suspension of the Sinking Fund.[16] The possibility of a revenue
tariff was discussed but, in deference to the deep-seated divisions within
the labour movement on the issue, no recommendation was made. Above
all else, the General Council remained obdurately opposed to the proposal
of cuts in wages and unemployment benefits, thus incurring the dis-
pleasure both of the eventual defectors to the National Government and of
Sidney Webb, who dismissed them as 'pigs'.[17] In contradistinction to the
programme advanced by the General Council in its discussions with the
ailing Labour administration, the Economic Committee of the TUC, in a
report endorsed by Congress two weeks before Britain left the gold
standard, advocated the policy of devaluation once more. Although not a
panacea, such a course of action was regarded as 'an important and even an

[13] Ibid., p. 286.
[14] *The Life and Times of Ernest Bevin*, vol. I, pp. 432–4; 'Trade Union Reactions to the
Economic Crisis', pp. 106–7; M. Stephens, *Ernest Bevin – Unskilled Labourer and World
Statesman 1881–1951*, London, Chaucer Press, 1981, pp. 78–9, Donald Winch, *Economics
and Policy: A Historical Study*, London, Hodder & Stoughton, 1969, pp. 137–8.
[15] *TUC, 63rd Annual Report, 1931*, pp. 286–7.
[16] Ibid., pp. 77–84, 456–66, 512–20.
[17] The full comment made by Sidney Webb (Lord Passfield), Colonial Secretary, was:
'The General Council are pigs; they won't agree to any cuts of unemployment insurance
benefits or salaries or wages.' Margaret Cole (ed.), *Beatrice Webb's Diaries, 1924–1932*,
London, Longmans, 1956, p. 281, cited in *The Life and Times of Ernest Bevin*, vol. I, p. 485.

essential factor in recovery'.[18] The inconsistency of the TUC during the crisis can be attributed to a failure of nerve rather than a lack of foresight.

With the introduction of the exchange equalization account in April 1932 and a supporting policy of cheap money, the management of the currency no longer preoccupied the TUC as a major issue. In September 1932, exactly a year after Britain had left the gold standard and devalued, Congress noted with some satisfaction that the dire prediction of five to ten million unemployed, made by Snowden to the TUC leaders during the crisis, had not been fulfilled in practice.[19] From the trade-union movement's point of view, Britain's departure from gold had successfully undermined the rationale for wage-cutting demanded by the canons of economic orthodoxy. In addition, the export trades had been relieved from the burdens of an adverse exchange rate. However, the TUC did express concern at the disruption in trade caused by the inevitable collapse in the international system of exchange following Britain's secession from the gold standard. Thus, throughout the remainder of the interwar period, it continued to call upon the government to support initiatives to reconstruct an international system of exchange that would stabilize rates without any of the in-built deflationary mechanisms and pressures of the old standard. Any suggestion of a reversion to the pre-1931 system was rejected out of hand.

In contrast to its explicit formulations on currency and monetary matters, the TUC was less than forthright in its policy towards tariff barriers and protectionism. Prior to the slump of 1929–33, the trade-union movement had traditionally subscribed to a free-trade policy which became increasingly outmoded by the growth of protectionism, as individual countries attempted to insulate their own economies from foreign competition and external deflationary pressures. The General Council was, however, reluctant to initiate a change in policy due to the deep divisions within the movement between unions in trades apparently suffering from import-induced unemployment and others in sectors of the economy dependent on exports, who feared retaliation and the loss of markets if Britain adopted protectionism. In order to defuse this potential source of friction within its ranks, the policy orientation of the TUC throughout the period became one of calculated ambiguity. The principle of free trade was neither explicitly abandoned nor the alternative of import restrictions and protectionism officially endorsed.

The only consistent line of policy pursued by the TUC in the sphere of international trade was the desire to cultivate the empire and dominions

---

[18] *TUC, 63rd Annual Report, 1931*, pp. 263–4.
[19] Ibid., p.83, and *TUC, 64th Annual Report, 1932*, p. 196.

both as a market for British exports and as a potential basis for a self-sustaining trading bloc. A policy statement made by the Mond–Turner group, in its second joint interim report, had in fact advocated the creation of a development agency to channel capital investment into the colonies and open up market opportunities as a means of stimulating demand for Britain's depressed export industries.[20] Partly in response to this recommendation, the new Labour administration passed the Colonial Development Fund Act in 1929 and appointed an advisory committee, which included Bevin, to supervise the allocation of grants benefiting both the recipient colony and the home economy.

In view of its limited but successful influence on government policy, the TUC continued discussions on the matter with the FBI. As a result, its 1930 conference adopted a comprehensive report, which argued in favour of the expansion of inter-imperial trade to compensate for the loss of markets elsewhere.[21] The report, drawn up by the Economic Committee, noted that the pattern of international trade was displaying an increasing tendency towards the development of 'informal' trading blocs. After discounting the possible advantages for the British economy of an alignment of trade with either Europe or America, it argued in favour of a regulated and structured expansion of trading links with the empire. This was justified on the grounds that the supply of raw materials would be assured and market opportunities offered in a period of declining international trade. The thorny question of formalizing the proposed trading arrangement with a common tariff agreement was studiously avoided. Moreover, strenuous efforts were made to deny that the policy had been influenced in any way by Beaverbrook's Empire Free Trade crusade. When the report was discussed by Congress, it unleashed one of the most contentious debates of the interwar period, thus underlining the deep rift of opinion on the subject between right and left, free trader and protectionist. But the real significance of the report was the fact that the TUC had tacitly accepted the case for protectionism. In spite of its protestations to the contrary, a substantial reorientation of trade towards the empire and dominions could only be achieved with an intra-imperial commitment to unfettered exchange within the bloc and a concomitant policy of protectionism against external rivals. Furthermore, the report asserted that the validity of the general case for or against protectionism was irrelevant in the prevailing circumstances as a source of guidance for government policy. The imposition of tariffs, it argued, had to be assessed on the ground of expediency and potential net advantage rather than

[20] *Interim Joint Report adopted by the Full Joint Conference on 4th July, 1928*, pp. 15–16.
[21] *TUC, 62nd Annual Report, 1930*, pp. 208–18.

'approached with preconceptions based on the belief that certain fundamental principles or traditions must at all costs be adhered to'.[22]

The pragmatism of its approach and the explicit acceptance of the case for at least selective import controls ensured that the TUC was to remain largely uncritical when the National Government subsequently imposed general protection first as an emergency measure and then as a permanent feature with the Import Duties Act in February 1932. In a detailed investigation into the subject of tariffs and protectionist measures which coincided with the government's legislative initiatives, the TUC welcomed the regulation of foreign trade as a potentially progressive step towards the planning of the economy, but, in a remarkable piece of fence-sitting, asserted that it was premature to pass any judgement on the advisability and economic implications of the government's general tariff policy.[23] Thus it appears that the General Council was bereft at a crucial stage of any policy on a major issue affecting the British economy.

In reality, the TUC was merely applying the same tactic of deliberate ambiguity that it had adopted two years earlier to limit dissension within its own ranks. The stance of apparent neutrality was a means of tacitly endorsing the policy of protectionism without inciting antagonism and disquiet amongst its affiliates. This approach was underlined by the fact that the TUC continued to lend explicit support to the more limited but now much less contentious policy of imperial preference that was eventually adopted by the Ottawa Conference in August 1932. Indeed, prior to the conference, the TUC drew up a joint memorandum with the FBI which welcomed the Ottawa initiative as a measure that would increase the volume of trade between the participants while offering the opportunity for the eventual reconstruction of the system of multilateral exchange.[24] Thereafter, for the rest of the 1930s, the TUC made no further definitive statement on the issue of trade. It simply became a *de facto* and passive convert to protectionism.

UNEMPLOYMENT

Although the trade-union movement was engaged in the task of developing policies to deal with issues such as trade and the management of the currency, it was considerably more preoccupied with the pressing and intractable problem of how to tackle unemployment by direct means. A concern that was dictated not only by the social consequences of mass

---

[22] Ibid., p. 216.
[23] *TUC, 64th Annual Report, 1932*, pp. 202–6.
[24] Ibid., pp. 220–2.

unemployment but also by the threat that it posed to trade-union rates and conditions for those still in work and, indeed, to the viability of trade-union organization itself. However, as cyclical mass unemployment began to take its toll with the rapid increase in the numbers out of work rising from one and a quarter million in 1929 to nearly three million[25] at the nadir of the slump in 1932–3, the TUC continued to advocate an eclectic programme of palliatives. Many features of this programme had been drawn up in response to the problem of the stubborn and residual million unemployed of the 1920s. The emphasis was on the redistribution of existing jobs and on easing the plight of those unable to find work, rather than on schemes for the creation of more employment. During the slump of 1929–33, this redistribution–relief programme remained unaltered with the exception that the rationale offered in defence of certain policies became slightly more sophisticated than had previously been the case. The dictum that desperate situations call for desperate remedies did not hold good in the period, or at lease not for the TUC.

Throughout the 1930s, as in the previous decade, the General Council persisted in calling upon government to grant adequate relief to mitigate the hardship associated with unemployment. The demand for comprehensive and sufficient relief was based largely upon the moral conviction that those suffering from involuntary unemployment should not be punished further by having the burden of the economic crisis placed upon them. Moral rectitude apart, the attitude of the trade unions to relief was also informed by an ulterior consideration: that if the position of the unemployed was rendered so marginal, then employers would encounter little resistance in imposing significant wage cuts on those in work. Thus the TUC campaigned consistently in support of its case for effective relief by submitting extensive evidence to the various royal commissions which had been appointed to investigate the organization, costs and methods of financing unemployment insurance and benefits. At the same time the General Council availed itself of every opportunity to protest to the Ministry of Labour and government about the iniquities associated with the relief system such as the manner in which the 'genuinely seeking work' clause, the means test and the Board of Referees were used to deter claimants and penalize those entitled to benefits.[26]

---

[25] The official figures excluded those who had exhausted their benefits and those who had ceased to claim benefits as well as several categories of workers who remained outside the national insurance scheme. The actual number of unemployed may have been as high as three and three-quarter millions by late 1932. S. Pollard, *The Development of the British Economy*, 2nd edn, London, Edward Arnold, 1969, pp. 243ff.

Given that the prime concern of government in the 1930s was not the question of the adequacy of relief but the cost and the actuarial implications that it had for the Treasury and 'sound finance', it was not unnatural that the issue was a constant source of friction between the TUC and successive administrations. It was on this very point that relations between the General Council and the second Labour government were soured[27] even before the complete rupture that occurred during the sterling crisis of August 1931: a rupture due, most of all, to Snowden's insistence that unemployment payments had to be cut as the major part of the proposed package of 'economies'. It is also worth noting that, when the Unemployment Act of 1934 established a central Unemployment Assistance Board and replaced transitional benefits with a new scheme (which, in many instances, cut existing levels of payment), on this solitary occasion the TUC broke with its insistence on consitutional politics and endorsed, to some extent even encouraged, direct protest against government policy. This contrasted dramatically with the General Council's complete opposition to the NUWM's political and organizing activities amongst the unemployed and its deep suspicion of the avowedly apolitical Jarrow March of 1936.[28]

In conjunction with the demand for adequate relief, the TUC also sought to remedy unemployment by creating a redistribution of existing employment opportunities. At the forefront of this programme were the demands for the raising of the school-leaving age, the provision of a comprehensive system of state pensions to induce earlier retirement and, most important of all, a reduction in the basic working week from 48 hours ranging to 44 and eventually 40 hours. The raising of the school-leaving age and the provision of pensions were regarded as practical and desirable measures for eliminating surplus competition in the job market by stemming the inflow of labour at both ends of the age span.

The 'young and old' policy had been advanced vigorously by the General Council, under the influence of Bevin, since the late 1920s and had secured the assent of the employers in the Mond–Turner discussions

---

[26] Ibid., pp. 92–6, 300–4; *TUC, 62nd Annual Report, 1930*, pp. 124–8; *TUC, 63rd Annual Report, 1931*, pp. 69–79, 174–5, 342–4; *TUC, 64th Annual Report, 1932*, pp. 108–20, 268–73; *TUC, 65th Annual Report, 1933*, pp. 284–8.

[27] Robert Skidelsky, *Politicians and the Slump: The Labour Government, 1929–31*, Harmondsworth, Penguin Books, 1970, pp. 293–301.

[28] *TUC, 66th Annual Report, 1934*, pp. 243–8; *TUC, 67th Annual Report, 1935*, pp. 119–20; *TUC, 68th Annual Report, 1936*, pp. 123–5; W. Hannington, *Unemployed Struggles 1919–36*, London, Lawrence & Wishart, 1979, pp. 159–60, 173–4, 219–20, 310–12, 326–7; E. Wilkinson, *The Town That Was Murdered*, London, Gollancz, 1939, pp. 191–213.

and inclusion in the Labour Party's 1929 election manifesto. During the course of the second Labour government, the legislation for the raising of the school-leaving age was thwarted by a wrecking amendment passed on its third reading, before eventual rejection by the House of Lords, in early 1931. The proposals concerning pension schemes designed to encourage the withdrawal of older workers from the labour market were examined by an interdepartmental committee and eventually rejected by the Cabinet on the grounds of financial cost, administrative difficulties and equity.[29] In spite of these setbacks and the election of an even less sympathetic administration after 1931, the TUC continued to press its case. Discussion and resolutions on the school-leaving age and pensions remained on the agenda of virtually every Congress during the rest of the 1930s. However, in spite of the TUC's endeavours, the only legislative initiative adopted by government consisted of permissive legislation passed in 1936 for raising the school-leaving age to 15. In the event, even this measure proved to be inoperative, since the legislation specified September 1939 as the date for extending the school-leaving age, making it effectively the first casualty of the war.

Although the TUC's efforts came to nothing, there is little doubt that the measures it proposed would have had a significant impact in reducing the official unemployment statistics. As early as 1929, in a commentary on the Mond–Turner talks, Ernest Bevin calculated that the extension of compulsory education to the age of 15 and the provision of pensions at 20 shillings for a single person and 35 shillings for a couple per week would have reduced the number of unemployed by 600,000.[30] Returning to the subject four years later in his pamphlet 'My Plan for 2,000,000 Workless', which became the reference point for all trade-union and Labour Party discussions on the subject, it was estimated that with extension of education to 16 rather than 15, the provision of compulsory retirement pensions at 65 and optional and invalidity pensions at 60, the unemployment figures could be reduced by a total of 1,160,000. In an appendix to the pamphlet, Colin Clark estimated that all this could be achieved with a consolidation of certain funds and increased individual contributions at a net cost of only £30 million to the Treasury.

Whilst the proposals were perhaps economically and socially viable as welfare measures, they were fundamentally flawed as a means of solving the unemployment problem. If enacted, the scheme would have resulted, at best, in a redistribution of employment to those in the age span of 16 to

[29] *Politicians and the Slump*, pp. 113–19.

[30] E. Bevin, *Statement on Melchett–Turner Unemployment Report*, London, TGWU, 1929, pp. 3–7.

60, at the expense of young and old workers. In spite of Bevin's blithe optimism, there was no guarantee that the proposed pension payments would provide a sufficient incentive for those in gainful employment to retire on an income which he admitted was 'the absolute minimum upon which a pensioned person could possibly exist.'[31] Similarly, the raising of the school-leaving age from 14 to 16, even with a compensatory child allowance of 5 shillings per week grudgingly advocated by the trade unions,[32] was likely to encounter widespread working-class resistance, an opposition based largely on the fact that the incidence of unemployment in the 14–16 age group was not particularly high because employers readily utilized a cheap supply of labour and took advantage of the fact that insurance contributions were not payable until the age of 16. Besides, many parents depended heavily upon the wages from the children of the family and, even with a compensatory allowance, were unlikely to approve of the transformation of an economic asset into a liability on an already depressed income. Most importantly, the 'young and old' scheme would have contributed little to combating the cyclical mass unemployment and economic slump of 1929–33 and was even less appropriate for tackling the persistent regional unemployment arising from the continued structural decline of the staple industries thereafter. In any event, neither the second Labour administration nor the National Government regarded the political advantages that would accrue from the manipulation of the unemployment figures as sufficient reason for overruling the inevitable Treasury opposition based on financial and actuarial considerations.

The TUC's other major demand for the redistribution of work through a reduction in working hours without the loss of pay, by legislation rather than collective bargaining, was similarly deficient as a method of tackling unemployment. During the 1930s the General Council's case for the statutory regulation of a maximum working week rested upon three principal arguments. The first was based on the simple calculation that, if a shorter maximum was strictly enforced, significant numbers of the unemployed would be reabsorbed into industry by the resultant work-sharing. Ernest Bevin, in his 1933 pamphlet mentioned above, conservatively estimated that the application of a universal 40-hour week

[31] E. Bevin, *My Plan for 2,000,000 Workless*, London, Clarion Press, 1933, p. 11.

[32] In contrast to the Labour Party view, the TUC opposed the payment of cash sums to parents in the form of a family allowance on the grounds that the financial resources required would have a far greater impact on national welfare if disbursed collectively on schemes such as a child medical service, nursery provision, etc. The only exception to collective expenditure it was prepared to endorse was the payment of a maintenance allowance for the additional year at school once compulsory education had been extended to 15. *TUC, 62nd Annual Report, 1930*, pp. 217–21.

would lead to the re-employment of at least 700,000. The second argument was linked to the demand that any reduction in hours achieved should be secured without the loss of pay. The TUC believed that the re-employment caused by cutting working hours would lead to a sizeable increase in the aggregate volume of wages which would provide a much needed stimulus for the economy in the form of demand generated by extra purchasing power. The final rationale was based on the widely held conviction in the trade-union movement that rationalization, whether in the form of industrial reorganization by amalgamation or of the introduction of new techniques and machinery, had resulted simultaneously in increased output and the displacement of labour. The TUC therefore demanded that the new developments in industrial efficiency should be used to improve the conditions of labour in the affected branches of production, rather than create unemployment.

The TUC's attitude towards rationalization and the purpose of the statutory regulation of hours had undergone a marked change in comparison to the views that it had expressed on the same subjects in the 1920s. In the Mond–Turner talks, the trade unions openly agreed to assist the rationalization of industry in exchange for inclusion in negotiations on the process and certain minor guarantees for discharged or affected labour. Such a policy of cooperation, it was argued, in conjunction with a 'sound' monetary policy, would lead to the restoration of economic prosperity. As Pollard has pointed out, the Mond–Turner agreement was effectively a bargain struck between both sides of industry wishing to avoid further industrial strife in the aftermath of the general strike.[33] The substance of the bargain was a tacit understanding that the unions would no longer resist the dismissal of workers caused by the introduction of labour-saving machinery in exchange for the employers' promise not to attack wage levels. The result was a compact, designed to serve the interests of the employers by achieving more cost-efficient production without friction and to benefit the trade unions by providing a means of stabilizing the wages of those in work, albeit at the expense of the unemployed. The outcome was hardly surprising given that the leadership of the TUC was no longer predisposed towards confrontation of any kind and given that the employers represented in the Mond group were precisely those who would benefit most from an industrial truce and labour cooperation in the modernization of industry.[34]

Similarly, the demand for the statutory regulation of a 48-hour maxi-

[33] Pollard, 'Trade Union Reactions to the Economic Crisis', p. 106.

[34] Howard F. Gospel, 'Employers' Labour Policy: A Study of the Mond–Turner Talks, 1927–33', *Business History*, 21, 1979, pp. 184–90.

mum week, advanced during the 1920s, was regarded as a way of permanently consolidating the gains of labour made in the immediate postwar period, rather than as a means of reabsorbing the unemployed into industry. After the war industrial labour had secured an almost universal reduction in working hours from 54 to 48 per week. Furthermore, Lloyd George's coalition government had promised to ratify the International Labour Organization's Washington 48 Hours Convention by enacting parallel domestic legislation. In the event, neither it nor successive Conservative and Labour governments were prepared to confer a legal status on the *de facto* reduction, in spite of public declarations to the contrary and considerable pressure from the TUC.[35]

In the case of the second Labour government, an unequivocal election commitment had been made to ratify the Washington Convention. A Bill to that effect received its first reading in Parliament but, due to the opposition of the employers and drafting difficulties, was quietly allowed to drop on the pretext that other measures had priority in an already congested legislative timetable. Even as late as 1931, the government delegate to the ILO was disingenuously promising that the difficulties in the way of ratification would be surmounted shortly and legislation enacted.[36] However, by this stage the TUC's preoccupation with the Washington Convention had been superseded, first by its demand for a 44-hour week passed at its 1930 Congress, and then by the demand for a 40-hour week adopted a year later and subsequently endorsed by every Congress up to 1937.

This shift in policy had been induced, in part, by the intransigent opposition of the employers to any measure designed to improve the welfare of workers, but it was induced mainly by the extent of the post-1929 economic collapse and the spectacular rise in the numbers out of work. Thus the reduction in working hours, by international agreement and commensurate domestic legislation, was now regarded as an urgent measure to stem the tide of rising unemployment. Likewise, rationalization, previously embraced by the trade unions as a potential source of economic prosperity and a mechanism in defence of wages, was now widely viewed as a major source of impoverishment for labour and a significant factor in the diminution of employment.[37]

In every instance, the TUC's reformulation of policy followed, step by

[35] R. Lowe, 'Hours of Labour: Negotiating Industrial Legislation in Britain, 1919–39', *Economic History Review*, 35, 1982, pp. 225–59.

[36] Bureau Internationale du Travail (BIT), *Conférence Internationale du Travail, 1931*, vol. I, pp. 50–4.

[37] TUC, *62nd Annual Report, 1930*, pp. 334–44; TUC, *63rd Annual Report, 1931*, pp. 219–21.

step, the initiatives undertaken by the International Federation of Trade Unions in the field.[38] When the IFTU embarked upon a concerted international campaign to secure a 40-hour convention through the ILO, the previously insular British labour movement became one of its most vigorous exponents. The reason for the TUC's enthusiasm for the campaign was not newly found internationalism, but calculation based on simple expediency to quell the inevitable opposition of the employers and government at home. The British employers' federations, the NCEO and to a lesser extent the FBI, were opposed in principle to state intervention in business affairs and especially interference in an industrial issue as fundamental as the regulation of working hours. Moreover, their economic logic dictated that, in a period of depression with declining markets and intense competition, industrial costs, including wages, had to be lowered as much as possible. Any shortening of the working week, especially without the loss of pay, was regarded as nothing short of a prescription for the economic suicide of industry as a whole and the export trades in particular.[39] Similarly, the National Government, which had refused to give the matter any serious consideration before it was raised at the ILO, rejected the case for legislation on the pretext of the employers' opposition and suggested that the issue was one to be resolved through the normal channels of collective bargaining, without government interference.[40] Nevertheless, the General Council believed that in both cases the opposition of government and the employers could be overcome by the adoption of an international convention. Through securing an agreement under the auspices of the ILO, it was argued, labour conditions would be standardized throughout the major industrial countries, thus eliminating

[38] The IFTU adopted a resolution in favour of the 44-hour week at its Triennial Congress held at Stockholm in July 1930 and the TUC followed suit at its Congress in September 1930. Similarly, at its Executive Meeting held in September 1930, the IFTU decided to embark upon a campaign for the reduction of working hours through ILO. The proposal for a 44-hour week was subsequently replaced with a demand for a 40-hour week drawn up in conjunction with the Labour and Socialist International in January 1931. The TUC later adopted both policies at its Congress in September 1931. *The Activities of the IFTU 1930–32 submitted to the Sixth Ordinary Congress, Brussels, 1933*, Paris, 1934, pp. 74–9; IFTU, *Fighting World Economic Crisis and Unemployment*, Amsterdam, 1931, pp. 14, 17–18.

[39] ILO, *Tripartite Preparatory Conference to Study the Question of the Reduction of Hours of Work as a Remedy for Unemployment*, Stenographic Record, vol. 2, CPT/PV 11, pp. 71–100; BIT, *Commission de la réduction de la durée du travail dans l'industrie du fer et de l'acier, 1936*, Procès-Verbaux, Session II, pp. 1–4, Session III, pp. 6–9.

[40] BIT, *Conférence Internationale du Travail, 1932*, Compte Rendu des Travaux, XVI Session, pp. 427–8; ILO, *Tripartite Preparatory Conference*, vol. I, CPT/PV3, pp. 30–50, vol. 2, CPT/PV14, pp. 1–30; BIT, *Conférence Internationale du Travail, 1934*, Compte Rendu des Travaux, Session XVIII, pp. 71–3, 478–9; BIT, *Conférence Internationale du Travail, 1935*, Compte Rendu du Travail, XIX Session, pp. 237–8.

'unfair' competition and the employers' objections about increased costs handicapping competitiveness. By the same token, the British government would be compelled to follow the example set by other countries under the force of moral persuasion and out of concern for its standing in the international community.

The quixotic expectations of the TUC were entirely misplaced. That which the government and employers refused to yield in a national context, they were even less likely to concede within the forum of the ILO where they could operate in conjunction with others of a similar disposition. Thus, in spite of the IFTU's efforts in the Governing Body and the annual conferences of the ILO, it was not until January 1933 that a Tripartite Preparatory Conference on the issue of a 40-hour convention was finally convened and then only as a result of an initiative by the Italian government. From the outset, the British employers adopted an obstructionist stance and became the focal point of opposition for other employers' delegations by initiating disruptive tactics such as the boycott of subsequent discussions between 1934 and 1936. The British government used similar methods, short of boycott, to obstruct and delay discussions as much as possible whilst consistently voting against any proposed convention, provoking Bevin to comment bitterly,

> What I cannot understand is, that when you propose to deal with a problem internationally the British Government nearly always puts up a strong opposition and then when you attempt to deal with the problem nationally you are told it is impracticable because it must be dealt with internationally.[41]

Much to the TUC's chagrin, the international campaign for a reduction in working hours proved to be an almost total failure. The quest for an effective general 40-hour convention was abandoned in 1935, in favour of an industry-by-industry approach, after a vacuous 'convention of principle' had been adopted. At the same conference a 40-hour convention for the glass-bottle industry was passed followed by similar measures for public works in 1936 and the textiles industry in 1937.

Apart from the problems associated with employer and government opposition, the 40-hour week coupled with the maintenance of wages was a very dubious solution to the economic crisis and the problem of unemployment. The TUC's demand for a reduction in working hours was merely a modification on the practice of work-sharing which had already

---

[41] ILO, *Tripartite Preparatory Conference*, vol. 2, CPT/PV13, pp. 1–50; *BIT*, Conférence *Internationale du Travail, 1935, Session XIX, pp. 525–6.*

been established in a number of industries during the slump. The result was not that more workers were brought back into employment but that fewer numbers were laid off as the situation worsened. It was only after the nadir of the depression had passed in 1933, when a cyclical upturn was already occurring, that work-sharing could have had an impact on the level of existing unemployment. In Italy, for example, where economic recovery had been slow, the government decided to implement the proposal for a 40-hour week on an experimental basis, following an agreement between the two confederations of industrial employers and workers in October 1934. Within three months over 200,000 workless had been re-employed and the experiment was considered so successful that in February 1935, the Fascist General Council of State decided to embody the reform in permanent legislation.[42] The reduction in hours was, however, accompanied by a corresponding reduction in pay.

In advocating a shorter working week, the TUC had not been interested solely in reducing the level of unemployment through the artificial means of sharing a given amount of work amongst a larger labour force. It also believed that if wages were maintained at their existing levels, and where possible increased, recovery would be stimulated by an extension of the purchasing power in the hands of re-employed consumers. An engineering delegate, speaking in favour of a 40-hour resolution at the 1932 Congress, declared,

> The reduction of hours would put into employment another 260,000 men in the metal trades, but that does not finish there. Every man is a consumer, every man is a market . . . The effect of employing more men is cumulative; it does not stop at the door of the factory as every man signs on. The newly-employed engineer eats more, buys more, wants more; and the more he buys, the more he eats, the more he wants, the greater the number of other workers he throws into employment. To save British industry the markets for British goods must be increased.[43]

Although the idea of increasing aggregate demand as a solution to the crisis was perfectly sound, as evinced by Keynes's *General Theory*, the TUC's conviction that it could be achieved by hours-reduction was completely misplaced.

In the two instances where policies similar to the TUC's proposals concerning wages and working hours were implemented, they proved notable only for their failure as recovery measures. Roosevelt's National

---

[42] Royal Institute of International Affairs, *Unemployment: An International Problem*, Oxford, OUP, 1935, pp. 358–9.

[43] *TUC, 64th Annual Report, 1932*, p. 415.

Recovery Act (NRA), for example, legislated in June 1933, contained provisions for both a reduction in working hours and an increase in the general level of wages. Its impact as a reflationary measure proved to be negligible, because any increase in purchasing power achieved by the re-employment of idle labour and higher wages was cancelled out by an increase in the price of commodities. Higher labour costs were passed on to the consumer in the form of higher prices, a process assisted by the price-fixing arrangements allowed for industry under the provisions of Title I of the Act. As a consequence between March and September 1933 the wholesale price index rose by 17 per cent and in the first year of the NRA's operation the cost of living increased by 9.6 per cent, whereas wages rose by only 8.6 per cent.[44] Similar policies proved to be equally unsuccessful when applied in France during the Blum experiment. By neglecting the view that higher wage costs would cause and be absorbed by higher prices, the TUC also failed to take into account the effect its proposal would have on export industries, particularly in the absence of an international agreement. The British economy's ability to compete in the sphere of international trade had already been seriously hampered by the prevailing level of protectionism. Increased prices caused by higher labour costs would thus only have served to diminish the competitiveness of the nation's export trades further. The potentially disastrous consequences of this course were quickly seized upon by the employers as a justification for their obdurate opposition.

Despite its effects, the TUC's proposal did contain incisive and valuable insights. The assertion that an increase in the volume of wages, through higher pay or work-sharing, would boost purchasing power and thus stimulate recovery was a direct challenge to the orthodox remedies of governments and employers. Even after the slump, there were those who pinned the blame for the unemployment problem essentially upon high, inflexible wages and who prescribed deflation as the correct solution.[45] However, in the slump years, the most urgent necessity was to encourage measures to expand demand, without which the crisis would have been deepened.[46] Although the unions' theory of wages was defective, in that the purchasing-power aspect of pay was emphasized at the cost of the cost aspect, it did at least provide an adequate rationale for preserving wage rates in the face of deflationary pressures. Higher wages and reduced hours may not have been a unilateral solution to the problems of the

[44] H. W. Arndt, *The Economic Lessons of the 1930s*, London, Macmillan, 1944, pp. 42–6.

[45] *TUC, 63rd Annual Report, 1931*, pp. 260–2; L. Robbins, *The Great Depression*, London, Macmillan, 1934, pp. 82ff.

[46] *TUC, 63rd Annual Report 1931*, pp. 69–70, 283–4, 459. See also *The Daily Herald and Higher Wages* (London, The *Daily Herald*, 1932), pp. 3–7.

British economy in the early 1930s, but neither were deflation and wage-cutting.

PUBLIC WORKS

Compared with the energy and enthusiasm expended on the futile campaign for the reduction of working hours, the TUC placed surprisingly little emphasis on public works, either as an important measure for directly tackling unemployment or as a focal point for a counter-cyclical strategy to overcome the slump. The posture of indifference towards work-creation schemes had been established as early as 1929. In the Mond–Turner discussions, the TUC accorded greater priority to monetary policy, assisted emigration and a whole series of minor palliatives other than public works as measures for reducing unemployment. The demand for a State Development Fund to provide employment, particularly during times of a depression, and the speeding up of national construction programmes were added almost as an afterthought. The conservative stance of the trade unions was further betrayed by their response to Lloyd George's expansionist proposals outlined in his programme, 'We Can Conquer Unemployment'. Far from embracing Lloyd George's scheme, the General Council in its election manifesto issued in support of the Labour party commented cynically, 'The Liberal Party . . . now claims to be able to conquer unemployment – in a year. But Mr. Lloyd George was in power during the years in which unemployment rose to a point never reached before or since. You cannot trust him again.'[47] The only concession to the Liberals' initiative was a pledge that the trade unions would consult with the government 'in the preparation of sound, constructive plans for creating useful public works'. Otherwise, Lloyd George's proposals were simply ignored, on the ground of guilt by association. They were discredited by the connection with the politician, in whose name they were advanced.

Despite the massive rise in the level of unemployment after 1929, it was not until a full three years later that trade-union interest in public works revived. In the intervening period, neither the General Council nor the Economic Committee discussed the issue at any length and the Annual Congress omitted to refer to public works at all.[48] The barren silence was

---

[47] TUC Manifesto, General Election, May 1929, reprinted in *TUC 61st Annual Report*, *1929*, pp. 252–4.

[48] The only substantive reference to public works during the three-year hiatus was in the form of a complete copy of the IFTU–LSI Zurich Resolutions submitted to Congress in

finally broken at the 1932 Congress with the adoption of a composite
resolution which included amongst its provisions the demand that the
government should pursue the:

> planning of large-scale developments such as housing schemes, slum
> clearance and other public works which will provide long-term employment
> and purchasing power for persons now unemployed.[49]

The resolution was, however, advanced without conviction. In his speech
as proposer of the motion, George Hicks argued that the problem of
employment could never be fully solved under capitalism. Furthermore,
the little emphasis he placed on public works was expressed in the form of
a demand for the restoration of various construction schemes which had
been curtailed by the government's economy programme. This theme was
subsequently taken up in the TUC's pamphlet, 'Workless: A Social
Tragedy', which delivered a blistering attack upon the government's
'economania'. However, the central point of the TUC's criticism was still
that government economy measures had resulted in 'not only the
destruction of new opportunities of employment, but [also] the actual
dismissal of workers already in work'.[50] Thus, as late as 1932, the trade-
union movement continued to regard public works as peripheral to the
solution of unemployment. The TUC was prepared to criticize the
government's policy of financial stringency because of the adverse effect
upon the primary level of employment, but declined to attach much
importance to work-creation schemes as a central feature of a counter-
cyclical strategy. The constellation of financial and practical counter-
arguments consistently voiced by successive administrations, the Treasury
and contemporary economists had undermined the trade unions' confidence in the recuperative powers of public works. Accordingly, little
attention was paid to the question of how to finance such schemes or to the

---

[49] TUC, *64th Annual Report, 1932*, pp. 280–6.
[50] TUC, *Workless: A Social Tragedy*, London Co-operative Printing Society, 1932,
pp. 5–7.

1931. TUC, *63rd Annual Report, 1931*, pp. 127–34. In his article, Pollard mistakenly
identifies the IFTU–LSI resolution on public works and state expenditure as a policy
statement by the General Council, 'Trade Union Reactions to the Economic Crisis', p. 111. A
comprehensive memorandum was drawn up by the TUC General Council Research
Department on the public works policy of the Government, Mosley and the Liberals in
March 1931. The report was purely factual and contained no recommendation or comments
on the viability of the schemes and methods of finance. TUC Research Department,
Confidential Report on Schemes for Promotion of Employment and Economic Development in UK,
dated 26 March 1931, pp. 1–17.

generation of secondary employment by the multiplier effect, in spite of the fact that an understanding of the latter was already implicit in the TUC's own analysis of the wages–purchasing-power–underconsumption nexus.

The diffidence of the TUC's approach was finally transformed by the example of Roosevelt's massive expenditure on public works in the New Deal and the public debate between economists, including Keynes, in the run-up to the World Economic Conference, held in London in June and July 1933. In a memorandum submitted to MacDonald shortly before the conference convened, the General Council boldly declared that public works financed by loan were the best means of generating demand and stimulating economic recovery. However, both the government's response and the outcome of the conference proved to be very disappointing. The conference foundered on the inability of the major participants to agree on the proposed stabilization of exchange rates, and in the course of deliberations on public works Runciman, the President of the Board of Trade, declared, 'We have terminated our schemes for dealing with unemployment by way of capital expenditure works, and we shall not reopen these schemes, no matter what may be done elsewhere.'[51] With the newfound zeal of a convert, the TUC remained undeterred. At the Brighton Congress held two months later, Walkenden in his presidential address condemned Runciman for his intransigence, and Citrine, warming to the theme, assailed the deflationary policies of the government by drawing unsettling comparisons with the expansionist precepts of the New Deal. Following the speeches of the fraternal delegates from the American Federation of Labour, a resolution expressing wholehearted support for the measures of the New Deal, including a demand that the British government should emulate Roosevelt by implementing a programme of 'public works financed by the use of national credit', was passed with acclaim.[52]

The interest in and enthusiasm for public works proved to be purely transient. The TUC neglected to develop its proposals further and no campaign to bring about an alteration in government and public attitudes was embarked upon. By the time of the 1934 Congress, work-creation schemes, loan-financed or otherwise, did not even merit a mention during the entire proceedings. A year later, public works, although referred to, had been reduced to a supplementary measure for tackling the persistent high unemployment in the depressed regions.[53] Furthermore, a special

[51] Cited in *Economics and Policy*, p. 210.
[52] *TUC, 65th Annual Report, 1933*, pp. 70, 261–7.
[53] *TUC, 67th Annual Report, 1935*, p. 489.

committee appointed by the General Council to investigate services for unemployed workers, in a report endorsed by Congress, concluded that 'they could see no series of work schemes or economic readjustments in the near future, whether introduced by a Conservative or Socialist Government, which would absorb the majority of workers who were at present deprived of their livelihood'.[54] The TUC's attitude to public works had turned full circle.

The support of the British trade-union movement for a programme of deficit-financed public works was not only erratic but also relatively late and unsophisticated, when compared with the record of the IFTU and its other affiliated national labour movements. As the problem of cyclical mass unemployment became more acute, the federation attached increasing importance to the role of work-creation schemes in securing economic recovery. During 1930–1 it adopted a twofold strategy to propagate its ideas. The first part of the strategy was to press for a programme of large-scale international public works through the ILO with the assistance of Albert Thomas, its sympathetic director. The second part was to develop and refine the federation's own policies to assist its international campaign and the programmes of the affiliated national trade-union movements. By early 1931, the IFTU had come to the firm conclusion that the only way to arrest further economic decline was through a massive programme of public works financed by international credit. However, the thorny question of how to raise such loans, at a time when the international system of finance was racked by crisis, remained unresolved. At an executive meeting of the federation held in November 1931, it was therefore decided to convene a committee of financial and economic experts to discuss the problem.

The committee met at Berlin in the following month and drew up a plan for securing international loans based on two sets of proposals submitted by Léon Jouhaux, the president of the Confederation Générale du Travail and the German trade-union federation, the Allgemeiner Deutscher Gewerkschaftsbund (ADGB). The particpants in the committee included Wladimir Woytinsky, chief statistician for the German trade unions and author of the ADGB plan, who had by this stage published several tracts on expansionist policies and was fully acquainted with Kahn's concept of the multiplier and some of Keynes's earlier works.[55] In fact, Keynes had been invited to participate in the deliberations of the committee by Walter

[54] Ibid., p123.
[55] W. Woytinsky, *Stormy Passage*, New York, Vanguard, 1961, pp. 462–5; M. Schneider, *Das Arbeitsbeschaffungsprogramm des ADGB*, Bonn–Bad Godesberg, V.N.G., 1975, pp. 65–74; G. Garvy, 'Keynes and the Economic Activists of Pre-Hitler Germany', *Journal of Political Economy*, 83, 1975, pp. 396–9.

Citrine, both in his capacity as the TUC general secretary and in his capacity as president of the IFTU. In the event, Keynes politely refused the invitation on the pretext of a heavy work commitment coupled with a claim that his spoken German was inadequate – excuses which he subsequently repeated to Woytinsky in a separate correspondence.[56] Moreover, the TUC eventually declined to send a delegate on the ground that 'in the present state of Europe the insuperable problems involved in financing public works and international credit schemes would prevent any practical result from following the proposed meeting'.[57] A harsh assessment that was completely at variance with the TUC's own optimism and enthusiasm for the IFTU's campaign for the international reduction of working hours. In any event, the absence of British representation did not hinder the work of the committee.

The committee's deliberations started from the appreciation that expenditure on public works would have a multiplier effect upon aggregate demand and the level of employment. Secondly, such schemes had to be financed by credit alone, in recognition of the fact that capital expenditure from current taxation would result mainly in the transfer, rather than the creation of new, employment. Finally, it was acknowledged that to achieve the maximum counter-cyclical impact, public work schemes had to be carried out as part of a concerted plan of regulated, international, economic recovery to eliminate the potential adverse effect of reflation on the export trades and balance of payments of individual states. To raise the necessary capital, the ADGB-sponsored plan advocated an international agreement to increase the power of issue of the central banks by a multilateral reduction in the gold cover margin of each currency.[58] The plan argued that the additional supplies of money thus furnished should be transferred to the Bank of International

---

[56] The Keynes–Woytinsky correspondence is reprinted in full in Garvy, 'Keynes and the Economic Activists', pp. 400–1. In his article, Garvy mistakenly asserts that Woytinsky had invited Keynes to participate in the committee. Garvy also makes certain other claims — that the committee never met and that the IFTU refused to discuss Woytinsky's proposals – both of which are patently incorrect.

[57] *The Activities of the IFTU 1930–32*, p. 110.

[58] The gold cover margin was the legal stipulation by which a central bank was required to keep a minimum reserve of gold equal to a certain portion or certain amount of its domestic currency and credit. A reduction on the lines of the Woytinsky–ADGB proposal would have resulted in monetary expansion. During the course of the depression a number of countries did reduce their cover margins unilaterally, e.g. Argentina from 100% to 40% in 1929, Australia from 25% to 10% in 1930 and Denmark from 50% to 33% in 1931. In each case the gold reserves were used to finance a deficit in the balance of payments rather than for a domestic expansionist policy. See R. Nurske, *International Currency Experience*, League of Nations, Princeton, 1944, chs 2 and 4.

Settlements (BIS), rather than be allowed to go into free circulation within the domestic economies. The BIS would then allocate reconstruction loans for expenditure on public works commensurate with the scope of projects required to reduce each nation's level of unemployment. The loans would be free of interest and redeemable within a ten-year period. The provision of credit for public works thus achieved would 'strengthen the world market by furnishing additional possibilities of work and additional purchasing power'.[59]

The other plan examined by the committee, drawn up by Léon Jouhaux with the assistance of the French economist François Delasai, rejected the proposal for a reduction in the gold cover margin, as a source for raising international loans to finance public works, on the ground of political expediency. Instead it was argued that part of the gold reserves of the French, Dutch and Swiss central banks, which were far in excess of their needs for the statutory cover of their currencies, should be used as an alternative source of credit-creation. The essence of the plan was the suggestion that a sum of three milliard stabilized francs should be transferred to the BIS to serve as cover security for loans twice the value. The loans would then be allocated to other states to finance the wage and material costs of public works. The committee acknowledged the subtle nature of the Jouhaux plan, but criticized it for the inadequacy of the sums involved and the emphasis placed on cooperation between the three central banks with a surplus of gold reserves, at the expense of a wider international agreement. It was nevertheless recognized that the plan was both politically and psychologically important, largely because it emphasized the partial use of the French reserves which accounted for a quarter of the world's total gold. The committee therefore decided to incorporate certain features of the Jouhaux scheme into the ADGB plan and recommend the resultant combination as the most suitable means by which international loans for public works could be raised.[60] The proposals were subsequently ratified by the executive of the IFTU in January 1932 and used thereafter in submissions to the ILO, League of Nations and the ill-fated World Economic Conference of 1933.

Although the TUC's pessimistic view on the prospects of securing an international agreement to finance public works was partly vindicated by subsequent events, its refusal to participate in the committee and its

---

[59] For elaboration on these points see Woytinsky's article on public works written in late 1931 and published in January 1932; W. Woytinsky, 'International Measures to Create Employment: A Remedy for the Depression', *International Labour Review*, 25, 1932, pp. 9–15, and 'Richlinien zur internationalen Arbeitsbeschaffung', reprinted as Appendix I in *Das Arbeitsbeschaffungsprogramm des ADGB*, pp. 223–4.

[60] *The Activities of the IFTU 1930–32*, pp. 110–12.

failure to take note of the theoretical underpinning and prescriptions of the deliberations can be criticized on a number of counts. The fact that the IFTU and the German and French labour movements were engaged in developing such proposals is indictment enough when contrasted with the sterility of the TUC's own policies in the field. Moreover, the work undertaken by the French and German trade unions permitted them to adapt their policies for domestic use and advance them with conviction, once the prospects for international agreement had evaporated. The cautious pessimism of Citrine and the General Council was also marked by the failure to follow through a proposal for the multilateral reduction in the gold cover margin made by the TUC in its own submission to the Macmillan Committee. The proposal was based on an interim report of the Gold Committee of the League of Nations and advanced by the trade unions to fend off further deflation, rather than linked to the issue of raising loans for public works. It was the same League of Nations report and, indeed, the recommendation of the Macmillan Committee for international loans guaranteed by a joint fund that had been used by Woytinsky to devise the ADGB plan.[61] The shortcomings of the British trade-union leadership were compounded further by the fact that Citrine not only spurned the proposals of the IFTU, in spite of being the president of the organization, but also failed to respond when exposed to similar ideas advanced by Henderson and Keynes in the Committee on Economic Information (CEI).

Citrine had been appointed to the committee along with Keynes, Henderson and several other prominent economists in July 1931. Initially, the CEI had been created to service the Economic Advisory Council, but after the demise of the second Labour government it had assumed the role of a quasi-official brains trust, furnishing regular reports which often contained alternative perspectives to Treasury policy. The fourth report of the CEI adopted in July 1932 fully endorsed a scheme drawn up by Henderson for raising international loans to restore the international system of finance and induce recovery by the use of expansionist policies. The details of the scheme directly resembled the main features of the ADGB–IFTU proposals.

The focal point of the Henderson plan was that the BIS would be authorized, by international agreement, to issue notes acceptable as the equivalent of gold, which would then be distributed in the form of long-term, interest-free loans to governments to meet their external-debt requirements and finance domestic expansionist policies. The BIS loan,

[61] *TUC, 63rd Annual Report, 1931*, pp. 281–2, 285; 'International Measures to Create Employment', pp. 15–20; *Das Arbeitsbeschaffungsprogramm des ADGB*, pp. 72–3, 78–9.

anticipated to be in the range of £1000 million, would be allotted on the basis of an agreed criterion, perhaps calculated as a proportion of the gold value of exports and reserves, and then liquidated once pre-depression price levels had been restored. Participation in the scheme would be contingent on an agreement to establish a fixed parity for the major currencies and the removal of exchange restrictions. It was argued that once the scheme was in operation, it would help:

> in breaking through the present international difficulties. It would put the debtor countries into a position to meet their international obligations; it would thus make possible the abandonment of restrictions on exchange dealings, and contribute generally to 'unfreeze' the international position. At the same time it would facilitate credit expansion in the creditor countries, and would make it easier for their Governments to increase internal purchasing power by reducing taxation, by stimulating capital expenditure, or in other ways.[62]

Similar approval was expressed by Keynes when he made his version of the plan public in a series of articles published in *The Times* during March 1933, which were then subsequently reprinted in a tract, with other material on the multiplier, under the aggregate title of *The Means to Prosperity*.

The Keynes version of the plan differed from the Henderson original only to the extent that it attached explicit emphasis to the importance of expenditure on public works and that the note-issue loan involved would be the gold equivalent of $5000 million allotted to each country in proportion to their gold reserves of 1928, with a maximum ceiling of $450 million for each recipient.[63] When the Keynes–Henderson plan was submitted to the Treasury for scrutiny, prominent officials were compelled to admit that the idea was both economically and technically feasible. The only substantive objection that they raised, similar to the response of the TUC to the IFTU proposals, was the question of 'practical politics' concerning the dependence of the initiative on international cooperation. In fact, during the preparations of the World Economic Conference, the Treasury adopted a variation of the plan, in part because it regarded some form of international agreement to raise prices as a desirable accompaniment to the domestic policy of cheap money, but also

---

[62] Susan Howson and Donald Winch, *The Economic Advisory Council, 1930–1939: A Study of Economic Advice During Depression and Recovery*, Cambridge, CUP, 1977, pp. 262–81.

[63] J. M. Keynes, *The Means to Prosperity* (originally published in 1933) reprinted in *The Collected Writings of John Maynard Keynes*, vol. IX: *Essays in Persuasion*, London, Macmillan, 1972, pp. 355-64.

because it required some alternative initiative to counter the demands of France and other countries that Britain should return to the gold standard.[64] However, on the few occasions that the Treasury half-heartedly raised its version of the Keynes–Henderson plan during pre-conference bilateral negotiations, it met with complete opposition from the French and American governments and was therefore quietly dropped.

It is a matter of speculation to suggest that, had the TUC shown greater enthusiasm for the IFTU precursor of the Keynes–Henderson plan, when the latter was made public by Keynes in March 1933, trade-union backing could have helped to persuade the British government and the Treasury to champion the plan more vigorously at the World Economic Conference – which, after all, was the most promising occasion of the 1930s for international action to combat the slump. Although the TUC's pessimistic belief that the prevailing environment of mutual suspicion and economic nationalism militated against international action proved well founded, it does not alter the fact that such initiatives, if implemented, would have been thoroughly beneficial in restoring economic prosperity. To fail whilst striving to achieve a goal is not the same as failure to strive at all. Nor does it alter the fact that even the Treasury, widely regarded by the trade unions as the fount of the reactionary policy of 'economania', gave support to a policy position which was far more progressive than the stance of the TUC – in spite of the exposure of Citrine and the General Council to the same ideas, advocated first by the IFTU and subsequently by Keynes and Henderson. The myopia of the trade-union leadership was a failure of political will and economic vision.

The same indictment can be levelled at the TUC for its lack of imagination towards economic planning. The British trade-union movement possessed none of the ingenuity displayed by its counterparts in Belgium, France, Holland and other countries in devising a comprehensive package of measures which offered the prospect of immediate relief from the economic crisis, in addition to opening up the possibility for the gradual transformation of capitalism into a planned economy. Its attitude remained traditional and predictable; whenever planning was discussed, the TUC continued to operate on the assumption that greater rationality under capitalism could only be accomplished by an extension of

---

[64] Howson and Winch, *The EAC*, pp. 114–16. The Treasury version, the Kisch plan, named after Sir Cecil Kisch, Secretary of the Financial Department of the India Office, strongly resembled the Jouhaux proposal submitted to the IFTU because it stressed redistributing surplus gold stocks in the form of loans to debtor nations, via the Bank of International Settlements. Ibid pp. 116–21; C. P. Kindleberger, *The World in Depression 1929–39*, Harmondsworth, Penguin Books, 1973, pp. 204–16.

central state direction based upon the cumulative nationalization of industry. Furthermore, nationalization was justified less on the ground that it provided the foundation of a socialist economy and more in terms of the pragmatic consideration that it offered the best possibility for the regeneration of declining industries which had been stricken by mismanagement under private ownership. Hence, the TUC expended considerable effort on the formulation of detailed proposals for the reorganization and nationalization of specific trades such as iron and steel (1934), cotton (1935) and coal (1936) but failed to place these in the context of a wider strategy for the management of the economy as a whole.[65]

The only concession to a more subtle form of economic regulation was made in a report on the depressed areas drawn up by the Economic Committee in 1935. The content of the report indicated that the TUC was beginning to think along the lines of regional planning and a vigorous location of industry policy. However, the recommendations contained no original ideas and were mostly a reworking of the first public report issued by the two commissioners appointed under the 1934 Special Areas Act. Otherwise, the trade-union movement remained preoccupied with the question of nationalisation. Thus in the early 1930s the TUC spent considerably more time at its annual congresses debating the question of workers' participation in public corporations than the question of unemployment. In this instance, the problem was finally resolved in 1933 when the trade-union movement came down firmly in favour of Morrison's views that direct responsibility for managerial decisions should be left to those appointed on the basis of 'expertise'.[66] Many of these and subsequent debates were highly important in laying the foundations for the future programme of selective nationalization implemented by the postwar Labour government, but they had little bearing on the immediate problems facing the British economy in the 1930s.

The TUC's attitude towards planning was, in fact, symptomatic of the general conservatism it displayed in approaching the major economic problems of the period. Far from attempting to construct a coherent alternative to the policies pursued by the National Government, it responded to the slump and the intractable problem of mass unemployment with proposals that were little more than temporary expedients and improvisations on well-established themes. This lack of

---

[65] *TUC, 66th Annual Report, 1934*, pp. 189-201, 359–66; *TUC, 67th Annual Report, 1935*, pp. 202–9, 400–2, 467–70; *TUC, 68th, Annual Report, 1936*, pp. 210–13, 419–23.

[66] *TUC, 63rd Annual Report, 1931*, pp. 433–9; *TUC, 65th Annual Report, 1933*, pp. 369–79; *TUC, 64th Annual Report, 1932*, pp. 389–97.

vision was most evident in the British trade-union movement's refusal to embrace the coherent expansionist programme offered by the IFTU and its French and German affiliates. It was compounded by the failure of the TUC to challenge the precepts of economic orthodoxy in any systematic or decisive way. It is therefore surprising that historians such as Pollard and Bullock have attributed a degree of perception and innovative thought to the trade unions which they manifestly did not possess. The TUC may have played a constructive role in the sterling crisis of 1931 by opposing the damaging package of economies proposed by Snowden, but its analysis of the gold standard and its concomitant prescriptions were an isolated *tour de force*. The rest of the trade-union movement's policies for tackling the slump were mediocre, conventional and lacking in imagination. They were based on reflex actions tempered by the cautious 'realism' of Bevin and Citrine. The TUC's contribution to the propagation of a viable alternative economic strategy was therefore negligible.

6

The Labour Party Economic Programme
in the 1930s

We have noted that, as the 1931 crisis unfolded, the Labour Party leadership had nothing to offer in economic policy-making beyond clinging to the manifestly inappropriate shibboleths of free trade, the balanced budget and the gold standard. The convinced socialist path had been rejected with the persistent refusal to adopt any of the ILP's *Living Wage* programme; the convinced reformist strategy had also been cast aside in the failure to adopt the message of the Mosley Memorandum. It was only fitting, therefore, that the Labour government should disintegrate in the midst of a financial crisis which was to crush each piece of the institutional framework which the party had cherished so carefully.[1]

The manner of the Labour government's going did have a considerable impact on the formulation and content of Labour's economic programme for the next decade. Firstly, the party suffered an electoral rout. Although the popular vote held up remarkably well, falling by only a quarter, there was a calamitous drop in the representation in Parliament from 289 to 46. Not surprisingly, the tiny Parliamentary Labour Party (PLP) was also very short of talent. The only Cabinet Minister returned was Lansbury, and Attlee and Cripps were the only surviving junior Ministers. Secondly, the TUC became much more interested and involved in Labour Party economic policies. The Labour Cabinet had disintegrated on the question of cutting the levels of unemployment benefits. The TUC quite rightly regarded cuts in unemployment benefits as a signal to employers to reduce wages, a course it regarded as anathema throughout the interwar years. Accordingly, the TUC had urged the Labour Cabinet in its last weeks to find alternatives to cutting benefits, but without success. However, there was much less resistance from the weakened, post-election Labour Party

[1] A spirited defence of the Labour Cabinet, largely along the lines that orthodoxy was the only option, can be found in Ross McKibbin, 'The Economic Policy of the Second Labour Government', *Past and Present*, 68, 1975.

to the TUC's moves to prevent a recurrence of what it saw as attacks on wages. The General Council of the TUC revitalized the National Joint Council (NJC), which was intended to coordinate policies between the two bodies, but had met only rarely during the 1920s. The composition of the NJC was now changed to give the TUC as many representatives as the combined total of the PLP and Labour Party National Executive Council (NEC), and the General Council won the right to 'initiate and participate in any political matter which it [deemed] to be of direct concern to its constituents'.[2] Moreover, the NJC now began to meet regularly and often, indicating that the TUC wanted a bigger role in the Labour Party's affairs. Indeed, the 1933 Labour Party conference decided that no Labour leader should agree to take office as Prime Minister until he had received the support of the PLP and the NJC, and that during periods of office three Cabinet Ministers should be appointed to maintain close contact with the NJC. Conference's acceptance of these conditions illustrates a further aspect of trade-union influence over the Labour Party, the domination of conference by the bloc-voting system. The TGWU alone controlled almost 10 per cent of all the votes cast. The unions did not always act as a unit, but their collective power to mould the party's policies was immense. In fact, the fields in which they exerted the most decisive influence were non-economic: the TUC took the lead in the NJC's opposition to dictatorship of the left and of the right; and it helped wean the Labour Party away from the pacifist foreign policies favoured by so many of the socialist intellectuals of the 1930s.

In economic policy, stronger TUC leadership was a very mixed blessing for the Labour Party. The TUC's bias was towards the same moderate, pragmatic policies it had favoured during the late 1920s. But the TUC was not the body to take the Labour Party along either of the two logically consistent paths open to it. As we have seen, the TUC paid little heed to the blueprint of the IFTU, which represented one of the best available reformist programmes of the interwar period. Nor could the Labour Party expect to move towards the socialist path under trade-union leadership. The TUC General Council had an almost neurotic fear of contamination by communism; it took the lead in opposing any form of 'popular front' of the British left and fought bitterly to expel communists from TUC-affiliated unions. The TUC could not help the Labour Party to resolve its identity crisis.

---

[2] Henry Pelling, *A History of British Trade Unionism*, Harmondsworth, Penguin Books, 1963, p. 196 (quoting a memorandum by Walter Citrine, General Secretary of the TUC).

FOR SOCIALISM AND PEACE

The Labour Party's loss of direction between 1929 and 1931 seemed to have been solved in the immediate aftermath of the 1931 collapse by a considerable and predictable swing to the left. With its right-wing former leaders now in the coalition Government, there was little doubt that the Labour Party would reaffirm its socialist faith.

The 1931 conference took place after the collapse of the Cabinet, but before the general election. The party's most urgent need at this time was to close ranks and offer a united party, almost regardless of the content of its economic policies. Unity was achieved at the conference with the rallying cry of 'The banks versus the people'. Conference demanded control of the financial sector which, in the minds of the Labour rank and file, clearly bore the most of the responsibility for the events of the summer. The other significant development at the conference was the preference for a greater emphasis on planning in economic policy. In the event, these half-formed ideas could not prevent the electorate from turning against Labour in the 1931 general election. Indeed, in the circumstances, nothing could have saved Labour from a rout at the polls.

Defeat did give the party the opportunity and the time to turn these rather vague ideas (which had already been more fully developed by some of Labour's political opponents)[3] into something more coherent. Accordingly, in December 1931 the NEC established a Policy Committee to equip the party with a new programme to bring before the electorate. This committee itself established a number of sub-committees which produced reports for debate at the 1932 and 1933 conferences. In turn, these reports constituted the draft of what became the major policy statement of the decade, *For Socialism and Peace*.

The final version of *For Socialism and Peace* was a wide-ranging document, covering foreign policy, 'economic reorganization', industrial legislation, the social services, national economic development, and the preservation of political democracy. Nevertheless, at least until 1935, it was economic policy which occupied most of Labour's energies and the development of the alternative economic strategy which most animated the annual conference.

The strategy developed in *For Socialism and Peace* rested upon a determination to 'apply a policy of full and rapid Socialist economic planning under central direction', but the document was very unclear how this

[3] The similar proposals of the New Party and Mosley are discussed in chapter 1, and those of the Tory planners in chapter 3.

central direction would operate. It called for the establishment of a National Investment Board which, utilizing its corps of expert economists and statisticians, would 'organise the mobilisation and allocation of that part of the national wealth which is available for capital investment, and will license new capital issues. It would prepare annual estimates of the national income, showing what new money was likely to be available for investment.'[4] The board also had the function of coordinating existing investment projects in the public sector and of proposing additional schemes. The board was thus to be the major planning agency of any future Labour government, but the party had not yet paid attention to the relationship between this board and other, similar bodies suggested to oversee, *inter alia*, transport, agriculture, imports, water, electricity and agriculture, nor even about the relationship of these boards to existing government departments. As at earlier stages in the evolution of Labour's economic policies, there was a distressing tendency to propose new machinery and to pay very little attention to the actual measures which would be needed.

This depressing lack of vision and coherent thought is evident throughout the economic sections of *For Socialism and Peace*. The passages on industrial policy were equally superficial. The programme produced a long list of sectors to be reorganized – banking and credit, transport, water, coal, electricity, gas, agriculture, iron and steel, shipping, shipbuilding, engineering, textiles, chemicals, insurance – and indicated that in most cases nationalization, with fair compensation to the owners, would be the favoured method of reorganization.[5] But many of these industries were heavily involved in exporting, and the document was much less sure how public ownership would assist these industries to regain lost export markets. Even for the home-market industries, Labour was not really sure how the change of ownership would help counter the most pressing problem of lack of demand. The best the document could do was to return to one of the slogans of the age – the need to exploit science more forcefully – and the impossibility of achieving this under capitalism:

> There has been a phenomenal increase in modern productive capacity; and to release it for the common good must be the primary objective of any rationally-organised society. The relation of this release to the public ownership of the means of production has already been emphasised. Upon that basis the advantages to be derived from improved technique become

[4] Labour Party, *For Socialism and Peace: The Labour Party's Programme of Action*, London, The Labour Party, 1934, p. 17.

[5] *For Socialism and Peace*, pp. 14–20.

available to the community as a whole. Reorganisation, from the point of view of productive efficiency, must aim at six objectives:

(a) The introduction of efficient methods of production.
(b) The organised purchase of raw materials.
(c) The establishment of effective selling agencies.
(d) The elimination of all unnecessary charges.
(e) Reasonable wages and conditions for the producers.
(f) Reasonable prices for the consumers.[6]

Labour's point seems to have been that the unemployment problem was one of lack of competitiveness rather than of structural imbalance. The emphasis throughout Labour's industrial policy was on *efficiency*, not mobility, and the passages dealing specifically with unemployment policies vaguely hinted that sufficient jobs would be created in the depressed industries to absorb most unemployed coal miners, shipyard workers, cotton operatives, and so on.[7]

Labour's industrial policy was based on a belief that the private entrepreneur no longer had the ability to direct his business efficiently. This thesis certainly underlay Morrison's faith in the public corporation, a model which was first presented to conference in 1932 to undertake the public control of transport and electricity. Morrison's view was that private owners lacked the intelligence and ability to run their concerns effectively. Replace them with boards selected solely on merit and relevant expertise, and industries would regain their competitiveness. He told conference, 'Our industries must succeed; Socialism must be successful. The workers must not be made the victims of incompetence of socialised undertakings as they are made the victims of incompetence in the cotton industry and other industries today.'[8] Indeed, there was a strong, romantic trend in interwar socialism that the simple replacement of private by public ownership would solve all the problems of lack of markets, ruthless foreign competition and decline in trade.[9]

[6] *For Socialism and Peace*, p. 15.

[7] Specific mention was made of re-equipment of the socialized industries and of concentrating public spending on 'the development of publicly-owned and publicly-controlled economic resources' (p. 29). Nothing in *For Socialism and Peace* recognized that even after early retirement and later entry into the labour force, there might be more workers than jobs in certain industries.

[8] *Labour Party Conference Reports*, London, The Labour Party, 1932, p. 212.

[9] In a speech on financial policy to the 1932 conference, Frank Wise assumed quite naturally that under public control both cotton and coal would again become sufficiently prosperous to absorb all the workers seeking jobs in these industries. *Labour Party Conference Reports*, 1932, p. 185.

These vague statements of faith were both a great strength and a source of great weakness for the Labour Party. By such heroic assertions, Labour managed to retain the appearance of unity, despite great pressure from the left for a more explicitly socialist commitment, by virtue of an equally determined resistance from the moderate leadership. Labour (just) managed to avoid having to make the potentially crippling choice between these two competing philosophies. But, with debate conducted at, or rather restricted to, this level of broad banality, Labour suffered a lack of credibility with the electorate. The party could not work out in detail any of its policies, because to do so would expose fundamental divisions.

These problems were also very obvious in the expansionist parts of Labour's programme. The party's longstanding commitment to public works for the unemployed reappeared in *For Socialism and Peace*, but with the emphasis upon slum clearance and council housebuilding. The financing of the programme was to become a major source of division. In the 1920s, Labour's expansionist intentions had been baulked by the party's orthodox financial ideas and its total faith in the gold standard and free trade.[10] After 1931, the party began slowly to free itself from these self-imposed manacles. Overall, the greatest strides were made in external financial policy.

Not surprisingly, Labour was quick to renounce its allegiance to the gold standard after 1931. Like so many radicals of the previous decade (including J. M. Keynes, E. M. H. Lloyd, Mond and Mosley),[11] the party began to favour a monetary policy which would stabilize internal prices rather than uphold the stable exchange rates of the gold standard. By the time of *For Socialism and Peace*, external policy was to be in the hands of Import and Export Boards to extend 'planning' to foreign trade. Further, Labour hoped to work through the League of Nations and the International Labour Organization to bring about planned international economic development, international agreement to stabilize prices and exchange rates, and reductions in tariffs. The trade proposals were much more fully developed than those for international finance, but in many respects exchange-rate policy was already following principles of which Labour approved. When it had abandoned the gold standard in 1931, the National Government had formed the exchange equalization account in the Treasury to try to manage the exchange rate in accordance with the other objectives of economic policy. The pursuit of a stable internal price

---

[10] See above, pp. 29–32.
[11] For Mond, see above, pp. 80–7; Keynes's ideas are discussed in chapter 8, and those of Mosley and Lloyd above, pp. 21–6, 30–4.

level was no longer a radical proposal; Labour did not have to hammer the point home in any great detail in *For Socialism and Peace*.

However, there were cross-currents in this stream of Labour thinking. Many of the proposals for economic policies in *For Socialism and Peace* came from the party's Finance and Trade Committee under Dalton. This committee laboured diligently and minutely over the whole field of economic policy and Dalton used its deliberations as the basis for his own version of socialist economic measures, *Practical Socialism for Britain*. Dalton favoured a policy under which all currencies would be stabilized on a commodity standard, being fixed in accordance with the prices of certain agricultural products. More positively, since the commodity standard was probably administratively unworkable, he raised the prospect of a large initial devaluation to boost the price competitiveness of Britain's exporters.[12] Dalton should have known that the government shared this objective, but was finding it exceptionally difficult to exert any control over long-run exchange-rate strategy in the conditions of floating exchange rates and severe competitive devaluations in the early 1930s. There is no doubt, however, of the much greater coherence in this external area of Labour's economic programme.

But when we turn to domestic finance we see yet another example of Labour's internal splits producing a bitter, protracted debate over new machinery, distracting attention from actual policies. In this instance, the point at issue was the extent to which the banking system should be nationalized. After the debacle of 1931, the Labour Party sought a financial policy which would enable it to pursue two policy goals: first, to expand the domestic economy to reduce unemployment; and, secondly, to control economic development rather than be at the mercy of economic and financial events. Socialist economic planning was to fulfil this latter role. For the first objective, the whole movement wanted the nationalization of the Bank of England. There were no divisions on this point. There was no one prepared, as Snowden had been before the 1928 conference, to argue that political control of credit policy was dangerous and threatened national collapse. But, for the left, the nationalization of the Bank of England was not enough. Control of the central bank might enable a Labour Chancellor of the Exchequer to reduce interest rates, but it would not ensure that industry and local authorities would borrow, nor would it ensure that investment would flow in socially useful channels, that is into the projects designated for expansion in the national economic

[12] Hugh Dalton, *Practical Socialism for Britain*, London, Routledge, 1935, pp. 194–5.
[13] This point was made most clearly by Frank Wise at the 1932 conference; *Labour Party Conference Reports*, 1932, p. 188.

plan. Nationalization of the whole banking sector would be essential if these objectives were to be achieved.[13] Sidney Pollard has shown that, although numerous other arguments were put forward to justify nationalization of the joint-stock banks, basically:

> the political drive for bank nationalisation stemmed from the alleged role of the banks in the debacle of 1931; economically, it derived from the growing conviction, before the publication of Keynes's *General Theory*, that a counter-cyclical and employment policy was necessary and possible and required ownership and control of the credit mechanism.[14]

However, the party leadership did not share this analysis of the necessary conditions for an employment policy. To Ernest Bevin, nationalization of the Bank of England was sufficient. The joint-stock banks would have to dance to the tune called by the nationalized Bank of England. To John Wilmot, any proposal to nationalize the joint-stock banks would raise the same electoral scare has had the rumour in 1931 that the Labour Cabinet had planned to raid the Post Office Savings Bank to pay unemployment benefits.[15]

The left was fortunate in that this topic was debated at the 1932 conference at Leicester, before the leadership could control conference decisions. Thus the NEC was defeated and *For Socialism and Peace* contained a pledge not only to nationalize the Bank of England but also to amalgamate the joint-stock banks into a single Banking Corporation to be 'run by a small directorate appointed by the Government on grounds of ability and willingness to carry on the work. The Government would indicate the general lines of banking policy and would require the Corporation to co-operate with the publicly-owned Bank of England and a National Investment Board.'[16] Obviously, under this sort of system private enterprise had only a residual role to play. The left seemed to have won the decisive battle. The leadership was, however, unhappy with this commitment (even though Attlee had been one of the first to champion the policy),[17] and eventually secured its disappearance from the party's immediate objectives. The debate rumbled on for a number of years, absorbing much time and intellecutual energy. Unfortunately, the party

---

[14] Sidney Pollard, 'The Nationalisation of the Banks: The Chequered History of a Socialist Proposal', in David E. Martin and David Rubinstein (eds), *Ideology and the Labour Movement: Essays Presented to John Saville*, London, Croom Helm, 1979, p. 177.

[15] *Labour Party Conference Reports*, 1932, pp. 190, 192.

[16] *For Socialism and Peace*, pp. 16–17.

[17] See C. R. Attlee and Stafford Cripps, *The Joint Stock Banks*, Labour Party Policy Paper 102, January 1933. A copy can be found in Hugh Dalton's papers, IIA, 2/1.

did not discuss how credit policy was to be conducted, be it through a privately owned, mixed or nationalized financial sector. In *For Socialism and Peace*, the finance of the expansionist public works programme was not specified in any detail, but there is a strong suspicion that the party still believed that finance should come out of the ordinary budget and that that budget should balance. Certainly, one of the arguments in favour of reducing unemployment was that budgetary stringency would thereby be relaxed.[18] If it was intended that the finance would come through the nationalized banking sector, there were no indications of where or how such sums could be found.[19]

Dalton's own ideas were no clearer. In 1933 he had edited a survey of several capitalist countries, entitled *Unbalanced Budgets*. At this stage, he was clearly still held by the chains of orthodox finance. In his introduction, he wrote:

> a world where so few budgets balance, in spite of the moral precepts and orthodox traditions of Treasuries and money markets, is in a bad way. Unbalanced budgets on this world-wide scale are just a vivid symptom of world-wide disorder, both in economics and finance.[20]

The preference for orthodoxy is obvious, but Dalton did allow himself some radical proposals. Following the Liberal Yellow Book, he suggested that a separate capital account should be established, that statutory sinking funds should be placed outside the ordinary budgetary accounts even if the idea of the capital account were rejected, and that balancing over a longer period than the single financial year be considered.[21] Of course, such measures would have brought substantial help to Britain's unemployed only if the capital account were in persistent deficit, representing a large loan-financed programme of public works. Dalton came to support this view by the time of *Practical Socialism for Britain*. He argued that the next Labour administration should come to power with a massive public works programme ready for immediate implementation, and that it should raise the funds from the public by a loan.[22] At the same time, the monetary authorities would take steps to hold down interest rates through open-market operations and restrictions on the export of

---

[18] *For Socialism and Peace*, p. 29.

[19] In this respect, it is worth noting that Labour did not intend to force private industry to channel into the National Investment Board the undistributed profits which were such a potent destabilizing force. Dalton, *Practical Socialism for Britain*, pp. 228–9.

[20] Hugh Dalton (ed.) *Unbalanced Budgets: A Study of the Financial Crisis in Fifteen Countries*, London, Routledge, 1934, p. 12.

[21] *Unbalanced Budgets*, pp. 13–15.

[22] *Practical Socialism for Britain*, ch. XXV.

capital. In fact, Dalton was outlining in 1935 the approach to budgetary policy he was to adopt, under very changed international and domestic economic conditions, while Chancellor of the Exchequer between 1945 and 1947. In these very different circumstances, Dalton's combination of low interest rates and vigorous public spending greatly increased inflationary pressures and perpetuated the system of wartime controls.[23] If these measures had been tried during the 1930s, Dalton would undoubtedly have found a more immediate problem, how to raise funds from a deeply conservative and orthodox financial sector. The last three sentences of the following extract from his book seem to anticipate these problems:

> The money to pay for all these things will come, partly from the money which is now being paid to the unemployed, who will be reabsorbed into useful work; partly from the savings which are now running to waste, financing losses instead of new investment; partly from the new money which will be created in the form of additional currency and additional bank credits, in pursuance of the monetary policy . . . whereby the level of prices is kept steady and purchasing power expanded as production expands . . . There will of course be a limit to the total programme which can be financed during any given period. But this limit will be elastic, rather than rigidly fixed. It will depend on the savings, both individual and corporate, available for investment, the corporate savings including those of public bodies and socialised undertakings.[24]

Indeed, these same problems faced the left during the phase of transition to the socialist, command economy. Thus both sides of the Labour Party stood to gain from a discussion of the practical difficulties of engineering deficit finance, especially since the calamities of 1931 had taught the power which finance possessed. Indeed, the tone of *For Socialism and Peace* surely multiplied the suspicions of rentiers and financiers. But Labour chose instead to indulge itself in a simmering row over machinery – how much of the banking sector should be nationalized – in the naive belief that all practical problems would disappear if government took effective control. For the majority of the Labour Party, nationalization was a cure-all, for finance as much as for industry.

Labour's problems went deeper than the failure to work out the details of their policies. The leadership looked towards a programme of limited nationalization and a much enlarged public sector. The final goal might be 'socialism', but that goal was distant and presupposed a change of attitude and outlook for the individual in society. In this respect, little had changed

---

[23] Alan Booth, 'The Keynesian Revolution in Economic Policy-Making', *Economic History Review*, 2nd ser., 36, 1983, pp. 119–21.

[24] *Practical Socialism for Britain*, pp. 261–2.

from the party of MacDonald and Snowden. What had changed was the party's official programme, which was very different both in immediate policies and in final objective from that of Dalton, the leadership's leading spokesman on economic policy. Thanks to the efforts of Frank Wise and the Socialist League, Labour's alternative economic strategy now seemed to commit the party to the convinced socialist path. In many ways, *For Socialism and Peace* does appear to be a very radical document. We have noted the calls for very extensive 'reorganization' of industry, with the implication that 'reorganization' would mean nationalization. Extensive control over the financial sector was implicit. There was a strong sense of urgency in the document, with suggestions that guillotines and emergency powers would be used to secure the quick enactment of a substantial socialist legislative programme. Even the House of Lords stood doomed to abolition within the first term of office of a future Labour government. To understand how the leadership came to accept a document which went further along the socialist path than the party had ever gone before, we must survey the influence of the left on the party.

THE SOCIALIST LEAGUE

In the wake of 1931 the left appeared to have been routed. The ILP had become embattled during 1930 in its attempts to push MacDonald towards socialism, and chose to fight the 1931 election under its own programme, *Socialism in Our Time*. This was the first move towards the ILP's eventual disaffiliation in 1932. However, the left was split and a substantial minority of ILPers, led by Frank Wise and containing most of the party's intellectuals, were determined to remain within and change the official Labour Party.

The rising discontent with the performance of the MacDonald government had also led G. D. H. and Margaret Cole to form the Society for Socialist Inquiry and Propaganda (SSIP) to campaign for a more thorough socialist commitment from the Labour Party. Negotiations began between SSIP and Wise's group about amalgamation, which went ahead with the formation of the Socialist League in 1932, despite the opposition of SSIP's chairman, Ernest Bevin, and a number of its younger members.[25]

---

[25] Margaret Cole, *The Story of Fabian Socialism*, London, Heinemann, 1961, p. 232; Patrick Seyd, 'Factionalism within the Labour Party: The Socialist League, 1932–1937', in Asa Briggs and John Saville (eds), *Essays in Labour History, 1918–1939*, London, Croom Helm, 1977, p. 206; Ben Pimlott, *Labour and the Left in the 1930s*, Cambridge, CUP, 1977, pp. 44–6.

The National Council of the new Socialist League was dominated by middle-class intellectuals. The League had a highly structured organization and set out to become a body to propagandize for socialism, but it soon took up a position as the major critic of the NEC. Its major successes came at the Leicester conference, immediately following its inauguration. Sir Charles Trevelyan, Sir Stafford Cripps and Frank Wise all spoke with considerable effect, and helped push the Labour Party not only to nationalization of the joint-stock banks, but also to the immediate introduction of socialist measures by an incoming Labour administration. The NEC was taken by surprise, but was able to regroup for later conferences.

The Socialist League did not help itself. It began to direct its propaganda not at the broad labour movement, as had been the tactics of SSIP, but very directly at the Labour Party, much as the ILP had done before 1931. A number of the SSIP group resigned, and the League moved further left. The League, like the ILP before it, became increasingly sceptical of the tactics of gradualism. William Mellor proclaimed that the League should be 'an instrument for co-ordinating what I would call Marxist opinions and action within the wider Labour Movement'.[26] Thus, for the Labour Party's 1934 conference, the League submitted 75 amendments which sought to make *For Socialism and Peace* much more explicitly socialist. The League wanted more nationalization, workers' control rather than the public coporation for nationalized industries, and above all a specific programme of socialist action to be put before voters at the next general election. Cripps, who had become the League's leading spokesman, wanted a full commitment to the socialist path. Indeed, Pat Seyd has shown that sections of the League had concluded from the events of 1931 that any socialist government would meet capitalist sabotage and should therefore be prepared for conflict and force, even to the extent of exploiting political unrest outside Parliament.[27]

But this time the NEC was prepared. Firstly, it gave the appearance of making concessions to the left's point of view. Thus *For Socialism and Peace* contained, as we have noted, the threat to introduce emergency powers if an incoming Labour government felt itself faced by 'an emergency situation'. At the same time, the document made it explicit that these powers would be taken for only a limited period and that the Labour Party remained committed to constitutional means. The League's proposal was so watered to be almost inconsequential, but the gesture had

---

[26] Cited by Pimlott, *Labour and the Left*, p. 54.
[27] Seyd, 'Factionalism within the Labour Party', pp. 215–16.

been made. In the same way, there were many industries to be 'reorganized', but relatively few explicit commitments to nationalization. Secondly, the League's 75 amendments for conference were rolled up into 12 composite resolutions which looked both threatening and vague. The unions were suspicious and antagonistic, and each of the 12 resolutions was decisively beaten.

After these defeats, the Socialist League committed itself to a course which led to its eventual disaffiliation and dissolution. The League decided to turn its attentions from 'programme making' to 'immediate day-to-day activities', in other words, to socialist agitation. As Seyd and Pimlott both note, this was a decisive shift, taking the League into competition with the Labour Party for the support of socialists.[28] The League began to move towards the ILP and the Communist Party, neither of which was affiliated to the Labour Party, with Cripps taking a leading role in the discussions. The 'unity campaign' could produce only one response from a Labour Party in which the TUC had a decisive voice, the disaffiliation of the Socialist League. Indeed, opposition to the Socialist League was now absolute. The NEC refused to endorse as parliamentary candidates any of those known to favour an alliance with the ILP and the communists. It even refused to allow at conference any resolutions on the 'united front'.

Thus, despite the apparently socialist phraseology of *For Socialism and Peace*, the Labour leadership had remained faithful to its traditional blend of moderate socialism. The absence of any real change was underlined in the party's next major policy pronouncement, *Labour's Immediate Programme*.[29] Once again, the approach of a general election (which was due at the latest by 1940) led to a considerable watering of the socialist content of the party programme. *Labour's Immediate Programme* described itself as 'a programme of measures of Socialism and Social Amelioration, which a Labour Government would carry out during a full term of office'. Most of the proposals for which the left had fought had been formally discarded. The Socialist League call for complete socialization was dropped in favour of a 'commanding heights' programme of public ownership for the energy and transport sectors. The proposal to nationalize the joint-stock banks disappeared without trace. The only other major commitment in economic policy was to set up a National Investment Board to mobilize and allocate finance, to develop public enterprise in high technology industries and to sponsor research and development. As before, Labour was very strong in its commitment to

[28] Ibid., p. 219; Pimlott, *Labour and the Left*, p. 55.
[29] London, The Labour Party, 1937.

extend and improve social welfare benefits, to reduce the working week, to slow introduction into and accelerate retirement from the workforce, and to make holidays with pay compulsory. Once more, the demands of the unions were given special prominence at a time when Labour was drafting a programme which might be put before the electorate.

The only new policy in *Labour's Immediate Programme* was for a battery of measures to help the regions of high unemployment. But the Labour Party could scarcely claim any credit for the early development of regional policies. Even though the depressed areas tended to be those in which Labour had managed to hold seats in 1931 or might legitimately expect to regain some of its losses at subsequent elections, the party had not turned its attentions to regional policy before 1934. It was preoccupied with the question of general strategy and the debate over its socialist programme. *For Socialism and Peace* did not even include any regional slant to the major public works programme. However, the depressed areas did become the centre of public attention, as the result of a campaign led by *The Times*, and the government was forced to introduce a proto-regional policy with the Special Areas Act of 1934.[30] From this very modest beginning, the government was carried along by a tide of public opinion which was determined to see active government support for the regions. To a very large extent, Labour was dragged in the government's wake. Labour established its own depressed areas commission, significantly under Dalton, toured all the unemployment black-spots, and dutifully brought forward measures of national scope (in particular, the central control of industrial location) and specific projects for each region.[31] However, there was nothing in the Labour plan which had not been suggested already by the government's own advisers, the Commissioners for the Special Areas.

So the policies outlined in *Labour's Immediate Programme* were for the most part those for which the party had fought throughout the interwar period. However, considerable progress had been made in Labour's understanding of the economy since the 1920s. With the departure of MacDonald, Snowden and Thomas, Labour had lost a leadership which had sought to combine a misty-eyed, emotional commitment to socialism with an unquestioning acceptance of orthodox principles of finance and administration which, for all practical purposes, made any progress towards socialism impossible. Those who came to the forefront after 1931

[30] For a fuller discussion of the Special Areas policy, see Alan Booth, 'An Administrative Experiment in Unemployment Policy in the Thirties', *Public Administration*, 56, 1978.

[31] Labour Party, *Labour and the Distressed Areas: A Programme of Immediate Action*, London, The Labour Party, 1937.

were, as a result of the shift to the left in the party and the campaign of the Socialist League, compelled to choose between socialism and the managed capitalism of the mixed economy. Almost unquestioningly, they opted for the latter. Paradoxically, this meant a firmer commitment to some measure of nationalization and to other policies which had been championed by the left. By 1937, not even the anticipation of a general election could provoke in the leadership an attack of sufficient nervousness to remove nationalization from the programme completely. The commitment to planning was now also firm, especially where regional development was concerned; the leadership had also accepted that a National Investment Board was to be the principal planning agency. None of this had been possible under the leadership of MacDonald and Snowden. It looked forward to the post-1945 mixed economy, to Labour's preference for 'planning' in both 1945–51 and 1964–70, to its vigorous regional policies, and to supply-side devices such as the Industrial Reorganization Corporation and the National Enterprise Board. After 1931, the left certainly gained widespread support for a broad range of its economic policies, but the real progress was made by those who preferred to mould these policies to make them bolster rather than destroy capitalism.

EXPERTS, INTELLECTUALS AND THE REFORMIST STRATEGY IN THE 1930s

Paradoxically, the disasters of the MacDonald government boosted the reformists as much as the left and, in the longer run, it was the centre–right of the party which gained most from the Cabinet's obvious problems with unemployment after the winter of 1929. The inability of the government to tackle this problem brought intellectuals and experts into the party's policy-making debates to try to educate the movement in economic and financial affairs. This influx had a considerable impact on the shape of party policy in the 1930s, comparable with that of the left. The greatest influence, however, came after the war, as many of the expert recruits of the 1930s entered Parliament in 1945–51 and occupied prominent positions in the party during the 1950s and 1960s. In recruiting and directing this new generation of socialists, great credit must be given to G. D. H. Cole and Hugh Dalton.

Cole was the 'talent scout', drawing young, radical Oxford undergraduates into a lively discussion group which he and his wife had established in the 1920s. When Cole became unhappy about the performance of the MacDonald government, he began to investigate ways of winning support for more socialist measures within the Labour Party. The result was the formation of two new bodies; one, SSIP, which we have noted above, was to be a propagandist organization; the other was the New Fabian Research Bureau (NFRB), to conduct research along socialist lines, much as the Fabian Research Department had done at an earlier stage in Labour's development. Into the NFRB, Cole recruited many of the Oxford-educated socialist intellectuals whom he had already drawn into his own circle. Hugh Gaitskell became assistant secretary of the NFRB and chairman of its 'economic section'. Also active in the NFRB from Oxford economics were Colin Clark, Evan Durbin, Eric Nash, Christopher Mayhew, James Meade, Erich Roll, E. F. Schumacher and in the later 1930s, Douglas Jay.

The NFRB was very much Cole's child. After the collapse of his early beliefs with the final demise of guild socialism, Cole was beginning to find his socialist way once more at the end of the 1920s. Gradually, his ideas came to focus upon three proposition: "that the British economy needed rational planning and reorientation, that the problems of unemployment and finance were the keys, and that they could be approached only through an evolutionary, Parliamentary socialism'.[32] His position was set out in *The Next Ten Years in British Social and Economic Policy*, published in 1929. In many ways it was a most unsatisfactory book, full of contradictions, half-grasped ideas, yet containing in it the basis of Labour's demands in economic policy from the 1930s to the 1950s.[33] But *The Next Ten Years* at least raised a broad range of questions for socialists to consider, and this, in essence, was also the function of the NFRB.[34] The NFRB issued pamphlets over a wide range of policies, particularly on foreign and economic affairs. In economic policy, the main focus of attention was public enterprise and nationalization. The NFRB produced studies of possible socialization of iron and steel and electricity supply, a long, unpublished piece on socialization of the gas industry, and a book, *Public Enterprise*, edited by W. A. Robson, showing how existing, publicly controlled industries operated. As the NFRB grew in numbers and

[32] L. P. Carpenter, *G. D. H. Cole: An Intellectual Biography*, Cambridge, CUP, 1975, p. 134.

[33] His main proposal, a national labour corps, looked very much like the militarization of the unemployed; he tried to work out the financial aspects of the public works schemes he proposed, but in no authoritative way. He was unsure whether public works should be financed out of a balanced budget or by borrowing. He assumed a mixed economy, yet explicitly called for the nationalization of the banks, which could only lead to a comprehensive system of nationalization. Yet he did anticipate the NEDC, Department of Economic Affairs, NBPI, and the 'Little Neddies'.

[34] Margaret Cole, *The Story of Fabian Socialism*, p. 237.

expertise, it also mounted larger-scale research studies which were not published until after the outbreak of war. The unifying theme of much of this work was the use of techniques of planning in specific sectors of the economy.

However, there was no NFRB study of planning in the aggregate. This was Cole's own task.[35] He undoubtedly made a great contribution to the literature of planning and clearly anticipated much of the machinery of economic planning introduced in Britain after 1945. Moreover, he can claim realistically to have made a distinctive contribution, by building his own strong preference for workers' control and decentralization into the machinery of economic planning. Cole's was a particularly democratic and responsive model of planning. But none of this (nor, indeed, of the work of other socialist writers on economic planning of the period) had any great impact on the development of Labour Party policy. Labour had been committed to the concept of economic planning long before the publication of any of Cole's major studies. The forces pushing the party in the 1930s towards planning were considerable. The proposals of the ILP, which had been the most powerful proponent of planning during the 1920s, resurfaced in the demands of the Socialist League. The experiments with planned economies in various countries attracted much attention and sympathy from various shades of British political opinion. Other opposition groups rapidly devised their own models of the planned economy, and even the government seemed ready to adopt some of these ideas, albeit in a much-weakened fashion. Most importantly, 1931 had taught the whole Labour Party that the free market would have to be regulated and guided in key areas if a future Labour government were to succeed. The Labour Party of the 1930s would have been committed to planning even without G. D. H. Cole (and Barbara Wootton). Moreover, its most significant decisions on the nature and scope of planning (among which the proposals for the joint-stock banks were paramount) reflected power struggles within the party rather than any intellectual debate. Where the NFRB did help shape opinion was to point out to moderates that limited schemes of nationalization were possible and that a mixed economy with a larger public sector could be an ultimate goal. Curiously, Cole's own work pointed in the opposite direction. His work on planning was avowedly utopian, and assumed a fully socialist society. Thus, despite the weight of academic literature on socialist planning during the 1930s, its impact outside the very small world of the socialist intelligentsia was minimal.

[35] G. D. H. Cole, *Principles of Economic Planning*, London, Macmillan, 1935; and *The Machinery of Socialist Planning*, London, Hogarth Press, 1938.

When we consider expansionist policies, however, a rather different picture emerges. In this field, Dalton was the vital link between Labour and the experts. Like Cole, Dalton was very keen to further the careers of young socialists of ability, often by drawing them into work for the party. Gaitskell, Durbin and Jay were certainly marked by Dalton for this type of work, and acted from the mid-1930s as economic advisers to Dalton's committees. Moreover, in financial policy, Dalton could count himself an expert, lecturing at the LSE on public finance and being the author of a well-known textbook on the subject. However, it was his political role as chairman of the NEC's finance and trade committee which gave him influence over Labour's economic policy-making.

From the very formation of Dalton's committee, it was clear that financial policy would be a major preoccupation. As we have seen, following a vague commitment to the public control of banking and credit at the 1931 conference, the Socialist League led the next year's conference to a pledge to nationalize both the Bank of England and the joint-stock banks. The tone of these debates indicated a definite absence of goodwill towards the financial sector. Mutual suspicions persisted throughout the decade. Labour firmly believed that bankers would sabotage the plans of a future, democratically elected Labour government. The City believed the party was bent on revenge for 1931. To the small number of City socialists, this was an unacceptable state of affairs. Consequently, a small group of financiers and financial journalists sympathetic to Labour's views formed the XYZ Club. The pioneer was Vaughan Berry, an assistant manager with the Union Discount Company, and among its members were Francis Williams, George Strauss, John Wilmot and Charles Latham. After 1934, XYZ added its first economists, Durbin, Gaitskell and Jay. The first meeting took place in January 1932, and continued in a clandestine fashion thereafter. Contact was quickly made with the Labour Party and Dalton, who circulated XYZ papers to his committee.

In the first instance, XYZ offered Dalton explanatory papers, trying to educate the party's policy-makers about what the City did, how its markets functioned, and what changes would be necessary to implement its programme. From the XYZ papers to Dalton's committee and the published reminiscences of participants, it seems that XYZ adopted an essentially deferential role, working out the details of party policies (such as providing blueprints for Bills to nationalize the Bank of England and to

---

[36] See Dalton Papers IIA, 2/1; Francis Williams, *Nothing So Strange*, London, Cassell, 1970, pp. 112–13; Nicholas Davenport, *Memoirs of a City Radical*, London, Weidenfeld & Nicolson, 1974, pp. 75–7; Douglas Jay, *Change and Fortune: A Political Record*, London, Hutchinson, 1980, pp. 60–2.

establish a National Investment Board) or fleshing out the controls which would be needed over financial markets when Labour came to power.[36] It was essentially reformist in outlook, and appears to have had considerable impact on Dalton. Significantly, only those aspects of the party's financial policy which had been the subject of detailed investigation by XYZ were put into *Labour's Immediate Programme*.

But, why did XYZ not go further to work out details for an expansionist financial policy? The search for such a policy was undoubtedly occupying much of the time of the party's moderate experts. In fact, in the mid-1930s socialist intellectuals were involved in an extensive learning process, trying to apply economic theory with a socialist bias to a whole range of economic problems.[37] In effect, Labour was developing the reformist analysis to an extent never before attempted. The objective was to understand and correct the faults of capitalism. There was no central focus of this intense effort, but the prime movers were undoubtedly Dalton, Durbin, Gaitskell and Jay. However, the effect on policy was comparatively small. *Labour's Immediate Programme* was undeniably reformist, but no more so than could have been predicted following the collapse of the Socialist League and at a time when an election was thought to be near.

The main trouble for the reformists was the difficulty in reconciling the diverse economic analyses circulating within the Labour Party. At least four widely different views of budgetary policy, for example, were held at this time. The most powerful was undoubtedly Snowdenian orthodoxy, and Dalton its most powerful adherent at least until the mid-1930s. Donald Winch has bemoaned the 'tepid and uninformative' discussion of public works as a cure for unemployment in the first edition of Dalton's textbook on *Public Finance*.[38] The book remained unaltered up to the eighth edition, published in 1934. As we have seen, the position adopted in *Practical Socialism for Britain* was rather more favourable to public works, an attitude mirrored in the ninth edition (1936) of *Public Finance*. But, even at this stage, Dalton was not yet free of one important element of the orthodox position, the quantity theory. Winch notes that Dalton's discussion of the effects of budgetary deficits and and surpluses was conducted solely in terms of prices, not incomes. To Dalton, it was physical, economic planning alone which could reduce unemployment.[39]

---

[37] Such a discussion was certainly taking place in XYZ and NFRB, as Philip Williams's biography of Gaitskell makes clear (pp. 45–7, 65–7). He also lists discussion groups led by Dalton (p. 69), and a group which met at 'Bogey's Bar' (p. 46). Philip M. Williams, *Hugh Gaitskell: A Political Biography*, London, Cape, 1979.

[38] Donald Winch, *Economics and Policy: A Historical Study*, London, Hodder & Stoughton, 1969, p. 345.

[39] Ibid., p. 345.

While Dalton was still in his rigidly orthodox phase, another even more pessimistic view of the possibilities of monetary policy was circulating among the London socialists. Friedrich Hayek came to the LSE in the early 1930s, and his lectures had a profound influence upon a number of his professional colleagues. Evan Durbin, also of the LSE, seems to have been particularly impressed by Hayek's analysis that the trade cycle was caused by the tendency of the capital goods sector to become over-expanded in the upswing of the trade cycle. In these circumstances, a public works programme would merely make matters worse by extending the capital sector still further. Durbin was driven to very pessimistic conclusions.

> It is not possible for us to enjoy an easy road to salvation in the cure of the Trade Cycle. We must choose between the relief of inflationary policies and temporary prosperity or settle down to a cure which is slow, which is devoid of spectacular success, and which in the first instance is as painful as the disease. It is unlikely that the opinion of democracy has yet reached a sufficiently high stage of reason to permit the execution of a policy which involves the continuance of immediate distress and whose benefits can only be reaped in a period as long as ten or twenty years ahead. Particularly this is so when the way to immediate relief is at hand. But that is no reason why we should not attempt to face the truth.[40]

Thirdly, there was the view that monetary expansion by deficit finance could raise output (in contrast to the 'later Dalton' belief that planning alone could cure unemployment and that monetary expansion was merely a necessary accompaniment to the public works element of socialist planning) provided that controls were imposed on the financial sector and that the government was expanding employment elsewhere in the economy. This was Mosley's analysis at the time of *Revolution by Reason*, and was considered by Colin Clark in a very interesting collection of essays on money edited by G. D. H. Cole.[41] In what is by post-Keynesian standards a very curious chapter, Clark did recognize that an economy could be in equilibrium at less than full employment and that budgetary deficits could raise incomes and employment. However, such was the stupidity of bankers that, according to Clark, deficit finance would be effective only if government could control exchange dealings by some

[40] E. F. M. Durbin, *Purchasing Power and Trade Depression: A Critique of Under-Consumption Theories*, London, Cape, 1933, p. 177.

[41] Colin Clark, 'Investment, Savings, and Public Finance', in G. D. H. Cole (ed.), *What Everybody Wants to Know About Money: A Planned Outline of Monetary Problems by Nine Economists from Oxford*, London, Gollancz, 1933.

device such as the exchange equalization account, control domestic banking to prevent an internal financial panic, and bolster financial confidence by undertaking large and successful projects elsewhere in the economy.[42] It would be safer, Clark concluded, to increase consumption by more progressive taxation and more generous social welfare benefits; that is, by redistribution within a balanced budget. Moreover, Clark also proved to his own satisfaction that the Keynesian multiplier principle would operate only if any new investment were undertaken by the government on public works. In all other cases, money pumped into the system would merely raise prices, much as Mosley had argued in the 1920s.

Finally, the Keynesian approach to budgetary policy was discussed within the group. Its most forceful proponent was James Meade, who was less politically and more university-oriented than Clark, Durbin or Gaitskell and thus tended to find himself on the fringes of the NFRB and Dalton's finance and trade committee. He had been in Cambridge in 1931, and became a member of the 'circus' which helped Keynes in the transition from the *Treatise* to *The General Theory*. In 1932 and 1933, Meade organized collective letters to *The Times* demanding expansionist policies. He fought the same campaign within the Labour Party. Dalton circulated to the finance and trade committee a paper by Meade on the form of a socialist budget.[43] In it, Meade called for cheap money, a separate capital account in the budget, and a National Investment Board to press forward with public investment. Under these conditions, expansionist finance need not imply the nationalization of the joint-stock banks. In *Practical Socialism for Britain*, Dalton adopted a similar position, though retaining his conviction that financial policy was less important than socialist planning in ensuring full employment.

In the NFRB, Meade (with some early assistance from Roy Harrod) did manage to draw both Durbin and Gaitskell away from much of the Hayekian analysis, at least in so far as short-term policy was concerned.[44] Durbin came to favour first expansion and subsequently deficit finance. Both he and Gaitskell dropped their earlier insistence on nationalization of the joint-stock banks as an integral part of any expansionist programme.[45] When Meade published his *Introduction to Economic Analysis and Policy*, a

---

[42] Ibid., pp. 433–4.

[43] J. E. Meade, 'Financial Policy of a Socialist Government During the Transition to Socialism', paper 189 for the Labour Party Constitutional Committee, in Hugh Dalton's papers, IIA, 2/1.

[44] Elizabeth Durbin, 'Evan Durbin and the Economics of Democratic Socialism', paper given to the 1982 History of Economic Thought Conference, Nottingham.

[45] Williams, *Hugh Gaitskell*, p. 66.

layman's version of Keynesianism which showed how many aspects of existing economic policies could be easily adapted to help reduce unemployment, he won still more converts.[46] Douglas Jay paid very generous acknowledgements in his own *The Socialist Case*.[47] Keynesian analysis was clearly gaining ground.

But the Labour Party was far from conversion. Nothing in *Labour's Immediate Programme* looked forward to Keynesian analysis or policies. In fact, the Labour Party was highly suspicious of Keynes, both for his previous association with such 'dubious' political characters as Lloyd George, Mosley and the Conservative planners, and for his unfortunate manner.[48] Keynes's personal relations with trade-union leaders (except Bevin) were never less than difficult. But Labour had the added problem of distinguishing its own expansionist policies from those favoured by Keynes and his dubious associates. Both required similar machinery: the capital budget, public works and an Investment Board. Thus Labour was under some incentive to go beyond these proposals to something distinctly 'socialist', especially as the party had moved to the left since 1931. Labour was hastened along this road because it had a comparatively dismissive view of the importance of finance, and certainly no clear understanding of the relationship between monetary and real variables. To some extent (and especially in the case of Dalton), these attitudes probably had their origins in adherence to the quantity theory of money. If one believes that pumping money into the economy will only raise prices, one is inclined to look elsewhere for the solution to the unemployment problem. Economic planning, dealing with real variables, seemed the logical way out, particularly as both the party and the unions had strong links with and a better understanding of the production process. The final barrier for the proponents of Keynesian policies was that of age; the intellectuals were part of the 'younger generation' of socialists in a party in which age and length of service to the movement certainly count.

Labour continued to see financial policy and economic planning as essentially separate activities, and did not integrate them as would have been the logical course for a party adopting a Keynesian approach. Labour remained weak on the balance-of-payments implications of increasing economic activity, something of which Keynesians were all too well aware.[49] Indeed, the only work on balance-of-payments policies under-

---

[46] James Meade, *An Introduction to Economic Analysis and Policy*, Oxford, OUP, 1936.
[47] Douglas Jay, *The Socialist Case*, London, Faber, 1937, pp. 123, 339–40.
[48] Pimlott, *Labour and the Left*, pp. 39–40.
[49] Meade had certainly recognized the problem: *Introduction to Economic Analysis*, Part V, passim.

taken by Dalton's committee was on measures to stem a crisis of confidence, work which had been prompted not by economic analysis but by fears of a repeat of 1931 and the later problems of the Blum Popular Front government in France. Thus, in this crucial aspect of the reformist strategy, Labour still had work to do to turn its expansionist desires into effective policies. Unfortunately, other, more pressing problems arose in the later 1930s to take the time and attention of many who had been involved in the economic debate. Questions of foreign policy to combat fascism and the fight to move the party from its pacifist stance began to preoccupy Dalton, Gaitskell and many of the party's unofficial experts. Financial policy remained the weakest link in Labour's economic strategy.

CONCLUSION

A fair school report on the development of Labour's alternative economic strategy in the 1930s would read: 'Encouraging progress, but still considerable room for improvement.' The broad avenues open to the party seem to have been perceived much more clearly than in the 1920s, perhaps inevitably after 1931. The Socialist League rightly reasoned that if socialism were the goal, a woolly, utopian party programme would not suffice. The League's strategy of building socialism by control of the entire financial system was almost certainly viable. What the socialist wing of the party did not come close to solving was how to win popular support for this type of programme at a time when economic and social conditions tended to breed apathy and accommodation rather than revolution.

The same problem faced the Labour Party. In many ways, the middle years of the decade saw encouraging, if belated, attempts to develop the reformist strategy. The programme was undoubtedly stronger, more coherent, and much closer to a realistic five-year programme than anything the party had brought forward before. The praise is deliberately faint in recognition of the considerable weaknesses in financial policy which were fully revealed to the 1945–51 government.[50] Labour may have had a better economic programme, but it had very few ideas about how to achieve office to put this programme into practice.

The Labour Party in the 1930s was in a very uncomfortable electoral position. It was still regarded by many as a sectional party for the working classes, yet outside its areas of traditional strength (inner London and the coalfields of Wales, Scotland and Yorkshire), it had great difficulty in

---

[50] Booth, 'The Keynesian Revolution', pp. 119–22.

mobilizing working-class votes, especially among women and even among the unemployed. The party had two choices: bid for middle-class allegiance, or make a more vigorous appeal to the working-class voter. Both options were discussed in the 1930s.

To woo the middle classes, Labour needed a compact with the centre radicals, which implied the dropping of the distinctively socialist parts of the programme. The Next Five Years Group did try to build just such a 'popular front of the centre', but, after some hesitation, Labour withdrew. Even though both sides had favoured expansion, planning and a larger public sector, Labour remained deeply suspicious of the early corporatist enthusiasm of many members of the NFY Group and the association of some of its leaders with MacDonald after 1931.[51] Indeed, many of the objections the party had to Keynesianism also applied to any centre progressive movement. These objections were strong enough throughout the party to baulk any such realignment, yet rumours of such a new grouping (with Morrison frequently named as a new leader) persisted during the later 1930s.[52]

To many on the left, and especially to members of the Socialist League, it was not the middle but the working class to which Labour should turn. We have noted the defeat of the Socialist League, but any consideration of mobilizing working-class votes must look deeper than mere factionalism within the Labour Party. As John Saville notes in 'May Day 1937', his incisive essay on the labour movement in the 1930s, any bid for working-class votes would have to have been led by a drive to organize workers into trade unions.[53] The connection between trade unionism and the Labour vote has always been strong. But the TUC of the 1930s was not adventurous, despite low levels of organization. The largest, most dominant unions were also the fastest-growing; there was no incentive from the leadership of the movement to undertake a major recruiting drive. Moreover, TUC conservatism made itself felt on the party in more direct ways. The party did nothing for the unemployed outside Parliament because the unions were afraid of communist infiltration of the unemployed workers' movement. The unions prevented the party from building a popular front of the left again because the TUC wanted nothing to do with the Communist Party.[54] This attitude, shared no doubt by the party's own leadership, helped defeat the Socialist League, but it also

[51] Pimlott, *Labour and the Left*, p. 146.
[52] Bernard Donoghue and G. W. Jones, *Herbert Morrison: Portrait of a Politician*, London, Weidenfeld & Nicolson, 1973, pp. 247–8.
[53] In Briggs and Saville, *Essays in Labour History, 1918–1939*.
[54] Saville, May Day, 1937, pp. 244–7.

helped condemn the party to an extended period of opposition. Thus the broader political and philosophical choices made by the Labour Party are evident in the debates on its economic policy during the 1930s. At both levels, Labour was not in good order at the outbreak of war.

7

The Webbs, Beveridge and Soviet
Economic Planning

Thus far, we have dealt exclusively with the economic ideas of organized groups in both the economic and political spheres. However, there were also notable and interesting contributions to the policy debate by individuals who were outside the formal structures of progressive politics. In the last two chapters, therefore, we turn our attention first to the writings on planning of the Webbs and Beveridge, and finally to Keynes's major role in the development of the expansionist case.

In the 1930s, the concept of planning assumed the same status in economic prescription as the philosopher's stone had done in medieval alchemy. It was widely proclaimed as the panacea for all economic ills. The extensive use of the term by politicians, businessmen, radicals and economic reformers resembled a contagion, which failed to respect the boundaries of either political or sectional interest. Previous chapters have illustrated the widespread adoption of 'planning', but the very breadth of this interest ensured that there was no common agreement on fundamental issues of form or content. The Labour Party and the TUC advocated a statist model, based upon the cumulative nationalization of key industries. The centre radicals tinkered with a corporatist version which attached minimal importance to central intervention. G. D. H. Cole devised blueprints which embodied his lingering commitment to the ethics of guild socialism, while Lloyd George and Mosley appear to have been prompted more by cynical opportunism than by ideological consistency. The substance of planning was as diffuse as the political affiliations of its exponents.

Despite this diversity, planners were bound together by common convictions: planning appeared to offer order where there was chaos; prosperity where there was collapse; and recovery in place of decline. This consensus was based on various degrees of despair about the ability of unregulated capitalism either to function effectively or to function at all. The depth of the slump, the prevailing levels of mass unemployment and the attendant threat of social and political instability indicated to many that 'radical' measures were required to transform the economic environment. The search for an alternative mechanism to the free-market economy via planning was therefore regarded as an urgent imperative. Underpinning this conviction, in a general, rather than specific form, was the widely held belief that the efficacy of planning had been proven in practice, by the contemporary example of the Soviet Union. For a variety of reasons, however, nearly all of the would-be planners opted for a hybrid species which combined the best elements of regulation and the free-market economy. This chapter will therefore concentrate on two exceptions to the rule; the Webbs, who regarded the Russian model as an exemplar of planning, and Beveridge, who gave serious consideration to all forms of planning, including the Soviet variant, but declined to endorse any.

THE FIVE-YEAR PLAN

When the Soviet regime embarked upon the first Five-Year Plan in late 1928, the scope and declared objectives of the project were greeted with widespread scepticism in Western Europe and Britain. Stalin had decreed that a decisive step towards the transformation of the Soviet Union, from a predominantly agrarian to an industrial economy, was to be achieved within the time period of the Plan. The material basis for 'socialism in one country' was to be provided by the implementation of a dual policy, of modernizing agriculture through collectivization and developing heavy industry, under centralized production planning.[1] The credibility of the Plan was further questioned when the regime revised the Plan targets upwards in a spectacular manner, to the extent that historically unprecedented growth rates were required, and then, in December 1929, announced that the entire project was to be completed in four instead of five years. However, when it became evident that the Soviet economy was achieving substantial growth, many of the critics were silenced. The First Five-Year Plan was duly fulfilled nine months ahead of schedule, at the end of 1932, and at a significantly higher level of production than had been envisaged.

According to the statistics of the state planning agency (Gosplan), the

---

[1] For a full discussion of Soviet economic planning see Maurice Dobb, *Soviet Economic Development Since 1917*, New York, International Publishers, 1966, chs 9–11; Alec Nove, *An Economic History of the USSR*, Harmondsworth, Penguin Books, 1975, chs 6–8; E. H. Carr and R. W. Davies, *Foundations of a Planned Economy*, London, Macmillan, 1969, vol. I.

economy had registered spectacular growth rates in all sectors. Under the aegis of Stalin's industrialization strategy, national income had apparently doubled, gross industrial production increased by more than twofold and the output of producer goods quadrupled.[2] In many industries such as electricity-generation, coal, oil, iron and steel, growth rates often exceeding twofold increases were not uncommon. Investment in heavy industry alone was nearly double the original estimates and accounted for 80 per cent of the total undertaken by the state. A total of 1500 new factories and metal plants had been built, in addition to the development of a massive virgin coalfield in Kazakhstan and the construction of the largest hydro-electric power station in Europe on the Dnieper. The statistics, however, concealed more than they revealed. The imperfections of the planning mechanism, the wasteful use of scarce resources and the manipulation of aggregate data to inflate the degree of success were all glossed over. Any mention of forced labour, extensive shortages in consumer goods and rural famine were naturally suppressed. Nevertheless, a major breakthrough in economic terms had been achieved. Agriculture was subordinated to industrial needs and an irreversible shift towards a diverse manufacturing economy had been secured. By 1933, the foundations of Stalin's industrial–military complex were laid to be built upon by the Second Five-Year Plan with its dual emphasis on 'consolidation' and a more technically efficient use of resources.

The dramatic success of the Soviet economy at a time when western capitalism was reeling under the effects of the slump transformed the initial response of incredulity towards the Five-Year Plan into interest and approval. The British intelligentsia, in particular, became increasingly receptive to the repetitive claims of outstanding success made by the Soviet authorities. The change-around in attitudes was not, however, entirely the product of persuasive Soviet propaganda. During the course of the 1930s, luminaries from intellectual, political, scientific and literary life visited Russia to witness the making of a new society at first hand.[3] From what they observed, many came to regard the Soviet Union as a massive laboratory in which experiments that provided pointers to the future of mankind were being conducted. Thus Julian Huxley was moved to describe Soviet planning as 'a symptom of a new spirit, the spirit of science introduced into politics and industry'.[4] Maurice Hindus, preferring the metaphor of the battlefield to the laboratory, asserted that the Plan was 'the first step in a Great Offensive for a new society, a new

[2] *An Economic History of the USSR*, p. 191.

[3] David Caute, *The Fellow Travellers*, London, Quartet, 1973, ch. 2.

[4] Julian Huxley, *A Scientist Among the Soviets*, London, Chatto & Windus, 1932, p. 50.

world, a new human personality'.[5] Even Robert Boothby was prepared to concede that economic experiments were being conducted in Russia 'which may well prove to be of infinite value to humanity in the future'[6] – a tribute which he admitted was prompted by the desire for collective security and increased bilateral trade! In most instances, the luminaries not only felt a compulsion to visit the Soviet shrine but also to publish glowing accounts of their experiences on their return. A veritable industry of books, pamphlets, articles and radio broadcasts on all facets of Soviet life sprang up as a result, the bulk of which verged on the sycophantic. The high point of apologia and uncritical support for Stalin and Soviet planning was not, in fact, reached until the publication of the Webbs' *Soviet Communism: A New Civilization?*

THE WEBBS' *NEW CIVILIZATION*

The Webbs, formerly implacable opponents of the October revolution,[7] visited the Soviet Union in 1932, and Sidney returned alone two years later to gather additional material for the book. Prior to their visit a series of 'hypothetical conclusions' had been drafted, based on extensive reading, including the works of Hindus and other pro-Soviet publicists.[8] As in the case of most experimenters whose results are known in advance, the 'hypothetical conclusions' remained substantially unaltered by their sojourn. When *New Civilization?* was eventually published, it consisted not only of elaboration upon their *a priori* findings, but also of extensive quotation from material provided by Soviet officials. The result was a tome of unrelenting tedium and condonation of the Soviet regime which fell short of hyperbole but never strayed onto the path of critical analysis – in spite of Margaret Cole's protests to the contrary.[9]

New Civilization? started from the viewpoint that the Soviet Union possessed a Fabian constitution, which enshrined the Webbs' long-

[5] Maurice Hindus, *The Great Offensive*, London, Gollancz, 1932, p. 22.

[6] 'The Congress of Peace and Friendship with the USSR', *Britain and the Soviets*, London, Martin Lawrence, 1936, p.. 5.

[7] Margaret Cole, *Beatrice Webb – A Memoir*, London, Frederick Muller, 1945, pp. 164–6.

[8] Margaret Cole (ed.), *Beatrice Webb's Diaries, 1924–1932*, London, Longmans, 1956, entries of 5 April and 17 May, 1932.

[9] After furnishing a series of excuses for the Webb's pro-Sovietism, Margaret Cole has consistently argued that only those who have not read *New Civilization* thoroughly could dismiss it as crude propaganda. *Beatrice Webb*, p. 174, and Margaret Cole, 'Beatrice and Sidney Webb', in Michael Katanka (ed), *Radicals, Reformers and Socialists*, London, Charles Knight, 1973, p. 250. In view of her defence of the Webbs, it would not be uncharitable to suggest that Cole has not thoroughly read the book either!

standing blueprint for a social order, based upon a tripartite division between Political, Vocational and Consumers' democracies.[10] The first half of the book was accordingly dedicated to a detailed examination of the state's administrative and political structures, followed by similar studies of the network of owner–producer and consumer organizations. In each instance, every effort was expended to sustain the illusion of mass democratic participation upwards through the pyramidal hierarchy of institutions, representing man in his separate capacities of citizen, producer and consumer.[11] Inconvenient facts such as candidates securing unanimous electoral support, the operation of systematic terror by the OGPU (Unified State Political Directorate), the suppression of trade-union bargaining rights and widespread resistance to collectivization by the peasantry were either disregarded or blandly stated. Where additional explanation was offered, it largely consisted of reciting, *ad nauseum*, the official version of reality propagated by the Stalinist regime. Thus electoral unanimity was accounted for by the careful selection of candidates to accord with the popular will. Readers were assured that trade unions retained extensive bargaining rights, even though they were superfluous, because management possessed no pecuniary inducement to cut wages. Resistance to collectivization, at least in the Ukraine, was dismissed as the work of counter-revolutionary émigrés and saboteurs.[12]

Critical inquiry fared little better in the second half of the book which dealt with social trends. Apart from the treatment of economic issues, a wide range of other topics was examined including health, education, sexuality, science and ethics. The technique of reciting the official Soviet line was adopted once more. If the USSR was not already the Garden of Eden, then it had the potential to become so! The Webbs' sycophancy was compounded when the question mark in the title of the original book was dropped from subsequent editions, thus indicating that their last remaining doubts about the New Civilization had been dispelled. Thereafter, the decline in their critical faculties knew no bounds. Beatrice asserted in her introduction to a reprint published in 1941 that Stalin could not be legitimately described as a dictator; he was only a duly elected representative of 'the most inclusive and equalised democracy in the world', who possessed nothing like the arbitrary power wielded by an

---

[10] *Beatrice Webb's Diaries*, entries for 4 January and 17 May 1932; and Sidney and Beatrice Webb, *A Constitution for the Socialist Commonwealth of Great Britain*, London, Longmans, 1920, pp. 101–4, 247–317.

[11] Sidney and Beatrice Webb, *Soviet Communism: A New Civilization?*, limited edition printed by authors, pp. 1128–30.

[12] *A New Civilization?*, pp. 41–3, 169–72, 187–8, 247–8.

American President![13] These and other incursions into crude propaganda were not, however, particularly effective. The most influential elements of the book remained those which dealt with economic questions and planning. Indeed, in a rare autobiographical insertion the Webbs confessed that it was:

> the deliberate planning of all the nation's production, distribution and exchange not for swelling the profit of the few but for increasing the consumption of the whole community . . . that induced us, despite the disqualifications of old age, to try to understand what is happening in the USSR.[14]

The attraction was based upon one of the Webbs' ideological constants: anti-capitalism prompted by moral rectitude and conservative rationalism. In their book, *Decay of Capitalist Civilisation* (1923), Sidney and Beatrice had denounced the existing economic order in a systematic critique which included condemnation of the parasitism of the rich, the prevalence of poverty, the detrimental effects created by a substantial inequality in income, the pursuit of monopolistic power by the few and the propensity of the system to degenerate into war.[15] The substance of the indictment was repeated in *New Civilization?* but this time the condemnation was directed to the 'warring contradictions' which had resulted in the slump. Thus apparent absurdities such as increased labour productivity leading to destitution in the midst of plenty, the simultaneous promotion and frustration of science and invention, and the denial of remunerative employment to millions whilst produce remained unsold and factories closed because of the lack of effective demand were all castigated as features of a 'decivilization' process.[16] All the evidence suggested to the Webbs that capitalism was both morally indefensible and irrational. In contrast, Soviet communism was viewed by the septuagenarian Fabians as a 'synthetic unity' calculated to maximize the realization of human potential and promotion of harmony through the planning of production for community consumption.[17] By abolishing the profit-making motive as the determining factor in economic relations the superiority of the Soviet order was assured.

[13] *A New Civilization*, 2nd edn, London, Longmans, 1941, Preface, VII–IX, xxxviii–xxxix.

[14] *A New Civilization?*, p. 602.

[15] Sidney and Beatrice Webb, *The Decay of Capitalist Civilization*, 2nd edn, London, George Allen & Unwin, 1923, pp. 10–44.

[16] *A New Civilization?*, pp. 138–40.

[17] Ibid., pp. 631–3.

In terms of immediate comparisons, the Webbs adduced three main reasons for the primacy of Soviet planning over unregulated capitalism. The first was simply that the USSR had devised an efficient economic structure capable of sustaining unprecedented rates of growth. Extensive quotations from Gosplan data were used to demonstrate that under central direction scarce resources had been exploited to the full in maximizing production. The Soviet Union's material progress as a result had not only been enormous but also proportionately greater than that of any other country in the postwar period. Moreover, its continued enrichment, at a time when the western industrial economies were racked by crisis, provided decisive empirical proof of the efficacy of planning.[18] The second reason was that planning guaranteed predictability in economic trends, thereby obviating both booms and slumps. Central regulation, it was urged, eliminated the disruptive effects of speculation and erratic changes in patterns of consumer demand. With implicit reference to 1931, even crises in currency and credit were ruled out as possible causes of fluctuations in economic performance. The result was a permanent equilibrium between production and consumption at the highest possible level.[19] The final reason, most emphasized by the Webbs, was that planning had resulted in the elimination of involuntary unemployment. It was pointed out that, in contrast to the prevailing levels of mass unemployment in the west, a scarcity of labour had developed in Russia to the extent that, by October 1930, the regime had discontinued the provision of unemployment benefits. With the degree of economic expansion engendered by the First Five-Year Plan, each citizen was guaranteed remunerative employment and security. Moreover, the guarantee was rendered permanent by adjustments in the planning process which ensured that sufficient purchasing power existed to provide a market for all commodities that were produced.[20] In each instance, the success of Soviet planning was attributed to the replacement of the profit-making motive with comprehensive central direction of the economy; for the Webbs there could be no separation of the gains from the means by which they were achieved.[21]

By focusing on planning's three major advances of economic growth, the obviation of booms and slumps and the elimination of unemployment, the Webbs summarized the basis of the attraction of the Soviet example.[22]

---

[18] Ibid., pp. 647–8, 651–9.

[19] Ibid., pp. 662–4.

[20] Ibid., pp. 664–8, 682–4.

[21] Norman MacKenzie, *The Letters of Sidney and Beatrice Webb*, vol. III: *1912—1947*, Cambridge, CUP, 1978, pp. 416–17, letter from B. Webb to Pigou, dated 19 January 1937.

[22] 'Now all this new structure and function in Soviet Russia would not be exciting

However, the utility of economic success was not the only consideration. In a perceptive insight into the intellectual milieu of the 1930s, Caute has suggested that the infatuation of liberals and 'progressives' with the USSR can best be explained as a 'postscript to the Enlightenment'. Stalin's Russia became an object of fascination because:

> It signified a return to the eighteenth-century vision of a rational, educated and scientific society based on the maximization of resources and the steady improvement (if not perfection) of human nature as visualized by objective, unprejudiced brains.[23]

It was precisely this positivistic social engineering inherent in the Soviet experiment and most fully expressed in the rational order of planning which appealed to the Webbs. Beatrice, in particular, believed that the Soviets were imbued with a new religion of 'Scientific Humanism' which acted as the impelling force behind the struggle to create a New Civilization. The precepts of Scientific Humanism were based on August Comte rather than Marx and expressed in a creed with:

> the avowed and inflexible purpose of using all the resources of theoretical and applied science in order to procure the state of society deemed most advantageous for Soviet Russia in particular, but also for the whole human race.[24]

Beatrice asserted that the new religion was significantly different from that of its predecessors because it substituted the service of man for the service of God and was carried into practice by 'the scientific method of making the order of thought correspond to the order of things'.[25] The agency by which this was accomplished was the high priesthood of the Communist Party (CPSU). The Webbs could spare no praise for this 'religious order' and its role as the decisive force in the transformation of the Soviet Union. In their view, the CPSU was 'a voluntary, but highly organized and strictly disciplined Vocation of Leadership'.[26] It consisted of a self-sacrificing and carefully selected minority bound by monastic

---

[23] *The Fellow Travellers*, p. 259.

[24] *Beatrice Webb's Diaries*, entry for 17 May 1932.

[25] Letter from B. Webb to Toynbee dated 20 May 1935 in *The Letters of Sidney and Beatrice Webb*, p. 406.

[26] *A New Civilization?*, p. 1130.

---

attention among intellectuals and social reformers of all countries . . . if it were not for the material and moral collapse of capitalism'. *Beatrice Webb's Diaries*, entry for 14 May 1932.

obligations of poverty and obedience, which provided guidance in public affairs. It was responsible for ensuring that science and technology were developed to the full as the source of material progress for the whole community. It persuaded industrial workers, by voluntary means, to increase production, and even compelled the backward peasantry to enter the twentieth century. Indeed, it enthused the whole Soviet populace with the task of constructing a new society, a new personality and a new future. Above all it assured that prominence was granted to the technocrat and expert in the *administration* of the entire economic and social system.

The lavish praise bestowed upon the CPSU by the Webbs was, in fact, a clear indication that they had found in Russia a realization of yet another of their ideological constants – the belief in the omniscience of the expert and technocrat and his ability to administer in a selfless and efficient manner. Pondering over their career in *Our Partnership*. Beatrice stated that both spouses had long:

> placed all their hopes in the working class, served and guided, it is true, by an elite . . . of experts who, without claiming any superior social status, would be content to exercise the power conferred upon them by their science and their long administrative experience.[27]

This hope had come to fruition in Russia, for the Webbs could find no evidence to contradict the view that the CPSU was a 'professional association' voluntarily qualifying itself for the function of the administratorship of public affairs — to that extent it was 'analogous to any other organized Scientific profession'.[28] Although the Webbs' characterization was patently absurd, it had a number of attributes in common with the aspirations of economic reformers in Britain. Their adulation of technocracy was not substantially different either from the assumptions which Herbert Morrison operated upon in drawing up his blueprint for the efficient managerial administration of nationalized industries or indeed from the progressive Conservatives' faith in the potential of the experts' contribution to economic recovery. The only real difference between the Webbs and others, in this respect, was that they found their exemplar in the Soviet Communist Party.

BEVERIDGE AND PLANNING

Whilst proselytizing on behalf of her discovery of a New Civilization in

---

[27] Cited in Marcel Liebman, 'The Webbs and the New Civilization', *Survey*, 41, 1962.
[28] *A New Civilization?*, p. 1131.

Russia, Beatrice Webb bitterly complained about the 'wilful blindness' displayed by English economists towards the Soviet experiment.[29] The only exception that she was prepared to make to her blanket condemnation was William Beveridge, whom she regarded as 'far more straightforward, scientific and practical than other theoreticians of the capitalist order'. It is apparent that during the course of the 1930s Beveridge did not share the same conviction about himself. According to his biographer, José Harris,[30] Beveridge suffered for several years from an intellectual malaise which resulted in both uncertainty of conviction and vacillation. He started the decade as an implacable free-trader and exponent of the economic supremacy of market forces, sharing many common beliefs with other orthodox economists, including the view that unemployment had been caused by trade unions generating rigidities in the wage structure. However, because of the extent and gravity of the slump, his faith in both orthodox economics and the free market were shattered. By 1932, Beveridge confessed that he was unable to explain the underlying causes of the economic crisis. Thereafter, he declared himself to be an agnostic on the:

> unresolved conflict of opinion between the planned economy (such as the Russians are trying to work out, though with many mistakes of their own) and an automatic system using the mechanism of prices and the motive of profit to adjust production to the wishes of the consumers through their use of purchasing power . . . I see the dangers and difficulties of complete socialism and complete laisser-faire.[31]

Furthermore, he declined to support any intermediate position between the polarities of these two economic philosophies and viewed with scepticism the tradition of collectivist liberalism articulated by Keynes, Salter *et al.* – a position that he maintained until the outbreak of the second world war, when he became one of its most forcible exponents. Thus the greater part of the 1930s was, for Beveridge, a distinct hiatus between the certitudes he possessed as an Edwardian social reformer and his future role as the architect of welfare capitalism and full employment.

As a longstanding friend of the Webbs, Beveridge had been relentlessly exposed to their enthusiasm for the Soviet experiment ever since the return from their sojourn in 1932. He was particularly dismayed by their

[29] Letter from B. Webb to S. Webb, dated 11 September 1934 in *The Letters of Sidney and Beatrice Webb*.

[30] José Harris, *William Beveridge: A Biography*, Oxford, Clarendon Press, 1977. This paragraph is heavily indebted to pp. 306–7, 324–7, 331–3.

[31] Cited in ibid., p. 326.

lack of circumspection and bland condonation of the repressive aspects of Stalin's regime. Thus, whilst he was prepared to maintain an open mind as to the technical feasibility of central planning, he spared no criticism of the coercive measures which accompanied it in the Soviet context. Much to the chagrin of the Webbs, Beveridge argued that there were substantial similarities between Russia and the fascist regimes of Italy and Germany. He also refused to share their view that the 'Vocation of Leadership' provided by the CPSU was the embodiment of an enlightened administration, claiming only that it had within it 'the seeds of great good for the human race – and of almost infinite evil'.[32] The differences between the two parties spilled over into the public arena on more than one occasion. In response to an article published by Beatrice in *The New Statesman and Nation*, which severely criticized W. H. Chamberlin's *Russia's Iron Age*, Beveridge cautioned the Webbs to turn their backs on Russia precisely because of the irrefutable evidence, provided by Chamberlin, of the systematic distortion of truth, terror and repression perpetrated by the Soviet authorities.[33] Similarly, when reviewing the Webbs' book, he warned that they had 'made out a case for their title "Soviet Communism: A New Civilization?" but not for leaving off the question mark at the end of it'.[34] His advice went unheeded in both instances.

Beveridge also took issue with a number of the other cherished beliefs the Webbs had in the Soviet Union and subjected them to a searching examination. In the same review of their work, he expressed a scarcely concealed astonishment at the authors' fascination for the material progress of Russia and argued that the much lauded 'achievements' were products of industrialization long enjoyed by other countries. The only unique feature, he conceded, was 'the attempt to bring about in one or two decades changes which elsewhere have been spread over one or two centuries',[35] otherwise, there had been no substantial improvement in the standard of living and Russia remained technically inferior to the west. Beveridge also professed his lack of faith in the veracity of the Soviets' claim that unemployment had been abolished. He contended that, despite certain favourable peculiarities in its economic structure, Russia continued to experience at least some degree of frictional, seasonal and

[32] William Beveridge, 'Soviet Communism', *Political Quarterly*, 2, 1936, pp. 352–3.

[33] Beatrice Webb, 'Soviet Communism', *The New Statesman and Nation*, 9 March 1935, pp. 322–3, and letter from William Beveridge, 'The Russian Famine', *The New Statesman and Nation*, 16 March 1935, pp. 378–9.

[34] Beveridge, 'Soviet Communism', p. 367.

[35] Ibid., p. 348.

technological unemployment. Moreover, he rejected the Webbs' analysis that mass unemployment had been eliminated by 'the universal distribution of effective demand among consumers'.[36] In his view, the most crucial factor had been the unlimited demand for labour generated by the state, for the purpose of investment and defence, irrespective of the *financial cost* and the *efficient deployment* of resources. He asserted, therefore, that if the same constraints were removed under capitalism an identical result would be achieved. It was for this reason that he attributed the persistence of mass unemployment in Britain to the paralysis of successive governments rather than to any inherent defect in the nature of capitalism.

After dismantling the major propaganda point in favour of the Soviet regime, Beveridge offered no quarter in his assessment of the Russian version of planning. Using the Webbs' material for confirmation, he asserted that:

> the Soviet experiment has shown at most that it is possible to direct production from the centre without actual breakdowns. So much was shown for the nation's food supplies in war by the British experiment of Food Control. But the decisions of the Soviet planners are still at the stage of being arbitrary and dictated largely by considerations other than economic . . . their experiment throws little light on the technique of planning.[37]

The cornerstone of his critique was the failure of the Soviet authorities to take into account patterns of consumer expenditure as a guide to the allocation of resources for production. It was for this reason that he judged the profit-making motive to be a more effective adjuster of economic activity than the Soviet method of planning. The profit motive both acted as an incentive to action and, by gain or loss, ensured production and resources were directed in accordance with patterns of consumer demand. In his view, therefore, the only way in which the Russian model could begin to approach or even exceed this economic efficiency was by the introduction of a 'gigantic detached system of audit of all productive institutions and a continuous consumers' referendum by spending'.[38] The critique, he stressed, was not a judgement on the efficacy of central planning *per se*, but on the Russian variant as it then existed.

In a series of addresses published under the collective title of *Planning Under Socialism* (1936), Beveridge consciously steered away from issues of

[36] Ibid., pp. 364–6.
[37] Ibid., p. 362.
[38] Ibid., p. 361.

immediate political contention and concentrated instead on presenting a measured assessment of the three types of economic system which were available for adoption – the free market, central planning and an admixture of these two polarities. To aid him in the task, Beveridge employed the didactic analogy of likening the economy to a machine which always operated at less than 100 per cent efficiency irrespective of the particular mechanisms selected for the allocation of resources. Under the free-market economy, he contended that the machine suffered from three major imperfections: liability to monetary disturbance which resulted in booms followed by slumps and widespread underemployment of productive resources; great inequalities in income which were potentially damaging and could not be justified as either reward or incentive; and the generation of antagonisms between management and labour as partners in production. In spite of these defects, it was asserted that the free market had stood the test of experience and had generally led to the enrichment of society. The onus was thus firmly placed on the rival systems to demonstrate that they could operate at a level of efficiency either equal to or greater than that achieved by the 'pricing process'.[39]

Beveridge believed that it was theoretically possible for central planning under socialism to pass such a test providing certain conditions were fulfilled. These included the preservation of consumer choice and its use as a guide to production; the maintenance of individual choice in the selection of occupation; the creation of a supreme economic authority in the state which had to be sufficiently well informed to make strategic decisions on rational rather than arbitrary grounds; and, finally, the limitation of the supreme authority's responsibility to significant rather than detailed decisions, in order to avoid the stranglehold of bureaucratic waste. He also envisaged that the economy would be run by several monopolistic corporations, subordinated to the supreme economic authority, which, by competition with each other for resources and consistent auditing of their use of the means of production, would assist the pursuit of efficiency. If a centrally planned economy operated along these prescribed lines, then it would be capable of surmounting the defects of the free market and, therefore, achieve technical superiority.[40] In reaching this conclusion, Beveridge stressed that he was not being prescriptive because the technical gains in efficiency could be outweighed by political costs such as the loss of liberty – all factors including the social and political effects of central planning had to be taken into account. The whole analysis, he confessed, was an abstract exercise for the consumption

[39] William Beveridge, *Planning Under Socialism*, London, Longmans, 1936, pp. 4–10.
[40] Ibid., pp. 11–24.

of academic economists, but, nevertheless, still of significant importance because it was precisely such elements that offered guidance in public affairs.[41] Furthermore, he emphasized that his analysis did not apply to the Soviet Union, which he dismissed as irrelevant as a guiding example for Britain.

In comparison, Beveridge was less than forthright in his assessment of the third variant; the compromise between free prices and planning. It was this model, characterized as the 'halfway house between Cobden and Lenin', which he expressed the most sympathy towards but had the most doubts about in terms of viability. In response to the rhetorical question of whether it was possible to secure the advantages of the free market and central planning, without the disadvantages of either, Beveridge stated:

> I have the uneasy feeling that one can't; that to keep the pricing process and capitalism, while abolishing competition or regulating markets by the power of the state, gives one the worst of both worlds, and not the best. The pricing process and central planning may be as different in economics as a steam-engine and an internal combustion engine are in engineering: I don't feel sure that the Conservative planners aren't putting water into an engine that needs petrol to make it go. I hope that I'm wrong.[42]

According to his assessment, there were two major factors which militated against the possible success of the synthesis. The first was the fear that if markets were regulated by 'preventing loss of capital, restraining cut-throat competition, putting the power of the state behind monopolies and cartels', then a significant loss in efficiency would occur because of the resultant decline in competition. The second was based on the calculation that once the price mechanism was interfered with, other distortions would develop, to the extent that the economy would be driven further down the road towards central planning than had originally been envisaged.[43] On both points, Beveridge was only prepared to offer the tentative conclusion that 'the one certain advantage which planning under capitalism appears to possess over planning under socialism is that it would be less difficult to abandon if it failed'.[44]

Returning to the same theme in *Constructive Democracy* (1938), Beveridge's tone was informed with a greater urgency prompted by the fear that war was close at hand. He argued that planning under democracy was fraught with the same difficulties mentioned above and likened it to

[41] Ibid., pp. 27–8.
[42] Ibid., p. 93.
[43] Ibid., pp. 26–7, 102–8.
[44] Ibid., p. 27.

'breathing under water', but this time he suggested it was imperative to adapt.[45] To eliminate the possibility that capitalist planning would lead to decisions that were both damaging to the democratic polity and calculated on arbitrary rather than rational grounds, Beveridge advocated the creation of an Economic General Staff (EGS), consisting of experts capable of offering informed advice to government. The creation of such an organ, he suggested, was an absolute necessity because certain features of British democracy militated against the efficient prosecution of planning. These included the fact that personnel engaged in government were already preoccupied with a range of important matters and were therefore unable to give consideration to wider issues. Moreover, they were generally old, cautious and prompted by political expediency to an extent that they were either incapable or unwilling to adopt a more considered perspective, especially on matters affecting the economy. Stripped of its euphemistic language, the creation of an EGS was, for Beveridge, an essential means of cutting through the Gordonian Knot of decreptitude, ineptitude and short-sightedness embodied in the politicians!

The proposal was not a new development in Beveridge's thought. He had advanced the same proposition in two articles published during the winter of 1923–4 in *The Nation and The Athanaeum*.[46] His interest in the idea had subsequently been revived when Lloyd George launched his 'New Deal' for Britain during 1935, which contained almost identical proposals to his own. In both instances, Beveridge's view was that the EGS should consist of a small number of experts with no other function than providing government with 'hard, continuous, impartial research . . . about economic problems',[47] in order to ensure that all policy decisions were both informed and beneficial. Although his idea had a long lineage, the important feature of its inclusion in *Constructive Democracy* was that it signified Beveridge's reluctant conversion to planning. By this stage, he had allocated an additional function to the Economic General Staff of bringing 'conscious direction into public affairs'[48] and to that extent his whole proposal came to bear a remarkable resemblance to the idealized version of the 'Vocation of Leadership' the Webbs had found in the Soviet Communist Party. Thereafter, Beveridge became a firm advocate of the need for comprehensive 'national planning' for both the

---

[45] William Beveridge, 'Planning Under Democracy', in *Constructive Democracy*, edited for the Association for Education in Citizenship by Sir Ernest Simon and Eva M. Hubback, London, George Allen & Unwin, 1938, pp. 135, 142–3.

[46] *William Beveridge*, p. 315.

[47] *Planning Under Socialism*, p. 38.

[48] *Constructive Democracy*, p. 141.

prosecution of the war and the tasks of peacetime reconstruction.[49] The wheel had turned full circle.

BRITAIN AND THE SOVIET EXAMPLE

E. H. Carr once described the story of the 1930s as 'a stampede of liberals and left intellectuals into the Soviet camp'.[50] A more accurate reflection would suggest less of a stampede and more of a temporary infatuation, for in spite of the extensive publicity given to the Soviet experiment in planning, it had no significant influence or lasting effect on economic thought in Britain. The reasons for this are not hard to cite. Apart from the works of John Strachey and the Webbs, there was no publication of systematic material on Soviet economics separate from the gamut of eulogies covering the broad sweep of Soviet life. Moreover, in the case of the Webbs, the most ardent admirers of the Soviet regime, their enthusiasm was tempered with reservation. They chose not to join the Communist Party, continued to reject the Marxist theory of class struggle and declined to advocate the duplication of Soviet planning as a solution to the economic ills of Britain. Trotsky was not wide of the mark when he stated in *The Revolution Betrayed* that:

> The Webbs found in the Soviet Union only an administrative mechanism and a bureaucratic plan. They found neither Chartism nor Communism nor the October Revolution . . . [their] friendship for the Soviet bureaucracy is not friendship for the proletarian revolution, but on the contrary, insurance against it.[51]

The Webbs' ambivalence was symptomatic of an attitude shared by nearly all of the fellow travellers — the modernization of Russia under the Five-Year Plans was an experiment to be admired from *afar*; it had no implications for either domestic politics or domestic economic management.

Another important factor was the numerical insignificance and relative isolation of the British Communist Party which inhibited its ability to act

---

[49] Although Beveridge became more sympathetic to Russia, he ruled out its example for application in Britain. William Beveridge, 'Freedom From Idleness', in G. D. H. Cole, H. J. Laski, W. H. Beveridge and L. F. Easterbrook, *Plan for Britain*, London, Routledge, 1943, pp. 89–90.

[50] E. H. Carr, 'The Russian Revolution and the West', *New Left Review*, 3, 1978, p. 29.

[51] Leon Trotsky, *The Revolution Betrayed*, New York, Pathfinder Press, 1972, pp. 302–3.

as a successful transmission belt for Soviet ideology. At its peak of membership in the interwar years, reached in 1937, the CPGB could number no more than 12,000 followers and this was precisely at the time of the Popular Front, when it was at its most conciliatory towards liberals and 'progressives'. Furthermore, the Communist Party proved incapable of building a base within the trade-union movement where its greatest potential for influence and fertile propagation of the notion of command planning lay. However, the most decisive reason was that the entire conception of planning in Britain consisted of short- and medium-term measures relating to the immediate management of the economic crisis. The extent of that crisis never reached such dimensions as to encourage significant elements to abandon the existing economic order altogether. Thus the Soviet experiment may have popularized the term of 'planning', but in the British context it contributed nothing to informing the content of the idea.

8

Keynes's Alternative Economic Programme

No survey of the opposition to interwar economic policy can avoid the figure of Keynes. *The General Theory of Employment, Interest and Money* is one of the most important works in economics, and his shorter, acerbic pieces are polemical writing of the highest order. Despite his eminence and the great influence of his ideas, Keynes's own interwar contributions to policy debates have been comparatively neglected, at least until recent years. His policy has been inferred from his theory or, worse still, from what has passed as Keynesian policy in the postwar years. Inevitably, myths about his policy stance have grown up – he was an inflationist, concerned only with global matters, and capable of breathtaking inconsistencies.[1] The publication by the Royal Economic Society of Keynes's *Collected Writings* has begun to redress the balance, and studies of Keynes's policy advice have begun to appear.[2] The time is thus opportune to draw together some of the threads of recent work. But our interest in Keynes goes beyond an exercise in teasing out the relationship between economic theory and policy. Keynes offers us a model of the intellectual in politics, a fascinating example of the ways in which an unorthodox thinker might seek to influence government policy. He attempted an enormous range of propaganda and persuasion techniques in his drive to change policy but without much success. We ought, therefore,

[1] A recent work on interwar policy writings implies that Keynes neglected structural aspects of unemployment by falsely contrasting the *policy* writings of 'pre-Keynesians' with the *theoretical* work of Keynes. Mark Casson, *Economics of Unemployment: An Historical Perspective*, Oxford, Martin Robertson, 1983, pp. 7–8.

[2] The volumes of *The Collected Writings of John Maynard Keynes*, London, Macmillan, 1972, are hereafter denoted as follows: *JMK* IV, for *A Tract on Monetary Reform*; *JMK* V and VI, for *A Treatise on Money* (2 vols); *JMK* IX, for *Essays in Persuasion*; *JMK* XIII, for *The General Theory and After: Part I, Preparation*; *JMK* XIX for *Activities 1922–9: The Return to Gold and Industrial Policy* (2 parts); *JMK* XX, for *Activities 1929–1931: Rethinking Employment and Unemployment Policies*; *JMK* XXI for *Activities 1931–9: World Crisis and Policies in Britain and America*.

to consider also Keynes's tactics and the political use he made of his economic ideas.

THE GOLD STANDARD

Keynes's first postwar interests were reparations and the Treaty of Versailles, but he soon turned his attention to the question of whether Britain should restore the gold standard. His approach to the problem which came to absorb so much of his time was always remarkably consistent; Britain *could* return to gold at prewar exchange rates, but it should do so only if the gains would outweigh the costs.

Such a calculation was necessary because Britain had been forced off gold in 1919. The postwar economy moved quickly into boom conditions under the stimulus of the inflationary financial policy of a Cabinet terrified of revolution and willing to buy off protest. Keynes was unhappy. He was one of the first to call for higher interest rates and monetary restriction to break inflation.[3] The exchange rate, which had stood at £1 = $4.76 during the war, fell quickly to a low of $3.40 in February 1920. In 1920, the boom collapsed, unemployment rose, wages and prices sank, and the exchange rate improved steadily, reaching $4.63 in late 1922. As this was close to the prewar parity of $4.86, the question of return was a real one. Keynes's first answer was to recommend a swift return to complete the adjustment to a new parity very quickly. A long and painful deflation must be avoided at all costs.[4] With unemployment so high, the monetary authorities were reluctant to take steps to exacerbate domestic economic conditions still further, but in July 1923 they did raise Bank rate from 3 to 4 per cent. British prices were falling, unemployment was severe, but the exchange had begun to fall. Having missed the quick return, the authorities were opting for a slow deflation towards the gold standard parity.

Keynes condemned the decision as 'one of the most misguided movements of [Bank rate] that has ever occurred'.[5] It could only damage the domestic economy. He elaborated the point in his *Tract on Monetary Reform*, published in 1923. The significance of the book for the development of Keynes's programme lies in one question. He recognized the significance of monetary stability, but asked whether it should take the form of stable internal prices or stable external exchange rates. For a country like Britain, heavily engaged in overseas trade, stable exchanges

[3] Susan Howson, *Domestic Monetary Management in Britain, 1919–38*, Cambridge, CUP, 1975, p. 19.

[4] *JMK* XIX, p. 61.

[5] Ibid, p. 100.

were important, but he opted for stable prices where the two were in conflict. It was assumed that the gold standard would give both, but Keynes argued that the economic environment had changed. America was the major economic power, and the international financial system was no longer a gold standard, but a dollar standard, managed by a central bank which lacked international experience and outlook. According to Keynes, Britain was better advised to continue with the system which had evolved since the war of 'non-flationary' finance, with price stability and an effective devaluation of between 10 and 20 per cent. [6] Slow deflation must be rejected. Falling prices rewarded the investor but depressed the entrepreneur. Business confidence, and hence production and employment, were harmed and the burden of debt on productive enterprise increased.

Policy-makers were, however, unconvinced, and Keynes's 'Notes on Finance and Investment' in *The Nation* failed to have the desired effect. He could not persuade the authorities to commit themselves to the existing exchange rate and this prospect of continuing deflation was, according to Keynes, damaging business confidence.[7] When Lloyd George used *The Nation* to launch his campaign for an attack on unemployment by public works, Keynes immediately saw a relevance for his own analysis. Public works programmes would raise business confidence and help restore a cycle of cumulative prosperity.[8] Finance was available for home investment, but the lack of dynamism at home simply drove savings abroad. He urged the Treasury to mobilize these funds into domestic projects. The pillars of Keynes's alternative programme – easier credit, public works and control over foreign lending – were now all in place.

The prospects of easier monetary conditions were, however, finally frustrated with the return to gold in 1925. Keynes had fought the decision in the press, in academic writing and by direct argument with policy-makers. His most sustained criticism appeared after the return in the second of his brilliant, peppery tracts, *The Economic Consequences of Mr Churchill*. As is very well known, the key to his case was his belief that the prewar exchange rate overvalued sterling by approximately 10 per cent. British prices and wages would have to be reduced *pro tanto*, initially in industries facing foreign competition, but also eventually in the 'sheltered' industries. Overvaluation meant prolonged deflation since the only way of forcing down British wages was to increase unemployment until British labour accepted lower wages. Direct attacks on wages could bring only social turmoil and injustice. The arguments were forceful, and undoubt-

[6] Ibid., pp. 212, 262–6.
[7] Ibid., p. 114.
[8] Ibid., pp. 219–23.

edly had more impact than his journalism, but the decision, once taken, could not be unmade, as Keynes well knew.

The return to gold did, however, enrich Keynes's policy programme by forcing him to concentrate on the structural dimension and, in particular, on the problems of the ailing export industries. Keynes acquired a policy for coal which, in 1925-6, included cartelization with the aim of concentrating production, a continuing, but tapering government subsidy, and the transfer of men out of the industry.[9] Similarly, Keynes often criticized the Lancashire cotton-spinners for failing to cut capacity in the face of falling postwar demand. He argued that to wait for market forces and bankruptcy was mistaken. All firms would suffer, and even the efficient might be forced out of business before capacity had been cut. Again, Keynes proposed cartelization, and on this occasion argued that the government might have to force the unwilling minority if a proposal were blocked by a small number of backward firms.[10] This proposal to 'rationalize' cotton-spinning brought Keynes much controversy, but his more general support of rationalization after 1925 as a method of increasing competitiveness and reducing costs demonstrates the way Keynes was willing to support any suggestion which would reduce British export prices without general deflation.[11] There is no reason to doubt Keynes's attachment to these measures and the need for a structural element in his programme. As we shall see, this aspect was retained both in the crucial period of the crisis and in the 1930s.

The second addition to Keynes's programme in 1925 was the idea of a 'national treaty', in effect a policy for incomes. He argued that the most equitable method of achieving the 10 per cent reduction in costs necessary after the return to gold was for government and unions to get together to reduce all wages by a uniform amount. In the interests of consensus, the unions were to be given a *quid pro quo* in higher taxation on unearned income which would otherwise have been unaffected. It would be wrong to call this an 'incomes policy' comparable to those which have emerged since 1947, but it would also be wrong to minimize the attractiveness of the idea to Keynes, as he revived it in his evidence to the Macmillan Committee.[12]

Thus by the mid-1920s Keynes had assembled an alternative economic programme which was broad and securely anchored to the problems of the British economy at the time. It comprised monetary reform, public works,

---

[9] Ibid., pp. 525–9.
[10] Ibid., p. 613.
[11] Ibid., pp. 727–8.
[12] *JMK* XX, pp. 102–5.

the limitation of foreign lending, rationalization and, in reserve, cuts in income by consensus. This was no academic treatment of the problem. Indeed, it is broadly agreed that Keynes's policy commitments were running far ahead of his ability to justify them in his theoretical work. [13] In the mid-1920s, Keynes was working on early drafts of the *Treatise* in which loan-financed public investment would 'do nothing in itself to improve matters' and might 'do actual harm'.[14] This clear divergence between theory and policy surely needs explaining.

Harrod has referred to Keynes's intuitive grasp, and Peter Clarke to the political presuppositions of the new liberalism to which Keynes had been attracted since before the war.[15] There is much in both suggestions, but we must add another. In twentieth-century conditions of a settled urban industrial society with comparatively slow population growth, Keynes doubted the validity of some of the assumptions of orthodox economics about labour mobility and wage flexibility.[16] If orthodox economics, rigorously pursued, might be a poor guide, he had only the unorthodox suggestions of those who wanted to avoid the waste of unemployment and lost production. As we have seen, such proposals were by no means confined to new liberal or even 'radical' circles. Keynes's programme was, therefore, almost inevitably derivative and constantly open to new ideas. Only monetary reform and the national treaty were distinctively Keynes's own contributions, and even on monetary reform his ideas ran closely parallel to those of the FBI. At this stage, Keynes was still collecting ideas. He had not yet fully applied himself to the work of the unorthodox intellectual – to work out how much of the old system he should jettison and how many of the new ideas he could usefully support. That task occupied most of the next ten years.

THE *TREATISE* AND THE MACMILLAN COMMITTEE

Between 1928 and 1931, Keynes involved himself in a second extra-ordinary, creative burst in economic theory, policy and propaganda. He was heavily engaged in the revamping of the Liberal Party economic

---

[13] R. F. Harrod, *The Life of John Maynard Keynes*, Hardmondsworth, Pelican Books, 1972, p. 415; Donald Winch, *Economics and Policy: A Historical Study*, London, Hodder & Stoughton, 1969, p. 156.

[14] *JMK* XIII, p. 23.

[15] Harrod, *Life of JMK*, p. 412; Peter Clarke, 'The Politics of Keynesian Economics, 1924–1931', in M. Bentley and J. Stevenson (eds), *High and Low Politics in Modern Britain*, Oxford, Clarendon Press, 1983, pp. 175–81.

[16] *JMK* XIX, p. 396 (in evidence to the Balfour Committee).

programme, he completed *A Treatise on Money*, and took a leading role in both the Economic Advisory Council (EAC) and the very important Macmillan Committee on Finance and Industry. He was consulted by Ramsay MacDonald, Oswald Mosley and Harold Macmillan. Britain had not seen such a public display by an academic economist for generations.

The self-assurance which Keynes needed to sustain such a role came from his belief that the analytical position of the *Treatise* could help solve the problems of the British economy. He presented this 'strict, logical treatment of the theory' to the full Macmillan Committee in his private evidence over five long sessions in February and March 1930, and returned to the analysis when the committee began to consider the shape of its report.[17] The main contribution of the *Treatise* was the distinction between savings and investment in a mature industrial economy. Decisions about investment, by which Keynes meant capital outlay, were taken by one group in the community, whereas saving, which was the difference between income and expenditure on current consumption, was undertaken by a different group. Established theory held that savings and investment were kept in equilibrium by changes in the rate of interest, but Keynes disagreed. If investment ran ahead of savings an inflationary boom would occur, and if savings exceeded investment there would be depression, unemployment and deflation. The dynamic factor was the method by which the flow of money incomes was divided between the purchase of consumer and capital goods. If public demand for consumer goods resulted in consumers' expenditure being lower than the sum earned in the production of consumer goods, then savings would be greater than required for the purchase of new capital goods, the price of consumer goods would fall, and excess savings would take the form of business losses. Keynes did not deduct business losses from savings, nor did he add the 'abnormal' profits which induced entrepreneurs to increase output. Keynes saw business losses and windfall profits as the dynamic elements in the economy, causing movements to either depression and deflation or expansion and inflation. The proper task of the monetary authorities was to ensure that investment, by far the most volatile element, was equal to savings by appropriate changes in the rate of interest and the availability of credit. The 'market' rate of interest had to be equated with the 'natural' rate – that which kept savings and investment in balance. In a closed, rapidly expanding economy, this was probably not an impossible goal, but, as Keynes told the Macmillan Committee in great detail, there

---

[17] Much of the material in this and the following five paragraphs is based on the extraordinarily detailed and developed arguments put by Keynes to the Macmillan Committee. See *JMK* XX, pp. 38–311.

were considerable difficulties for the British monetary authorities in 1930. They were faced by the problem of a mature, less dynamic economy in that the natural rate of interest was tending to decline as the most profitable investments had already been undertaken. Unfortunately, the British monetary authorities did not have the freedom to lower domestic interest rates because Britain was not a closed economy. It participated heavily in international trade and needed measures to protect its balance of payments with the rest of the world.

The balance of payments brought Keynes back to the workings of the gold standard which he painstakingly analysed for the committee. In the nineteenth century, the Bank of England had operated in conditions which made Bank rate a very effective policy instrument. If Britain were experiencing a balance-of-payments deficit, a rise in Bank rate would restore equilibrium in two ways. In the short term, a rise in British interest rates would diminish overseas lending and attract capital to London. This would give immediate respite, but any longer-term tendency for British goods to become uncompetitive relative to those of other nations was checked by the second effect of the rise in Bank rate. Businessmen would be less willing to embark on new investments. Additional unemployment would be created, and, in turn, there would be a small but necessary adjustment in the rate of wages. It was this sort of small adjustment which Bank rate had been asked to rectify in the nineteenth century, and the mechanism had been, according to Keynes, supremely efficient. He recalled that in 1925 restoration of the gold standard had involved an overvaluation of approximately 10 per cent. Bank rate now had to solve a problem of fundamental disequilibrium between British and world prices. From at least 1923 onwards, Bank rate had risen above the 'natural' rate of interest in an effort to force down the British price level to an extent which had no parallel in the previous century. The high rate of interest made businessmen reluctant to invest, with the result that business losses were accumulating. The answer, according to the *Treatise,* was to devise ways of lowering the interest rate and expanding credit.

Keynes offered the Macmillan Committee a series of measures to give the Bank of England greater flexibility to pursue domestic objectives in spite of external pressures. The Bank's reserves must be raised to give greater margins before it was necessary to raise interest rates. Keynes suggested that the Bank should hold higher foreign balances, that the clearing banks should hold more of their reserves as balances at the Bank of England, and that the Bank's Issue and Banking departments should be amalgamated. If the Bank would enter the market for forward sterling and widen the gold points, the effect would be to give foreigners the equivalent of interest-rate changes without changing internal rates. Control over foreign lending would also increase the freedom of internal action. In these circumstances, Keynes called for greater cooperation between the Bank of England and the clearing banks to ensure that the *volume* of internal credit should be appropriate to internal needs.

These proposals, directly suggested by the analysis of the *Treatise*, were an important part of Keynes's plan for an expansionary monetary policy under gold-standard constraints. But they represented his pre-crisis thinking, from a time when it was possible to argue that Britain was climbing out of the doldrums. The problem in 1930, as Keynes told the Macmillan Committee, was to cope with an international slump on top of Britain's domestic difficulties.

Here, too, he hoped that the *Treatise* could help. The problem was still that of savings exceeding investment. In order to restore equilibrium there were, according to Keynes, three strategies: 'either you must reduce the level of efficiency wages so that foreign investment can increase, or you must diminish saving, or you must increase home investments'.[18] He gave the committee seven methods of pursuing these strategies. The first was devaluation, but the most opportune moment had been missed in 1925. There was no likelihood of devaluation in 1930. It would be acceptable only under duress and would be expensive in terms of confidence and credit. The second remedy was the national treaty which was again unlikely in the circumstances of 1930. Thirdly, Keynes suggested a system of bounties or subsidies to export industries. Its greatest advantage was to permit 'uneconomic' wage levels in these industries, with the public as a whole subsidizing the difference between 'just' and 'economic' wages out of taxation. Fourthly, Keynes offered rationalization, which had only one drawback in the amount of time needed for it to be effective. Each of these four remedies would help reduce costs, and so earn a higher surplus on balance of payments, thus permitting those savings which would otherwise have run into business losses to go instead to foreign investment.

The next remedy was protection, a very difficult proposal for a lifelong free-trader like Keynes. He recognized that the free-trade argument was unchallenged when the economy was already in full-employment equilibrium. In 1930, however, free trade could bring equilibrium only by putting additional pressure on wages and employment. When he looked at protection, Keynes saw a series of immediate benefits. Keynes explained to the committee that the tariff would raise profits, especially in the unsheltered industries, and would depress real wages by raising prices. He considered both results desirable. As the crisis deepened, Keynes's

[18] Ibid., p. 82.

support for the tariff broadened. It would help to balance the budget and raise the confidence of investors.[19] All these arguments were for a short-term tariff, but Keynes also came to a structuralist, and probably longer-run, strategy of protection for the extremely depressed sectors like agriculture, for those with clear expansionary potential, and also as part of a levy subsidy plan for the export industries.[20] Not surprisingly, the publication of Keynes's support for protection provoked a storm of controversy and a debate in which Keynes believed that his opponents' dogmatism (contrasted with his own pragmatic approach) had forced him into a sterile argument: 'a peregrination of the catacombs with a guttering candle'.[21]

His sixth remedy was also highly controversial. Keynes restated the case for attacking excessive savings from the side of increasing investment by absorbing savings into public works. This was Keynes's own 'favourite remedy', and was the only option if it was impossible to cut imports and increase exports. The same effect could have been secured from an increase of private enterprise, but Keynes believed that business confidence was at such a low ebb that it would be necessary for government to set the ball rollling. At this stage, he saw the need for public works as only a short-term expedient to 'unjam' an economy stuck in the lower reaches of the trade cycle. Public works had, of course, been vigorously opposed by the Treasury in 1928–9, and Keynes now defended this remedy against the 'crowding out' hypothesis. If the programme began when idle resources were available, capital would come from business losses, not from other investment projects. He could not, however, deny that both profits and prices might rise as a result. But rising prices meant decreased international competitiveness. Although similar considerations had been at the root of his powerful analysis of the effects of overvaluation during the 1920s, Keynes did not appear to worry about increasing British wages when world prices were tumbling. He merely maintained that any deterioration in the balance of trade would be compensated by lower foreign lending.[22] He must have known that this reply was weak. In his analytical framework, 'foreign lending' included both long-term investment and movements of short-term capital.[23] The Macmillan Committee had uncovered a huge amount of short-term indebtedness in London, and Keynes knew that the prospects of controlling these funds under gold-standard rules were minimal. If Britain had pursued an

[19] *JMK* IX, p. 236; *JMK* XX, p. 501.
[20] *JMK* XXI, pp. 207–10; *JMK* XX, pp. 290–300, 416–19.
[21] *JMK* XX, p. 505.
[22] Ibid., pp. 72, 73, 141, 189, 236.
[23] Ibid., pp. 141–2; see also *JMK* XIX, pp 835–6.

expansionist strategy in 1930 the only result could have been a crisis of confidence. These weaknesses were shrewdly and subtly exposed by the Treasury witness before the committee, Sir Richard Hopkins.

The final element in the alternative programme which Keynes put before the committee was an international conference to try to get concerted action to raise world prices. What Keynes wanted was British leadership to encourage the raising of investment throughout the world by an all-round reduction of interest rates, a lowering in all countries of the gold proportion of their reserves, and the development of the Bank of International Settlements as a means of economizing on gold.

Keynes was completely committed to this package. He was most favourably disposed to home development, but he was trying above all to break the policy *impasse*. In his very detailed survey of Keynes's intense propaganda activity in 1930–1, Peter Clarke has shown how Keynes tried to alter the balance of the programme to suit the differing prejudices of the various audiences he addressed. The package as a whole, however, remained entirely consistent. But it is not the myth of inconsistency with which Clarke is most concerned. His primary interest is Keynes's persistent antipathy to wage-cuts and support for public works during the 1920s, a position which was taken, as we have seen, despite the arguments of Keynes's theoretical work. Clarke wishes to ascribe a primary role for Keynes's 'political predispositions' in this choice of policies. To Clarke, Keynes was acting as a new Liberal, seeking to build a radical, anti-Conservative alliance with Labour. In the light of these political influences, wage-cutting was most inopportune and public works were a much more attractive avenue. There is undoubtedly much in this analysis. Keynes certainly committed himself strongly to the rejuvenation of Liberal economic policy at this time and frequently argued that the ultimate aim of a reconstituted Liberal Party should be to permeate Labour with more intellectually solid policies. Keynes was a Fabian in reverse. But personal politics do not tell the whole story, and in a curious way Clarke has fallen under the sway of some of the stronger myths about Keynes's policy advice.

Clarke's analysis is subtly influenced by a view of Keynes as an incipient inflationist, preoccupied with macro-economic questions and policies, and as a purveyor of a nationalist political economy. These points are all interwoven, but might best be approached through the place of public works and inflation in Keynes's programme. In 1930, Keynes presented to the Macmillan Committee seven remedies for Britain's economic problems and was very keen that support should be given to any or all of them: 'The unforgivable attitude is . . . the negative one – the repelling of each of these remedies in turn.'[24] Clarke cites this quotation, but tends to dismiss most of the others to concentrate on public works almost to the exclusion of the other six. This does much less than justice to the range of policies Keynes had supported during the later 1920s, and in particular Clarke underplays the importance Keynes had given both to structural policies for coal and cotton and to the technical adjustments by which Keynes hoped to derive greater freedom to pursue domestic objectives in monetary policy.

Exaggeration of public works goes hand in hand with Clarke's subtle overplaying of the place of inflation in Keynes's analysis. It may be true, as Clarke suggests, that chapter 30 of the *Treatise* is 'virtually a hymn to inflation' and that rising prices were associated with expansion,[25] but he does not point out that Keynes tried to distinguish between credit expansion during an economic upswing, which he thought inevitable, and deliberate inflationary finance, which he rejected.[26] Keynes consistently favoured a regime in which prices were stable at much fuller employment than was the case in Britain in the 1920s.[27]

These points spill over into the major omission from Clarke's study, the weight Keynes attached to the dynamic interaction between Britain and the world economy. During the crisis, Keynes became convinced that Britain's problems could be solved only in the context of a rising world price level.[28] His proposals for domestic expansion were built upon a firm conviction that world prices *would* rise, in part because of what he saw as the inevitable impact of the gold flows to America during the 1920s. It is now forgotten that he opposed the gold standard because it would produce inflation during the later 1920s.[29] His belief that America would be forced to reverse the fall in world prices was not finally broken until the summer of 1930.[30] The international dimension was certainly not the fashionable platitude Clarke has implied,[31] and to ignore it inevitably means taking Keynes's ideas out of their context.

Of course, if one is waiting ever more anxiously for a rise in world prices

[24] *JMK* XX, p. 375.

[25] Clarke, 'The Politics of Keynesian Economics', p. 157.

[26] Keynes described as 'inflation' the expansionary forces in the upswing of the trade cycle when savings were insufficient to meet demands for investment (see *JMK* XX, pp. 80–1). However, he was also willing to throw out of office any Chancellor of the Exchequer who resorted to deliberate inflationary finance (*JMK* XIX, p. 257).

[27] *JMK* IV, pp. 125–41; *JMK* V, pp. 152–3, 267–8; *JMK* VI, p. 145.

[28] *JMK* XX, pp. 293, 453.

[29] *JMK* XIX, pp. 250–1, 259, 342.

[30] *JMK* XX, p. 605.

[31] 'The Politics of Keynesian Economics', p. 171.

the last thing one will want to see is an attempt by Britain (which still had pretensions to a leading role in maintaining the stability of the world economy) launch a round of beggar-my-neighbour deflationary policies. We shall argue below that Keynes's position on wages was highly flexible, but on one point he was resolute: Britain's domestic economic problems could be solved only in the context of rising world prices, and for Britain to begin a series of country-by-country wage reductions was a counsel of despair.[32] By the same token, at the time of the crisis Keynes was clearly hoping that the adoption of a public works programme in Britain would lead the rest of the world into expansionism. Donald Winch has criticized Keynes for his optimism during this period.[33] Keynes's optimism on prices looks, however, increasingly like desperation. His analytical position at this time associated recovery with rising prices. Professional economic opinion would undoubtedly have supported this link. Keynes was much more determined than most to look anywhere and everywhere for some stimulus to raise the world price level.

When it had become clear that the gamble of waiting for price rises had failed, Keynes did pronounce in favour of wage-cuts.[34] But this was only the last in a series of measures which he had championed to lower first real and increasingly money wages. As we have seen, half his policy suggestions to the Macmillan Committee were designed to reduce real wages. As the crisis deepened, he proposed the 'reform' of social security with the effect of cutting benefits.[35] Money wages could only have followed. Finally, he seemed almost to welcome a currency crisis as the only environment in which either a direct reduction in money wages (via a national treaty) or lower real wages (by a tariff or devaluation) would be politically possible.[36]

So Keynes scarcely ran away from the need to cut costs. Since 1925, the lynchpin of his position had been that a direct attack on wages would impose enormous economic and social costs and give mediocre rewards.[37] It would be wrong to see this as a 'new liberal' or 'Lib–Lab' position, as Clarke is wont to do. As we have seen, both progressive Conservatives and progressive industrialists adopted exactly the same stance. It is wrong to see Keynes's policy and theoretical position mainly as an attempt to build bridges to the moderate wing of organized labour. There is a strongly

[32] *JMK* XX, p. 292.
[33] *Economics and Policy*, p. 141.
[34] *JMK* XX, pp, 605–6.
[35] Ibid., p. 444.
[36] Ibid., p. 455.
[37] Ibid., pp. 60–4. The argument also features strongly in *The Economic Consequences of Mr Churchill*, *JMK* IX, pp. 218, 220–4.

pro-industrialist flavour to Keynes's programme during the 1920s. He was closest to the FBI on both currency and monetary policies. His initial support for public works was justified by its effects on business behaviour. Indeed, the *Treatise* presents entrepreneurial behaviour as the dynamic element in capitalist economies.

'New liberalism' and 'Lib–Labism' fail to explain other crucial parts of Keynes's programme. They cannot explain his long-term support for control over foreign lending (his 'little-Englander' tendencies were profoundly out of step with mainstream liberalism)[38] nor his support for protection, a proposal which was anathema to both Labour and the Liberals. There was nothing more likely to shatter the reconstructed Liberal economic policy than one of its architects defecting to tariff reform, and Keynes must have known this. It would be pointless to deny that Keynes's economics were shaped by his personal political beliefs, but it would be equally mistaken to overlook his technocratic perspective, his determination to find a practical solution to a complex unemployment problem.

If Keynes had outlined for himself in the mid-1920s a step-by-step plan to exert influence over economic policy, he could not have asked for much more than the actual pattern of events. By 1931, he had the ear of leading politicians, was regarded as the driving force on a number of expert bodies which appeared to be increasingly important in the resolution of conflicts within the policy-making elite, and he had ready access to newspaper proprietors for the public dissemination of his ideas. We know, however, that not only did he fail to have the impact he had anticipated, but in the following decade Keynes changed his style immensely by severely restricting his appearances on the public stage. It is to an explanation of this change of tactics which we now turn.

KEYNES IN THE 1930's

Keynes had sustained himself in the very public role he had taken since the late 1920s by his faith that the analysis of the *Treatise* was the best possible theoretical treatment of the dynamics of the modern economy. To the Macmillan Committee, he had made much of the favourable reception his ideas had received from his Cambridge colleagues and pronounced himself ready to have his head chopped off if his analysis was false.[39] This was rash. Within six months, Keynes had run into enormous academic opposition on the EAC Committee of Economists. This body had been

---

[38] Harrod, *Life of JMK*, p. 411.
[39] *JMK* XX, p. 351.

established at Keynes's suggestion to produce 'an agreed diagnosis of our present problems and a reasoned list of possible remedies'.[40] Keynes tried to win support for his savings–investment analysis, but met intense opposition from Henderson and Robbins. The committee was in disarray and, although it was able to produce a surprisingly coherent report as well as a minority report from Robbins, the exercise hardly confirmed Keynes's optimistic hopes for the *Treatise*.[41] The failure to carry professional opinion had also effectively denied Keynes the opportunity of influencing policy in 1931.

The problems for Keynes did not end with the EAC. Some of the academic reviews of the *Treatise* were very severe. Finally, the 'circus', a group of younger economics dons at Cambridge, began a lengthy critical appraisal of the book. One participant has argued that, within six months, the circus had formulated the questions that *The General Theory* set out to answer and that the whole process was welcomed and encouraged by Keynes himself.[42]

The failure to carry professional opinion with him has been blamed, in part, on the lack of time for academic writing which Keynes had permitted himself over the final drafts of the *Treatise*.[43] It is beyond question that Keynes was stung by his failure in 1931. He seems to have rearranged his schedule over the next five years or so to free more of his time and energies for academic work. As the publication date for *The General Theory* approached he even kept out of political controversy for fear of jeopardizing his serious academic reputation.[44] Keynes now believed that the way to change mass opinion was to convince the specialist first, and *The General Theory* is addressed to his fellow economists.[45] In contrast with the pattern of the *Treatise*, the pre-publication exchanges in 1934–6 were extraordinarily protracted and intensive as Keynes sought to win over some of his former critics. This is not to suggest that Keynes *abandoned* all other pursuits to concentrate on academic matters, but simply to note that his tactics in the 1930s were rather different and more narrowly focused than hitherto.

[40] Ibid., pp. 368–9, 402–66; Susan Howson and Donald Winch, *The Economic Advisory Council, 1930–1939: A Study of Economic Advice During Depression and Recovery*, Cambridge, CUP, 1977, pp. 46–72.

[41] Howson and Winch, *The EAC*, p. 72.

[42] Austin Robinson, 'Keynes and His Cambridge Colleagues', in Don Patinkin and J. Clark Leith (eds), *Keynes, Cambridge, and the General Theory*, London, Macmillan, 1977, pp. 25–38; *JMK* XIII, pp. 337–43.

[43] Don Patinkin, 'The Process of Writing The General Theory: A Critical Survey', in *Keynes, Cambridge, and The General Theory*, p. 8.

[44] *JMK* XXI, pp. 354–5.

[45] See the first line of its preface.

This subtle change of emphasis took Keynes into more abstract theorizing. Whereas the *Treatise* consisted of two volumes, one of which was concerned with the applied monetary economics of the UK and USA, in *The General Theory* policy questions were scarcely touched upon. The outstanding feature of *The General Theory* was its theory of effective demand. Aggregate demand comprised aggregate consumption and aggregate investment, and Keynes's distinctive contribution was to demonstrate that aggregate income, consumption and investment could be at equilibrium at conditions other than full employment, and to show how the equilibriating process worked via the marginal propensity to consume and the multiplier. As far as policy was concerned, the most important parts of the theory concerned the determination of aggregate investment. According to Keynes, the two main elements were the yield of any new investment and the cost of borrowing the money to finance it. He argued that yield could be properly assessed only over the lifetime of that investment, and in this calculation the most important factors were the amount of capital equipment already in place, the extent of its utilization and, Keynes's most original contribution, the expectations businessmen had of the future state of the economy. The last could be extremely volatile. If a slump were anticipated, prudent entrepreneurs would refrain from installing new capital equipment. The cost of borrowing, or the rate of interest, was determined by the supply and demand for money. Supply was under the control of the monetary authorities, but Keynes's discussion of the demand for money also broke new ground. He argued that people hold money for three basic motives – transactions, for their everyday purchases; precautionary, to meet unforeseen circumstances; and speculative, to take advantage of any profitable venture which might suddenly arise. Keynes argued that the first two were closely related to the money value of national income, but were largely unresponsive to changes in the rate of interest. The speculative motive, on the other hand, was much affected by both the existing and the expected rates of interest. If, to take the Keynesian interpretation of the 1930s, interest rates were low but popular opinion held that they would rise, people would prefer to hold cash and wait until interest rates rose rather than to hold securities. The final twist to this theory of liquidity preference had a direct policy implication. If the monetary authorities wanted to lower interest rates, normally they would simply increase the supply of money. However, at very low rates of interest, the behaviour of investors would continue to be dominated by this belief that low interest rates could not last. Any increase of money supply in these circumstances would result only in larger *pro tanto* liquid holdings for speculative purposes. In short, there was a level below which interest rates could not be forced.

The policy implications were not considered in any great detail, but were clear enough. The most basic yet revolutionary message was that governments could and should accept the responsibility of regulating or managing the national economy to achieve specific economic goals, such as full employment. If the range and reliability of economic statistics were improved, governments could, according to Keynes's theory, calculate with some confidence the scale of economic adjustments necessary for full employment. Keynes also gave broad indications about the most appropriate policy instruments. As we have seen, aggregate investment was the most volatile element and thus the most suitable for attention. The most likely method of raising investment was to lower the cost by reducing interest rates, but *The General Theory* suggested that cheap money might not be enough if interest rates were already low, if the supply of investment projects was drying up, or if entrepreneurial confidence about the economic future was shattered. In these circumstances, the state should intervene with programmes of public investment. Lo and behold! The message of *The General Theory* was the familiar one that cheap money and public works would help do the trick!

The exposition of *The General Theory* made many simplifying assumptions, the most important of which was to ignore the foreign trade sector. The theory applied to a closed economy. This does not indicate, however, that the strong nationalistic wave which swept through progressive–centre opinion after 1931 was carrying Keynes with it. The international dimension, which had been so crucial an element to his programme in the 1920s, was still an essential part of his outlook. His major policy statement of the 1930s, *The Means to Prosperity*, was constructed as a call for an expansionist policy (now strengthened by the inclusion of the multiplier analysis and a demonstration that considerable additional employment could be created by comparatively modest schemes of public works) for Britain and which could then be adopted by the rest of the world. Keynes was quite clear that a unilateral solution to Britain's problems was impossible. As we saw in chapter 5, Keynes took up the plan Henderson had presented to the EAC Committee on Economic Information to create additional international liquidity. The world as a whole was suffering from insufficient capital expenditure and low incomes. Essential steps in raising both investment and income were the reduction of interest rates around the world and a resumption of international lending. Central banks were reluctant to facilitate expansion because they lacked confidence in their reserves of world money. The problem could be overcome by the issue of new 'gold notes', based on national gold reserves at some agreed date, and equivalent to gold. Thus central banks would receive additional world money, international confidence would be fostered, and international lending could be reactivated. If countries were made to renounce restrictive trade and monetary practices as a condition of receiving gold notes, international trade would also be encouraged. Of course, in the depths of the world slump (*The Means to Prosperity* was published in 1933), this was scarcely an earth-shattering conclusion, but it was a comparatively isolated example of a liberal, multilateralist manifesto in the early 1930s when the tides of economic nationalism were running strongly. Keynes was undoubtedly justified in seeing this strategy as a better long-run bet for Britain's economic health given her enormous dependence on trade, but he was surely optimistic to expect success in the tangled, autarkic world of the early 1930s.

Keynes also carried from the 1920s his determination to achieve expansion without inflation. Early in 1937, he produced a series of articles which considered the impact of the government commitment to borrow for rearmament on the pace of economic recovery. Keynes had long been critical of certain aspects of Treasury monetary policy which he believed had the effect of raising the long-term rate of interest, and he reaffirmed his opposition to higher interest rates.[46] More interesting was his suggestion that, although the unemployment rate stood above 10 per cent, there should be cuts in other public spending programmes to permit faster rearmament without inflation. He feared that the structural rigidities of the British economy in the 1930s would produce inflation if demand were raised indiscriminately. Efforts to reduce unemployment further should take the form of *ad hoc* regional measures. When these articles were 'rediscovered' in the 1970s, the tone of caution amid so much unemployment created disappointment and controversy. However, the message should not surprise anyone familiar with Keynes's proposals of the 1920s. Fear of inflation, awareness of structural rigidities, and willingness to experiment with *ad hoc* policies to overcome structural problems were all well established as early as 1925.

The willingness to support regional *ad hoccery* underlines Keynes's ability to take matters of fashionable controversy, in this case the Special Areas programme, and shape them for his own purposes. Indeed, there are indications that Keynes so sympathized with radical opinion on the need for specific regional policies that he was prepared to give general support to the planning of industrial location as recommended by the Barlow Commission and others.[47]

What is so striking about Keynes's policy advice in both decades is the way it undermines the myths which have grown up since his death. The

[46] *JMK* XXI, pp. 312–17, 349–52.
[47] Ibid., pp. 590–2.

persistence of public works, cheap money and the international dimension as the main pillars of his programme give the lie to his reputation for inconsistency. His opposition to inflationary finance was always strong and his constant recognition of regional and structural rigidities went hand in hand with a willingness to adopt the suggestions of others to meet these specific needs. Thus a number of the most prevalent myths about Keynes's policy stance between the wars have precious little foundation. Recent academic writing on Keynes has, however, shifted from these concerns. Since the mid-1970s, economic historians have been pre-occupied with a myth which was already in decline, that Keynes had the answers to interwar unemployment. A major area of controversy is the employment creation effects of public works and, in particular, the value of the multiplier, one of the key elements in Keynes's defence of public works in the 1930s.[48] In simple terms, the value of the multiplier helps identify the amount of total income generated by injections of money into the economy (resulting, for example, from a loan-financed public works programme). If money is borrowed to support a labour-intensive project, most of the funds will go as wages to workers who will spend a large proportion of these wages on consumption goods, and save the rest. The amount spent on consumption goods would represent additional demand for workers in the consumer goods industries. These workers would then receive wages which would, as before, go to consumption and to savings, with the former creating another, smaller wave of income and employ-ment. By this process, diminishing increments of income and employment are created throughout the economy, and the total number of new jobs will far exceed those on the original scheme. The higher the proportion of wages going to consumption (of domestically produced goods), the higher the value of the multiplier, and the greater the number of jobs per pound of additional public works expenditure. The core of Keynes's position in the 1930s was that the multiplier was large, so that only a relatively modest programme of public works would be necessary to produce a significant impact on employment. However, recent work has suggested that Keynes's assumptions about the size of the multiplier were unduly optimistic, and that a unilateral solution to Britain's unemployment problem was at best unlikely.[49]

This work is exceedingly valuable and should revolutionize discussion of the options available to interwar policy-makers. However, there is a

[48] Sean Glynn and P. G. A. Howells, 'Unemployment in the 1930s: The "Keynesian Solution" Reconsidered', *Australian Economic History Review*, 20, 1980; T. Thomas, 'Aggregate Demand in the United Kingdom, 1918–45', in R. Floud and D. N. McCloskey (eds), *The Economic History of Britain since 1700*, vol. II: *1860 to the 1970s*, Cambridge, CUP, 1981, p. 346.

sense in which this literature is posing a question which Keynes did not ask. We have suggested that throughout the later 1920s Keynes anticipated a rise in world prices. Thus even his most domestically oriented programmes in this decade were premised upon a hope for increasing competitiveness in Britain's export industries. In the 1930s, when such hopes had been smashed, the need to expand world trade was an essential part of Keynes's programme. It is unlikely, therefore, that Keynes ever believed a purely domestic solution was possible. In the 1930s, the prerequisite of any international agreement was to persuade the USA, as the world's major economic power, to take the lead in restructuring world trade and finance. In this context, it is interesting to note that Keynes made a number of attempts both public and private to influence US opinion in this direction throughout the decade.

As far as the shaping of British policy was concerned, Keynes channelled most of his efforts through the Committee on Economic Information, an offspring of the EAC but more highly regarded than its parent, which it outlived. The committee, was a purely advisory body containing a number of specialist economists. It did not have a dramatic effect on policy, but it did bring specialist economic advice into Whitehall on a regular basis. It has been claimed that most of the committee's reports 'bore the impress of Keynes' and that Treasury officials gained much from this exposure to Keynesian economics.[50] It is worth noting, therefore, that the committee's identification of a probable rise in British unemployment in the late 1930s brought an interesting change in policy. The Treasury authorized local authorities to vary their public works expenditure contra-cyclically, and on the face of it were very close to Keynes. However, Peden has demonstrated that the Treasury policy was not 'Keynesian' in the sense of dependent on the analysis of *The General Theory*, and Rodney Lowe's researches have shown that it was not the Treasury but the Ministry of Labour (a department not in contact with Keynes and the Committee on Economic Information) which sealed the commitment to public works.[51] Indeed, the Treasury seems to have been much closer to Dennis Robertson, another Cambridge economist on the committee. Robertson had been a close collaborator of Keynes, but the two had differed over the *Treatise* and drew further apart in the 1930s, especially over *The General Theory*. Robertson was also an expansionist, but his ideas

[49] Sean Glynn and Alan Booth, 'Unemployment in Interwar Britain: A Case for Re-Learning the Lessons of the 1930s?', *Economic History Review*, 36, 1983, pp. 339–40.

[50] Howson and Winch, *The EAC*, pp. 108, 156–7.

[51] G. C. Peden, 'Keynes, the Treasury and Unemployment in the Later Nineteen Thirties', *Oxford Economic Papers*, 32, 1980; Rodney Lowe, *Adapting to Democracy*, forthcoming.

on interest rates and budgetary policy were closer to the immediate concerns of Treasury officials than were the theories of Keynes. Treasury officials began to take note of Robertson.[52]

Again, the difficulties facing the unorthodox intellectual are very clear. After 1932, Keynes had a much more persuasive theoretical justification for cheap money and public works than had been the case in 1930–1. His policy recommendations were, however, still distant from those of 'practical' Treasury officials. The chances of his persuading Treasury officials to accept his position depended again on his ability to deliver an economics profession united behind *The General Theory*. The differences between Keynes, Robertson and Henderson before the Committee on Economic Information merely underlined the divisions. Treasury officials turned instead to the more attractive views of Robertson.

Keynes had been correct to turn his attentions to academic opinion after 1931. With the construction and defence of *The General Theory* between 1932 and 1937, Keynes won the crucial support of the younger generation of academic economists and could hope for the *eventual* acceptance of Keynesian analysis within university economics departments. But the problem of how to bring public opinion behind these ideas had not been faced. Keynes was apt to think that no such difficulty existed because of the technocratic nature of the specialised advisory function.[53] Some of his younger supporters were more active propangandists and began to permeate the Labour Party as Keynes had operated through the Liberals in the 1920s. But progress was very slow, and almost ceased after 1937 with the rise of the foreign-policy issue. It was only the very different economic and political circumstances of the 1940s which created the conditions in which new policy ideas and priorities could prosper. Without the war, Britain may have had a 'Robertsonian evolution', but it might still be waiting for its 'Keynesian revolution'.[54]

---

[52] Howson and Winch, *The EAC*, p. 164.

[53] This element in Keynes's thinking was implicit in his constant calls for the improvement of official statistics, in the claims he was wont to make that the technicalities of monetary policy were understood only by a very small number of specialists, and in his assumptions that economic policy might effectively be formulated by a small group of specialist economists who would supply neutral advice to Ministers. These ideas surface most clearly during the war. See Alan Booth and A. W. Coats, 'Wartime Economists on the Role of the Economist in Government', *Oxford Economic Papers*, 32, 1980, pp. 190–2.

[54] It is worth pointing out that Robertson was brought from the Committee on Economic Information into the Treasury in the summer of 1939 to help prepare war economic and financial arrangements. Keynes was still less than fully fit, and so did not seek admission to Whitehall. His closest collaborator during the 1930s, however, Richard Kahn, was admitted as a temporary civil servant, on condition that he had no dealings with financial policy.

Conclusion

The previous chapters have explored the contribution of interwar progressive opinion to discussions of economic policy. We have attempted to show that the conflict between Keynes and the Treasury, which has absorbed so much of the energy of historians, was but one aspect of a wide-ranging reappraisal of the role of the state in the economy in which all aspects of economic life were legitimate causes for concern. Although this debate was conducted from all quarters of the political spectrum, it is possible to see common threads in the position of almost all the progressives on economic policy. There can be little doubt that the key stimulus was a loss of faith, albeit to varying degrees, in the efficacy of the market mechanism in regulating economic relationships.

PROGRESSIVE ECONOMICS

Dissatisfaction with unregulated capitalism and the assumption by governments of a limited, facilitative role in the economy was not, of course, new to the interwar period. Interventionist and collectivist doctrines had been evident long before 1900. These long-run forces undoubtedly had a profound effect on some of the contributions to interwar discussions, particularly from the Liberal and Labour parties, but they cannot account for the breadth and diversity of interwar progressives' suspicion of the market mechanism. To account for the immense shift of radical opinion away from the liberal market order in interwar Britain, the focus must be turned to more immediate aspects of the economic and political environment.

Unemployment and its corollary business depression was the single most influential factor in persuading progressives that market forces could no longer supply the dynamism or expansionism necessary for a prosperous economy. The need to confront unemployment and business depression was at the core of all the programmes we have considered. The second important influence was the general strike. The events of 1926 demonstrated that the benefits of a market solution in lower wages were far outweighed by the costs of class conflict, lost production, and political tension. As we have seen, there was an impressive flowering of alternative strategies from all shades of political opinion in the late 1920s, which may, in turn, have influenced the voters at the 1929 election. The final influence driving progressives away from reliance on market forces into alternative strategies was the slump. This unprecedented display of the destructive power of unregulated capitalism helped confirm a distinction in many minds between the chaos of markets and the orderliness and rationality of planning.

Progressives may have been united in the belief that free competition could not solve Britain's interwar economic problems, but there were disagreements about the extent to which the market should be eroded and about what to offer in its place. The most common response was to turn to the state. The collectivist bias of both socialism and new liberalism pointed in that direction, and the comparative success of state control in the wartime economy offered practical, *British* examples of what governments might achieve in economic affairs. This positive attitude towards an expanded role for the state in the economy touched all parts of progressive opinion to a greater or lesser extent. Even the Mond group, which had the greatest commitment to a rigid separation between the political and economic spheres, depended totally upon a friendly government for the core elements (protection, imperial development, easy credit) in their programme. At the other extreme were the statist planning models of the Labour Party and the TUC during the 1930s. In general terms, therefore, progressive opinion, which in the nineteenth century had seen state intervention in the economy as a threat to liberty and efficiency, had lost some of its inhibitions about increased state economic power.

Greater reliance upon the state implied the development of a more nationalistic political economy, and such trends are evident across the board, particularly in the 1930s. However, among the groups which led the search for a new role for the state in the interwar economy were those in which the international perspective had been strongest in the previous century. Liberal and socialist internationalism had been weakened, but not killed off, by the first world war, and remained to exert some influence over the development of alternative strategies in these quarters during the 1920s. The Liberal and Labour parties and the TUC tried to combine an international perspective of free trade and the gold standard with a strategy of state-promoted, domestic, national economic expansion. The two perspectives were not easily compatible, with the result that programmes of all three groups were weak on ways of overcoming an external constraint to national expansion. The problems were resolved by the slump, which effectively ended all hopes of a revival of the liberal international economic system.[1] Such problems were much less difficult for the social imperialists like Mosley and Mond, and the radical Conservatives. Mosley and many of the Mond group favoured an imperial rather than national political economy, but they advocated a very high degree of economic integration within the empire and almost complete isolation from the rest of the world. In a real sense, empire countries were expected to act as passive arms of the British economic system. The economies of empire countries would be directed from London and would have to respond to a strategy designed to meet the needs of British manufacturing industry. Under these circumstances, the distinctions between nation and empire are minimal. Macmillan and other radical Conservatives had even fewer problems. The strong nation state had long been an established part of Conservative party ideology, and progressives in this tradition were more accustomed to see state power as a possible instrument of national advantage.

However, progressives did not come to this more nationalistic, state-directed form without some reservations about the ability of the British state to make wise decisions in economic policy. The Mond group, for example, wanted to exclude the state from most areas of industrial decision-making, and the radical Conservative planners gained most of their early momentum from the call to free the economy from the palsied hands of the existing 'Old Guard'. There were, however, positive suggestions for improvement. Most progressives held that if the state's economic responsibilities were increasing, so should the quality of its economic advice. Almost every programme called for the introduction of specialist economic and business advice into elevated levels of the decision-making process. The cult of the expert was widespread, but the progressives also realized that the further their strategies moved from reliance on market forces, the more powerful and potentially threatening was the state economic machine they were proposing. The problem was especially acute for the planning movement of the 1930s. Planners had to devise ways of identifying the national interest and thus reconciling the claims of the nation with those of other groups within society. Most frequently, a solution was found in corporatist structures. Corporatist themes had the considerable virtue of being sufficiently flexible to be

---

[1] Of those considered in this volume, only Keynes retained a multilateral perspective, and it came to the fore once more during the war. See R. F. Harrod, *The Life of John Maynard Keynes*, Harmondsworth, Pelican Books, 1972, pp. 554, 720–2.

attractive to all shades of political opinion. Corporatism and quasi-corporatism appeared to offer harmonious ways of accommodating the demands of the nation with those of 'industry' (which could be defined as the owners, the owners plus the workers, or even as the owners plus the workers plus the customers, according to political taste).[2] Corporatist themes were thus almost a logical consquence of the post–1931 reaction against the market system.

The final influence which shaped most strands of progressive economic thought was the belief that scientific development could cure Britain's economic problem. Again, this was attractive both to the socialists, who could blame managerial inadequacies for the failure to adopt technological improvements, and to the non-socialists, who could blame the crisis of profitability induced by the anarchy of market forces. For both sides, the planned economy would create the stable conditions in which British technology could be harnessed to the British economy. Anti-market, nationalistic sentiment was evident even here.

There can be little doubt that these broad influences helped the radicals come to grips with Britain's interwar economic problem. We began this volume with an analysis of a dual economy, one side of which was constrained by demand and the other by cost. In these circumstances, it was suggested that policy-makers needed to promote higher efficiency on both sides of the dual economy and accelerate the pace of structural change to the demand-constrained, home-market sector. An industrial policy was the first prerequisite. It was suggested that this process was unlikely to produce full employment, especially during cyclical slumps, so the expansion of domestic demand (so arranged that it did not hamper the drive to efficiency and lower costs) and international action to promote greater world economic stability were essential accompaniments to domestic industrial policy. It should be added that these economic imperatives had to be applied in a political context of considerable, barely latent class conflict. Trade-union organization was resilient despite economic circumstances, and the general strike demonstrated very clearly that there were real tensions over the distribution of incomes between wages and profits. It was not enough for the progressives to pretend that unions did not exist or that economic policies would operate in an environment of social harmony and consensus.

The best of the interwar alternative economic strategies did accept the complexities of Britain's interwar economic and political problems and

---

[2] On the distinction between 'corporatism' and 'quasi-corporatism', see Luther Carpenter, 'Corporatism in Britain', 1930–45', *Journal of Contemporary History*, 11, 1976.

attempted to devise policies to meet those requirements. The need for structural adjustment was widely appreciated as was the necessity of increasing the efficiency of all sectors of British industry. Most progressives were also committed expansionists. Only in the crisis years of the early 1930s was stability given higher priority than expansion and growth. The interwar progressives anticipated, *inter alia*, deficit finance, industrial policies to promote both large-scale enterprise and structural change, incomes policies, growth planning, and an active location of industry policy. This reappraisal of economic policy in the interwar period pointed to many subsequent policy initiatives. Among the reformist strategies, the strongest were Mosley's *Revolution by Reason*, which was incisive on the absolute urgency of structural change; the Mond–Turner unemployment report, which contained an unequivocal recognition of the need for higher all-round industrial efficiency and an expansionist monetary policy; the mature version of Macmillan's programme, which was strong in all areas and saw a fruitful avenue for consensus politics in full employment, faster growth and econonomic redistribution; and, finally, Keynes's strategy of the 1930s, with its impressive combination of theoretical soundness and practical good sense. The best socialist strategy was the ILP's *Living Wage* programme, which devised the only serious interwar blueprint of the transition to socialism and contained the best picture of economic policy under socialism. All these programmes deserve much fuller attention than they have hitherto received and contain insights into the problems of policy-making which are of lasting significance. None of them was flawless, and interwar alternative strategies have an uncanny tendency to point to the weaknesses of policy in the years since the second world war.

The most persistent weakness was on external account. Almost every expansionist strategy failed to anticipate the balance-of-payments problems of higher levels of domestic activity, and the import/export boards of the planners carried even less conviction. In the progressives' defence, it should be noted that not only were interwar data on the balance of payments poor in coverage and unreliable, but there was also no clear-cut analytical scheme in which to fit the scraps of available data.[3] Economists, including Keynes,[4] were as weak as everyone else.

The second main weakness was a general tendency to fudge difficult policy areas by proposing new institutions rather than new policies. Not surprisingly, this criticism applies with special force to the efforts of planners to strengthen the balance of payments. Immense effort was

---

[3] Sean Glynn and John Oxborrow, *Interwar Britain: A Social and Economic History*, London, Allen & Unwin, 1976, p. 68.

[4] See above, p. 173.

directed to the construction of a wide range of new boards and institutions, but the actual problem of poor export commodity and market mixes reinforcing a lack of basic export competitiveness and an import requirement which was highly income elastic was never squarely faced. This trait was most deeply ingrained in the labour movement, anticipating some of the weaknesses of the postwar Wilson governments.

The same failing is evident in the tendency to see certain policies as cures for all economic problems. Progressive (and a large part of reactionary) industrial opinion undoubtedly saw the tariff as a panacea for many of their own competitive problems, and the Labour party regarded nationalization in much the same simple light. The most outstanding example of the retreat to panaceas rather than solutions was the planning movement. As we have suggested, many planners were engaged simply in vacuous exercises in the procedures of decision-making.[5] Actual economic problems were not allowed into the scheme. For many, planning was a barrier, not a stimulus, to constructive thought about the economic problem.

Finally, the progressives were weak on monetary policy. They were by temperament expansionists, but were also by intellectual persuasion or political necessity supporters of the balanced-budget doctrine and its major prop the quantity theory of money. The crude quantity theory which circulated in interwar policy-making circles held that any expansion of the money stock would act on prices rather than output. Only after the publication of *The General Theory* did the progressives have an academically convincing analysis which demonstrated that, starting from conditions of mass unemployment, an expansionist monetary policy could lead to higher output without inflation until full employment had been reached.[6] However, the progressives were not totally hamstrung by the quantity theory. Mosley, the YMCA Conservatives and the Liberals all called for deficit finance and had plausible explanations and ingenious devices to prevent inflation. The Labour party and the Mond group opted for expansion and hoped that financial experts might be swung behind the strategy if it was put before a Royal Commission. The progressives may have been weak in this area, but they did at least recognize the problem and were admirably resourceful in their efforts to overcome it.

Thus, despite the flaws, the progressive economic strategies, especially those which have been singled out for individual praise, did possess the

[5] See the comments on the Webbs and Cole, above pp. 151–6 and 139.

[6] Of course, very soon after the publication of *The General Theory* Keynes modified this theoretical analysis to accommodate the structural rigidities of the British economy of the 1930s. Above pp. 180–1.

Conclusion

basis of an attack on the complex, multi-layered unemployment problem of interwar Britain. This was a commendable achievement, but it is only part of the story. These strategies were designed for use, not for entertainment. A realistic assessment of interwar alternative economic strategies must consider also the politics of progressive opinion. How successful were these critics in changing policy?

PROGRESSIVE POLITICS

At first sight, the record of the progressives appears abysmal. The distinctive features of alternative strategies were expansionism and planning. Neither is very conspicuous in the actual policies pursued by interwar administrations. The most obvious omission from government policy for most of the interwar period is any deliberate attempt to reduce unemployment in the short term; after 1920, every Cabinet rejected expansionism, and even this short phase of deliberate expansionism was pursued in the interests of crisis management by a Cabinet fearful of revolution. The costs of crisis management were inflation and exchange-rate depreciation, but in the middle of this very difficult phase the Cabinet took a major strategic decision which was to dominate policy-making up to 1931. In December 1919, the Cabinet endorsed the Cunliffe Committee's recommendation to restore the gold standard at the prewar parity and at the earliest opportunity, and found itself, as we noted in the previous chapter, having to choose between an exchange rate and an employment objective.[7] As is well known, the exchange-rate objective was dominant. The Cabinet reversed its inflationary monetary policy, raised Bank rate to crush further inflationary expectations, and slashed public expenditure in 1921–2.[8] These deflationary measures coincided with a world recession, producing a dramatic rise in British unemployment. Faced by higher unemployment and a lower exchange rate than they desired, the British monetary authorities had to walk a tightrope. They persevered with monetary restriction to hold any appreciation of the exchange rate, but were unwilling to tighten the screw further because of the effects on 1930s and even implemented in 1918–20. Recent studies of Treasury officials have, moreover, emphasized the comparatively small part played by economic ideas in the formation of their policy advice.[14] Secondly, orthodoxy was not monolithic. Our survey of individual programmes has

[7] Susan Howson, *Domestic Monetary Management in Britain, 1919–38*, Cambridge, CUP, 1975, pp. 11–12.

[8] Ibid., pp. 25–9.

unemployment.[9] Their policy goals were inconsistent in the short term, but could be reconciled in the long run if restoration of the gold standard could be presented as part of a wider plan to reconstruct world trade and payments to revitalize the export industries in which most unemployment was concentrated. Governments, therefore, adopted a long-term strategy of export-led recovery.

Domestic action was possible as long as it complemented this strategy. In the 1920s, governments supported efforts to reduce costs in the export industries and became particularly involved in the restructuring of coal-mining. Other small measures were introduced to lower overhead costs in manufacturing. Although well intentioned and appropriate, these efforts were inconsequential in the face of mass unemployment. The policy objective of 1919, however, gave little room for manoeuvre. Getting back to and staying on gold meant high rates of interest, which in turn meant the commitment of a substantial proportion of government revenue to service the war-expanded national debt. To protect themselves against criticism that they were ignoring the immediate problems of the unemployed, governments could do little but point to their considerable efforts to provide maintenance for those out of work. Rates of and conditions for benefit could, however, be made more generous to defuse short-term political pressures. This combination of long-term strategy and short-term safety valve continued throughout the gold-standard period. The only major addition was the transference policy, introduced to help unemployed coalminers migrate to new jobs and areas. Workers were given assistance to move from areas where unemployment was so high that their departure would have a negligible impact on the local labour market. They were brought to areas where demand for labour was stronger, and where incipient labour shortage might have driven wages up. Not even the results of the 1929 general election, when parties favouring domestic expansion were in the majority, brought any real change.

Changes were, however, forced in 1931, when the external strategy perished in the slump. Britain was forced off gold and into protection. The fall in world interest rates made cheap money possible. The constraints against short-term expansion appeared to have been removed. However, governments of the 1930s persistently stood firm against deliberate domestic reflation. They held that recovery should come from the revival of the private sector. The tariff and cheap money clearly helped, but governments were very keen to avoid anything which might damage business confidence. Budget deficits and new government interventions

---

[9] Donald Moggridge, *British Monetary Policy: The Norman Conquest of $4.86*, Cambridge, CUP, 1972, passim.

were avoided. Governments did, however, bring experts into Whitehall, albeit in a merely advisory capacity, and used this forum, the EAC Committee on Economic Information, to consider the medium-term aspects of economic policy.[10]

The most important changes in economic policy came from the needs of national defence, especially after 1937 when deliberate budget deficits were introduced to accelerate rearmament. Despite initial fears that business confidence would be undermined, the experiment with deficit finance was successful, and led Ministers to authorize a programme of deficit-financed public works to counter an expected rise in unemployment after the rearmament programme had ended.[11] This was the clearest indication both of 'planning' and of short-term domestic strategy in the 1930s, but little was expected of the public works programme, even to ameliorate the anticipated unemployment problem.[12]

Thus in both decades governments were reluctant to make the short-term reduction of unemployment their highest priority, and there is precious little in either decade which can be seen as a 'planning' initiative. In this context, the progressives appear to have been a massive failure.

In a much-quoted passage of *The General Theory*, Keynes laid the blame for the failure of interwar governments to adopt expansionist or planning initiatives not on the weakness of the progressives but on the hold of outmoded, orthodox economic ideas. The grip of orthodoxy has, as we have seen, become the central concern of post–1945 Keynesian historiography of the interwar policy debate. Orthodoxy consisted of two main propositions: Say's Law of Markets, that supply creates its own demand, especially when interpreted as meaning that wages were fixed at too high a level as a result of interference in the wage adjustment process; and the Quantity Theory of Money; which held, as has been noted above, that changes in the money stock would affect only prices and not the real economy, and produced a preference for small balanced budgets.[13] Keynesian historiography has implied that the force of orthodoxy was particularly powerful within Whitehall and the policy-making elite.

There are a number of problems with this analysis. First, orthodoxy was not so powerful in the policy-making and administrative minds that it prevented short-term expansionist policies from being planned in the mid-

---

[10] Susan Howson and Donald Winch, *The Economic Advisory Council, 1930–1939: A Study of Economic Advice During Depression and Recovery*, Cambridge, CUP, 1977.

[11] Howson, *Domestic Monetary Management*, pp. 127–8.

[12] G. C. Peden, 'Keynes, the Treasury and Unemployment in the Later Nineteen Thirties', *Oxford Economic Papers*, 32, 1980.

[13] B. Corry, 'Keynes in the History of Economic Thought', in A. P. Thirlwall (ed.), *Keynes and Laissez-Faire*, London, Macmillan, 1978, p. 4.

shown how easy it was to combine orthodox and unorthodox ideas in varying proportions and still emerge with a realistic expansionist package. In general terms, the first proposition ceased to hold any real grip on progressive thinking after 1926, apart from the crisis years of 1931–2. The second proposition was more powerful, but we have already argued that it did not present an insurmountable barrier to expansionist commitments. Finally, orthodoxy did not have an inflexible grip over mass opinion. The 1929 general election, fought on unemployment policy, saw an enormous shift in public opinion from the party of orthodoxy to the parties of expansion. Our thesis is simple: in the right political and economic conditions, there are good grounds for believing that politicians, administrators and the mass electorate could favour (or, at least, not thwart) unorthodox policies. The implication of this hypothesis is that the progressives did enjoy successes (in 1929 and in the mid-1930s), but failed for most of the interwar period to fulfil their potential.

However, if we reject the Keynesian assumptions about the tightness of orthodoxy's grip, we are further away from explaining why interwar governments rejected short-term expansionist policies and so further from a considered assessment of the impact of the economic policy progressives. To obtain an answer, we need to look rather more deeply at the forces which shape economic policy.

At the most general level, the balance of social and political power is of decisive importance. This is not to argue that economic policies always follow the narrow interests of a 'dominant' class, but to accept that at crucial moments policy is determined not by consensus but by confrontation and that the outcomes of these conflicts can have lasting importance for the scope and objectives of all policies, including the economic. Turning to the economic aspect of policy-making, the second decisive influence is undoubtedly the economic problem to be faced and the way it is perceived, which is in turn partly determined by prevailing ideas about the legitimate boundaries of state responsibility for various goals of economic performance. British politial parties have different priorities and tend to perceive the legitmate boundaries of public repsonsibility in different ways, so we need to include a party-political element in the forces shaping economic policy. Parties in power have not only to pursue their own commitments, they have to avoid anything which might give political capital to their opponents. Finally, we must take

[14] G. C. Peden, 'Sir Richard Hopkins and the "Keynesian Revolution" in Employment Policy', *Economic History Review*, 36, 1983; Roger Middleton, 'The Treasury in the 1930s: Political and Administrative Constraints to the Acceptance of the "New" Economics', *Oxford Economic Papers*, 34, 1982.

account of administrative influences, of which the most important is the very time it takes to change policy; continuity in policy is thus always strong, and change invariably takes place at the margin. Under this administrative heading could be included the impact of the Whitehall machine and of pressure-group activity. This is in no sense a formal 'model of policy-making'; we are merely attempting to identify the main influences shaping policy.

This assessment helps explain the importance of the years 1918–21 to policy-making in the whole interwar period. In these crucial years, the militant wing of organized labour sought redistribution of economic power from capital and, after a brief period of success, it was decisively defeated in the second half of 1919.[15] The issues upon which the battles were fought were of enduring significance. Demands for the nationalization of specific sectors of private industry were rejected, and the experiment with a domestic orientation to monetary policy were abandoned in favour of restoration of sterling's international role. Industrial and finance capital had mobilized and fought to defend their interests.[16] They could not subsequently be expected to yield those rights which they had had to struggle to defend. The failure of labour to grasp the initiative in 1919 was confirmed by the defeats of trade unionism in 1921 and 1926 and the collapse of the Labour party in 1931.

This balance of socio-political power in turn helped determine the way the economic problem was presented. The triumph of those who wanted an international role for sterling made it inevitable that measures to regulate the international financial system and the avoidance of any steps which might weaken sterling's international acceptability would both loom very large in policy-makers' minds.[17] The sterling–dollar exchange rate and the maintenance of the gold standard became 'problems' of a magnitude equal to or greater than unemployment. This problem ought to have disappeared in 1931 with the collapse of the gold standard, but the authorities gained little additional latitude. Sterling was still an international currency within the sterling area. The authorities would have liked a low parity to ease the plight of the export industries, but they could not prevent a major appreciation of the exchange rate after the American devaluation. Of course, a deficit-financed expansionist programme could have caused sterling's exchange rate to fall, but for an international

[15] S. M. H. Armitage, *The Politics of the Decontrol of Industry: Britain and the United States*, London, Weidenfeld & Nicolson, 1969, pp. 159–60.

[16] See the discussion of the industrialists' case at the NIC, above pp. 78–80.

[17] This analysis owes much to Susan Strange, *Sterling and British Policy: A Political Study of an International Currency in Decline*, London, OUP, 1971, pp. 38–40.

currency such a tactic runs the grave risk of turning into a crisis. The rumours of a small deficit in 1931 were sufficient to provoke a near rout which shattered business confidence. Sterling's international position was a persistent problem for policy-makers, and one which often overrode domestic considerations.

Under these circumstances, the economic problem might have presented itself as a need to promote vigorously higher efficiency in the traditional staple industries and foster the expansion of new export sectors. To some extent, governments did follow a muted version of this strategy in the 1920s. However, the conflicts over nationalization made business very suspicious of government intervention in industrial affairs. On the whole, governments could intervene in the workings of an established, privately owned industry only after that industry had demonstrably failed to put its own house in order. Under these constraints, government industrial policy was certain to be limited in both ambition and extent.

This anti-interventionist bias was reinforced by administrative factors. Many of the alternative economic strategies required new political or constitutional arrangements at the level of Cabinet and Ministerial responsibilities. Progressive strategies also frequently implied shifts in the established pattern of the relationship between central and local government. Alternative strategies could be, and were, opposed on these grounds.[18] The Treasury was also a persistent stumbling-block. Top Treasury officials were far from dogmatic proponents of economic orthodoxy, but they were under enormous difficulty in finding revenue for existing government policies and had been scarred by their inability to control the money markets in the immediate postwar years. The corollary of flexibility of thought was an almost limitless supply of objections to any proposals which officials thought would worsen an already difficult environment for the conduct of public finance.[19]

Under no circumstances does this pretend to be anything more than a brief preliminary sketch of the socio-political, economic and administrative influences which shaped interwar economic policy. We believe, however, that the exercise is useful to appreciate the extent of the difficulties facing all those who hoped to push governments into more expansionist, interventionist and experimental economic policies in the

[18] Jim Tomlinson, *Problems of British Economic Policy, 1870–1945*, London, Methuen, 1981, pp. 88–90.

[19] See Howson, *Domestic Monetary Management*, for a sound survey of Treasury advice. This book should, however, be read in conjunction with Peden, 'Sir Richard Hopkins', and Middleton, 'The Treasury in the 1930s'.

interwar years. The influences considered thus far clearly interacted and reinforced one another to compel governments to attempt to rebuild Britain's position as a world financial power and, in the domestic sphere, to retain a strong bias against interventionism. Any assumption by governments of new economic responsibilities had to be a very slow and pragmatic process. The natural beneficiary of these 'realities of power' was the Conservative Party, which found its established ideological position almost perfectly in tune with the strong desire to preserve the full property rights of industrialists and financiers and with the preference for only cautious experimentation in economic policy. Baldwin's slogan, 'Safety First', admirably encapsulated the mood, and under Baldwin's leadership the Conservatives became almost the natural party of interwar government. Thus it is possible to offer an explanation of the failure of progressives to exert much influence over the shape of interwar economic policy without reference to orthodox economic ideas. It is clear, however, that orthodoxy did have an important legitimating role. Orthodox ideas provided intellectual justification for policies which were desirable on practical political grounds. The final, and perhaps most telling, obstacle facing the progressives was the fact that the cautious, anti-expansionist approach seemed to be successful, or at least it was not an abject failure. Unemployment fell in most interwar years. When it did rise, policy-makers could always point to extraneous shocks (usually a world economic downturn, but major strikes fell into the same category) which demonstrated that policy had not failed, but had simply been the victim of adverse circumstance. This concatenation of forces pulling government economic policy away from an expansionist, interventionist approach gave the radicals an almost impossible task.

The progressives were, however, not condemned entirely to ineffectual opposition, as the course of policy in 1918–19, the result of the 1929 general election, and the mildly expansionist plans of the mid–1930s all demonstrate. The progressives had one major asset, the persistence of mass unemployment. Government policy did tend to reduce unemployment, but at a depressingly slow pace. Unemployment was an issue that the progressives could and did exploit. Any assessment of the policital impact of the critics of intewar economic policies therefore revolves around the question whether persistent mass unemployment could have been exploited more forcefully to overcome the barriers to an expansionist, interventionist programme. In short, could unemployment have been used to sweep away Baldwin's consensus of 'safety first'? In theory, there were two possible methods. The first was confrontation, the tactics of 1918–19. The second was to attempt simultaneously to discredit 'safety first' and to build mass support for alternative strategies.

Confrontation was always unlikely after the collapse of postwar militancy. In conditions of mass unemployment the labour movement was almost certain to be more concerned with defence than with the possibilities of attack.

The second method was much more promising and conditions seemed favourable in both the late 1920s and the late 1930s. In both periods, there were issues which could have been exploited to weaken Baldwin's consensus. Thus in spite of Baldwin's best efforts, 'safety first' had not been able to prevent the waste and class conflict of the general strike. In the late 1930s, the record on rearmament and the attitude of the Conservatives to the fascist dictators inspired widespread criticism. In both periods, there also seemed to be good prospects for unity among progressive factions. In the late 1920s, the Labour and Liberal parties possessed very similar programmes, and there were real affinities between these and the Mond–Turner strategy. In the late 1930s, rumours of a centre-left realignment were rife. The key to progress clearly lay in closer agreement, but it is difficult to see how greater unity could have been managed. We have already noted that in both critical periods the extent of agreement was more apparent than real. To have pushed it further would have required either strong, charismatic leadership or the creation of an inclusive united front of the centre–left. The first alternative seems a possibility since there were leaders of real quality among interwar progressives. In the 1920s, the obvious choice was Lloyd George. In the following decade, the best candidate, Oswald Mosley, was outside the political pale. Macmillan and Morrison were possible alternatives, but the former had no real record of achievement before 1939, and the latter lacked national stature. We are left, therefore, to pin most of our hopes on Lloyd George, but, as we saw in chapter 2, he was most unwilling to pick up this challenge on the basis of an alternative economic programme. His performance between the publication of the Orange Book and the collapse of the Labour government in 1931 does not inspire confidence. Whether Lloyd George was already a spent force or whether he was afraid that he was vulnerable to criticism on economic policy from his record in 1918–22, the period in which the anti-expansionist, anti-interventionist stance was consolidated, is not clear. He was, however, an uninspiring leader on the economic issue. We must turn, therefore, to the prospects of a united centre–left front, a development which Marwick claims already to have identified in the group around Clifford Allen, Macmillan and the NFY supporters.[20] However, Marwick's centre–left conspicuously omits organized labour, which almost by definition had to be the major constituent of any broad centre–left realignment. Unfortunately, it is easy to see that persistent mass unemployment will always cause the organized labour movement to become introspective. Its left wing saw in interwar economic conditions evidence of the imminent collapse of capitalism and a signal to mobilize for socialist policies. The leadership of both the party and the unions, on the other hand, saw the breakdown of prosperity as a chance to seize power in the capitalist system. As a result, the labour movement spent most of the interwar period, as we have seen, contemplating and attempting to relocate its navel. Both the party and the TUC shunned alliances on all sides, from the Communist Party to the radical Conservatives. Both became more outward-looking in the years immediately before the outbreak of the second world war, but by this time the focus of attention had shifted from economic policy to the less divisive issue of the stand against dictatorship. We are left with a sneaking suspicion that it is comparatively easy to build alternative economic strategies during periods of economic weakness, but that it is desperately difficult to translate these ideas, however soundly based, into actual policy.

[20] See the comments above, pp. 72–5.

Index

DATE DUE